D0250460

PAUL

PAUL

An Introduction to His Thought

C. K. Barrett

WESTMINSTER/JOHN KNOX PRESS
Louisville, Kentucky

First published 1994
by Geoffrey Chapman
a Cassell imprint,
Villiers House, 41/47 Strand, London, WS2N 5JE, England

First American Edition

Published in the U.S.A. by Westminster/John Knox Press,
100 Witherspoon Street, Louisville, Kentucky 40202-1396

This book is printed on acid-free paper that meets the American
National Standards Institute Z39.48 standard.

2 4 6 8 9 7 5 3 1

Library of Congress Cataloging-in-Publication Data
Barrett, C. K. (Charles Kingsley), 1917–
    Paul : an introduction to his thought / C. K. Barrett. — 1st
American ed.
        p.   cm.
    Includes bibliographical references and index.
    ISBN 0-664-25541-8 (alk. paper)
    1. Paul, the Apostle, Saint.   I. Title.
BS2650.2.B374   1994
225.9′2 — dc20   94–1153
                                                          CIP

Cover picture: Rembrandt, *The Apostle Paul in Prison*

Typeset by Colset Private Limited, Singapore
Printed and bound in Great Britain by
Biddles Ltd, Guildford and King's Lynn

Contents

Editorial foreword

St Anselm of Canterbury once described himself as someone with faith seeking understanding. In words addressed to God he says 'I long to understand in some degree thy truth, which my heart believes and loves. For I do not seek to understand that I may believe, but I believe in order to understand.'

And this is what Christians have always inevitably said, either explicitly or implicitly. Christianity rests on faith, but it also has content. It teaches and proclaims a distinctive and challenging view of reality. It naturally encourages reflection. It is something to think about; something about which one might even have second thoughts.

But what have the greatest Christian thinkers said? And is it worth saying? Does it engage with modern problems? Does it provide us with a vision to live by? Does it make sense? Can it be preached? Is it believable?

This series originates with questions like these in mind. Written by experts, it aims to provide clear, authoritative and critical accounts of outstanding Christian writers from New Testament times to the present. It will range across the full spectrum of Christian thought to include Catholic and Protestant thinkers, thinkers from East and West, thinkers ancient, mediaeval and modern.

The series draws on the best scholarship currently available, so it will interest all with a professional concern for the history of Christian ideas. But contributors will also be writing for general readers who have little or no previous knowledge of the subjects to be dealt with. Volumes to appear should therefore prove helpful at a popular as well as an academic level. For the most part they will be devoted to a single thinker, but occasionally the subject will be a movement or school of thought.

The present volume takes readers of the series back to the very earliest days of Christianity—to the time before even the Gospels were written. And, as Professor Barrett says in his Preface, the only question to be raised at the thought of St Paul appearing in a series called Outstanding Christian Thinkers is: 'Should he not be described as the outstanding thinker?' The writings of St Paul comprise a large part of the New Testament. They laid the foundations on which much Christian thinking came to be built. And, as Professor Barrett shows very well, St Paul was very much a thinker.

Books on St Paul abound. But this book comes from the pen of one of his most distinguished twentieth-century commentators. Professor Barrett has spent many years thinking and writing about Paul. Readers of what follows will quickly see that they have before them a text to which they can turn for a solid and reliable guide to the thinking of Paul and to that of those directly influenced by him. Professor Barrett's book, written with clarity and vigour, will surely prove to be an enormous help to all students of Paul, both beginners and experts.

Brian Davies OP

Preface

If there is any question of Paul's place in a series of Outstanding Christian Thinkers it is whether he ought not to be described as *the* outstanding Christian thinker. He first gave the Christian movement a theology, and the greatest of his successors have known that they were building on his foundation. It is hardly to be hoped that the following pages will do justice to his achievement. They leave much unsaid; in particular they take much for granted, assuming answers to difficult and disputed questions of exegesis. I feel a certain freedom in this respect, because I have done my best to run away from none of these questions, and to take account of alternative views, in a number of commentaries: on Romans (Black's New Testament Commentaries, 1957; new edition 1991); on 1 Corinthians (ibid., 1968; new edition 1992); on 2 Corinthians (ibid., 1973); on the Pastoral Epistles (Clarendon Bible Commentary, 1963). I may mention also a study of Galatians (*Freedom and Obligation*; SPCK, 1985), and *From First Adam to Last* (A. & C. Black, 1962). I mention these books not because I think them the best available but because they supply the exegetical foundation of this exposition.

The short Bibliography is anything but exhaustive; it supplies references to a few excellent books on something like the scale of this one. They will enrich the reader's understanding of Paul; but there is no substitute for prolonged reflection on the text of the epistles.

Durham   C. K. Barrett
April 1993

ix

Bibliography

To have included commentaries on the several epistles would have expanded the Bibliography beyond measure; but good commentaries are among the best guides to Paul's thought. Only books available in English are included.

J. C. Beker, *Paul the Apostle* (T. & T. Clark, Edinburgh, 1980).
G. Bornkamm, *Paul* (ET; Hodder & Stoughton, London, 1971).
F. F. Bruce, *Paul: Apostle of the Free Spirit* (Paternoster, Exeter, 1977).
R. Bultmann, 'The theology of Paul' in *Theology of the New Testament*, Vol. I, Part II, pp. 187–252 (ET; SCM, London, 1952).
W. D. Davies, *Paul and Rabbinic Judaism* (SPCK, London, 1948).
M. Dibelius and W. G. Kümmel, *Paul* (ET; Longman, London, 1953).
W. P. Du Bose, *The Gospel According to St Paul* (Longman, Green, and Co., 1907).
V. P. Furnish, *Theology and Ethics in Paul* (Abingdon, Nashville and New York, 1968).
M. D. Hooker, *From Adam to Christ* (Cambridge UP, 1990).
R. Jewett, *Dating Paul's Life* (SCM, London, 1979).
E. Käsemann, *Perspectives on Paul* (ET; SCM, London, 1971).
W. A. Meeks, *The First Urban Christians* (Yale UP, New Haven and London, 1983).
A. D. Nock, *St Paul* (Thornton Butterworth, London, 1938).
E. P. Sanders, *Paul and Palestinian Judaism* (SCM, London, 1977).

E. P. Sanders, *Paul, the Law, and the Jewish People* (Fortress, Philadelphia, 1983).

A. Schweitzer, *The Mysticism of Paul the Apostle* (A. & C. Black, London, 1931).

A. F. Segal, *Paul the Convert* (Yale UP, New Haven and London, 1990).

K. Stendahl, *Paul Among Jews and Gentiles* (SCM, London, 1977).

J. S. Stewart, *A Man in Christ* (Hodder & Stoughton, London, 1935).

D. E. H. Whiteley, *The Theology of St Paul* (Blackwell, Oxford, 1964).

J. Ziesler, *Pauline Christianity* (Oxford UP, 1983).

1

Paul and his career

I think God has put us apostles on as last in the show, as men
under sentence of death, for we became a spectacle to the whole
world, angels and men alike. We are fools for Christ's sake, you
are sensible in Christ. We are weak, you are strong. You are held
in honour, we in dishonour. Up to this very moment we go
hungry, thirsty, and naked, we are cuffed, we are homeless, we
toil, working with our own hands. When we are abused, we
bless; when we are persecuted, we are forbearing; when we are
slandered, we speak kindly. We have become as it were the
world's scapegoats, the scum of the earth, to this day. (1 Cor
4: 9–13)

This is not a complete picture of Paul, but the words are his own,
and the facts were such that he did not need to exaggerate them. He
was one of the most hated men in the ancient world; and not without
reason. It was natural for Jews to think of him as a traitor. He had
betrayed their Law and therewith their national identity; he seemed
to have renounced the natural responsibility that he owed to
his fellow-countrymen by constituting himself an 'apostle for the
Gentiles'. Many even of the Jews who had become Christians
thought that he had given away too much in doing this: if Gentiles
were to be admitted to the people of God they should join the people
in the proper way. But if Paul was a bad Jew neither was he a proper
Gentile. In becoming a Christian he had not ceased to think of
pagan religion as Jews did. The pagans had their many gods and
many lords, but 'for us there is one God, the Father, from whom

1

come all things and to whom our own being leads, and one Lord Jesus Christ, through whom all things, including ourselves, come into being' (1 Cor 8: 6). Small wonder, to Paul, that pagan idolatry led to the horrors of pagan immorality (Rom 1: 24–31); and small wonder that he was not able — and indeed never attempted — to make himself universally popular.

It is harder to document the complementary truth that there were those who loved him. The preservation of his letters (by no means always flattering to the recipients), and their imitation by his followers, is enough to show at least a measure of admiration. There was a time when the Galatians would have torn out their eyes and given them to him (Gal 4: 15), and if in Galatia that time was now past, he could write to the Philippians of their 'fellowship in the Gospel from the first day up to now' (Phil 1: 5) — a fellowship that they had expressed in practical terms. There is no doubt that the author of the Acts of the Apostles looked upon him as the outstanding hero of the primitive mission. Clement of Rome, writing in the 90s of the first century, links him with Peter as (in contrast with those of the Old Testament) the greatest modern athletes of faith. How far he was understood, for example even by Clement, is another question. It is a question that we cannot answer because so few of his contemporaries have left us an account of their understanding of the Gospel, of its theological content and its practical expression. The evidence that we have, some of which will be considered in later pages, suggests that there were many who did not understand. This is not surprising. Paul is one of those men who are both simple and profound; he never had the leisure to sit down and write out a primer of Christianity specially adapted for beginners (though he might well have said that all his letters were written for such people). For the most part he was obliged to write in bits and pieces, partly because his writings were occasional, partly because the writing had to be fitted in with preaching, pastoral care, and working for a living.

Diverse attitudes to Paul have persisted through the ages, though in varying proportions. He has been hated and loved, understood and misunderstood, sometimes more hated, not very often more loved; often misunderstood, occasionally finding his way into the thought of a theologian, even of a church. It is hardly appropriate here to attempt to describe our generation as marked most by love or by hate, by understanding or misunderstanding; enough to say that among outstanding Christian thinkers Paul stands first — chronologically, without doubt; and perhaps in other respects also.

But what do we know about this loved, misunderstood man? This book is not about his life but his thought; the two, however, life and thought, are so closely integrated with each other that a certain amount of biography cannot be avoided. And the same sources deal with both life and thought.

For our knowledge both of Paul's career and of his thought there are two sources; at first sight each of them appears to be of the greatest value. They are the Acts of the Apostles and the corpus of letters bearing Paul's name. Closer and more critical examination raises questions with regard to their usefulness. Acts purports to give an outline of Paul's life from his conversion to Christianity in the vicinity of Damascus to the end of a two-year captivity in Rome. It looks back also, in a speech attributed to Paul (22: 3), to his origin in Tarsus and education in Jerusalem, and it refers several times to his inherited Roman citizenship. It recounts speeches, or sermons, given by him in Pisidian Antioch (13: 16–41), in Lystra (14: 15–17), in Athens (17: 22–31), in Miletus (20: 18–35), and in the Jerusalem Temple (22: 1–21), as well as a number of utterances made in courts and to legal and military officials. Between the beginning and the end of its story Acts describes Paul's work as a travelling evangelist, preaching and founding churches, round the north-eastern quadrant of the Mediterranean; he travels from Jerusalem, up through Syria, across Asia Minor, into Macedonia and Greece, and finally, after a stormy voyage and shipwreck, reaches Rome. Parts of these journeys are described in passages written in the first person plural; the most natural (though not necessarily the correct) interpretation of these is that the author of Acts, or at least, the author of one of the sources used by the author of Acts as a whole, was a companion of Paul, travelled with him, and had every opportunity of knowing him intimately. There are at least some points at which Acts is in direct contact with data derived from Paul's own letters, and to some extent it is possible to give, on the basis of Acts, dates to some of the events mentioned in the epistles. To provide a chronology of Paul's life is not one of the purposes of this book, though a little may be said on the subject below. It is perhaps fair to say that the author of Acts was better at dates than at theology – a fact that appears when we turn to our other source, the letters ascribed to Paul.

In the New Testament there are thirteen letters that bear Paul's name. In addition the Epistle to the Hebrews has been traditionally ascribed to him, but even the tradition is weak. 'Who wrote the epistle, God knows', wrote Origen; it is an opinion that may be affirmed in both its positive and negative sense. What of the rest? A detailed discussion of this question could easily fill the rest of this book; such discussions are easy to find[1] and need not be repeated here. The so-called Pastoral Epistles, 1 and 2 Timothy and Titus, are very widely (though not universally) rejected as Pauline documents. Their Greek style differs from Paul's, their theology is more developed but less profound, and they reflect a church order different from that which appears in the other letters. They (especially 2 Timothy) contain a few passages of historical reference and it has often been maintained that these or some of them come from Paul's hand and were incorporated by the author in his own work. The Epistle to the Ephesians presents a more difficult problem. The style is closer to Paul's but not identical with it; and the same may be said of the theology. Here however there is a distinction. If it may be said that Paul writes of Christ and the church one might say that Ephesians writes of the church and Christ. This is not to allege a contradiction, but the reader is aware of a change of emphasis. There are later touches, such as references to the 'holy apostles' and the hint that 'the apostles' now belong as definitely to the past as 'the prophets' (Eph 2: 20; 3: 5). There is a further problem in that the writer of Ephesians seems to presuppose that his readers do not know him personally (Eph 3: 2–4) whereas Paul had ministered long in Ephesus. This argument, however, loses weight in view of the fact that there is doubt whether the words *in Ephesus* were an original part of Ephesians 1: 1. Ephesians stands close to Colossians – indeed, its dependence on Colossians (and to a smaller degree on other Pauline letters) has been used as a further argument against its authenticity. The authenticity of Colossians itself is a difficult problem. In style, manner, pattern, and thought it is closer to the other letters than Ephesians is; there are however differences, and it is wiser not to use it as a direct source for Paul's own thought. The same is true of 2 Thessalonians. This leaves Romans, 1 and 2 Corinthians, Galatians, Philippians, and 1 Thessalonians, together with the short personal letter to Philemon. Doubts that have been expressed regarding the Pauline origin of these letters belong on the whole to the eccentricities of New Testament criticism. There is between them a sufficient unity of style and thought; one senses the same author confronted by various situations but dealing with them all on the basis of the same presuppositions and convictions. They fit together into a convincing picture of a single individual of unique mental and spiritual power, belonging to the first generation of Christians, and recognized — by no means always with approval — as a figure to be reckoned with in the affairs of the church. It is these epistles (with Philemon contributing but little) that will be used in this book as the primary sources for our knowledge of Paul as a thinker.

It is these epistles also that lead us to question Acts as a comparable authority. Minor differences in chronology need not concern us here, though they are bound to bear upon the question whether Acts was written by a travelling-companion of Paul. The most important considerations are the following.

Paul's letters are the first great theological product of the Christian faith; this is their essential greatness, but they are also a very notable literary phenomenon, marked by an individual, sometimes rough but always powerful, eloquence. They are anything but negligible simply as a piece of Greek literature. This was recognized by those who received and preserved them, and not least by Paul's adversaries. 'His letters are weighty and powerful, but his bodily presence is weak and his speech excites contempt' (2 Cor 10: 10). Paul was not indulging in fictitious self-flattery when he attributed these words to an opponent whom he does not name. Whatever he was like in person, his letters were forceful, and must have been one of the most effective and memorable elements in his ministry. But the reader of Acts alone does not know and would never suspect that Paul ever set pen to paper. On the contrary, he is represented as a powerful speaker; if to a heathen audience Barnabas suggested Zeus, Paul called to mind the figure of Hermes (Acts 14: 12). Paul may of course have been a better speaker than he in his modesty or a foe in his malice was prepared to allow; but it is hard to think that a travelling-companion can have been unaware of Paul's work as a letter-writer, and of the effect of the letters on their recipients. Acts was probably more remote from Paul than appears at first sight.

The form of the letters leads to their content and to a comparison of this with the speeches attributed to Paul in Acts. Paul's declaration in 1 Corinthians 2: 2 that when he opened his mouth in Corinth he resolved to know nothing but Christ and him crucified has in itself something of a preacher's exaggeration, but it is sufficiently backed up by the content of this epistle and the others. Paul's theme is Christ, and Christ is the directing authority in his churches. In Acts, Paul's first major speech is his sermon in the synagogue at Pisidian Antioch (13: 16–41, 46, 47). This perhaps sufficiently conforms to Paul's own canon, though the reference to justification in

13: 38, 39 gives the impression of a writer who knows that the great Pauline theme must get a mention though he himself is not quite clear on its meaning. The Areopagus speech in 17: 22–31 is a different matter. The argument is not simply a piece of Greek natural theology — there is too much of the Old Testament in it for that — but Christ appears in it only at the very end, and anonymously, and the controlling thesis lies elsewhere. It is hard to believe that Paul used the words attributed to him, hard to believe that the man who included them in his book, under Paul's name, was acquainted with Paul at first hand.

Another feature of the letters is controversy. This will be dealt with in some detail at a later point; here it is enough to remark that all the certainly genuine letters bear witness to it in some degree. It is at its most bitter in Corinth and in Galatia. In Corinth it seems that Paul, not without reason, almost despaired of winning back the loyalty of the church. They failed to stand up for him when he was attacked; they joined in the attack. They abused him personally; they abandoned the Gospel he had preached. In Galatia men who preached a Gospel so perverted that it was not a Gospel at all had won the ear and captured the heart of the Galatian Christians. Paul told them the true and by no means edifying story of the controversy; he argued theologically on the basis of Old Testament Scripture, and could not think what else he could do. The church at Philippi was loyal and loving, but at the place of writing (which may have been Rome or Ephesus) opponents sought to make Paul's imprisonment more painful by taking advantage of his absence, and the Philippians themselves were warned against 'dogs, evil workers, mutilationists' (3: 2). Things had not gone so far in Thessalonica (1 Thessalonians was probably Paul's earliest letter), but there were disorderly members of the church. Rome Paul had not visited when he wrote his letter, but the letter can be regarded as a pre-emptive strike in the battle that would one day have to be fought in the heart of empire. The Pauline literature is shot through with controversy; and it scarcely shows above the surface in Acts. Beneath the surface the traces are to be seen; there are those who take the line that without circumcision and the law there is no salvation, no membership of the people of God; one asks why the Jerusalem church did not more boldly take Paul's part in his long-drawn-out conflict with Jewish and Roman officials. But it seems that the conflict with those who would keep Christianity as a compartment of Judaism is very quickly stilled; indeed the conflict adumbrated in Acts 15: 1, 5 fizzles out with no shot fired. There is disagreement between Acts and the Epistles, and there can be no doubt which is the primary source.

The disagreement comes to a head in the accounts of the so-called Apostolic Council and in particular of the Decree which according to Acts 15 emerged from the meeting of apostles and elders summoned to look into the question of the relation between Christianity and the Judaism from which it arose. Was it or was it not necessary, in order to become a Christian, to be a Jew, whether by birth or by proselytization, which for a male convert would include circumcision? There is notorious textual variation in Acts 15: 29, but no text requires circumcision; the probably original text demands abstention from food offered to idols, from blood, from meat killed by strangulation (that is, killed otherwise than by the approved Jewish method), and from fornication. This conclusion appears to represent a compromise between the hard line that required full conversion to Judaism and the view that regarded affiliation to Judaism as irrelevant. According to Acts, Paul not only was a member of the Council that produced the Decree; he was entrusted with, and accepted, the task of propagating it. There is however no trace of the Decree in any of his letters. He discusses the questions of food offered to idols and fornication, and considers more generally the question of food regulations, but never mentions the Decree. It is moreover almost certain that if he had known it he would have thought it to be inconsistent with his deepest and strongest theological convictions. What can be made of a book whose author so misunderstood Paul as to represent him as not merely tolerating but advocating the provisions of the Decree?

This is not a rhetorical but a sober question, and if it is to be answered a distinction must be made. Paul was a great theologian; the author of Acts was not, and if on some important issues he misunderstood Paul he was certainly not the last to do so. As an exponent of Pauline theology he must be treated with reserve. He was however a popular historian of considerable gifts. He seems to have made a mistake (it was a very understandable one, but this is not the place to pursue the matter) over the Decree, but this does not exclude the possibility that he was substantially correct over the topography and chronology of Paul's journeys. These are not a primary concern in this book; if they were, Acts would be used much more.

In fact we have all that we need for an understanding of Paul's thought in Romans, 1 and 2 Corinthians, Galatians, Philippians, and 1 Thessalonians. The short personal letter to Philemon adds little of theological substance. The Deuteropauline letters are not to be totally ignored. They bear witness to Paul's continuing influence and to his reputation as a writer of theological and pastoral letters; they show (and more will be said of this later) how his thought was developing in the generation that followed his, and sometimes, as one projects a line back from the Deuteropauline material, are of use in casting light on what Paul himself thought. The Christology of Colossians, the doctrine of the church in Ephesians, the eschatology of 2 Thessalonians: these have their roots (or some of their roots) in Paul himself, and, though he might not have countenanced everything that his successors made of what they had inherited, their work (in addition to its own inherent value) sometimes helps the reader to understand Paul himself.

There is no other source of any value. There is an apocryphal Acts of Paul containing a number of narratives, and a Third Epistle to the Corinthians. According to Tertullian, the apocryphal Acts was written by a presbyter in Asia 'out of love for Paul'; it is historically worthless, though some of the names associated with Paul may have been drawn from traditional and possibly trustworthy sources — more probably, from folk memory.

If, as we learn from Acts 21: 39 and 22: 3, Paul was born a citizen of Tarsus in south-east Asia Minor and was educated under Rabban Gamaliel I in Jerusalem, there was little that the ancient world had to offer that he could not have learned; it is equally true that there is a great deal that he need not have learned had he been minded not to do so. Tarsus was a city of some importance that possessed a school or university said by Strabo to surpass in some respects those of Athens and Alexandria. Its two most important teachers, both called Athenodorus, were Stoics, and Stoicism was probably the prevailing philosophical fashion. It was there for Paul to study if he wished to do so, but it must have been equally possible for him to live within a Jewish ghetto, looking upon all Greek thought as heathen nonsense, or worse. He must have learned to speak and write Greek as a child; his Greek is too fluent, too eloquent, even if occasionally (according to the rules) incorrect, to be convincingly explained as picked up after he became a Christian missionary. His few allusions to Greek literature, however, do not prove profound acquaintance with it; they are confined to popular expressions that were on everyone's lips. In any case, if Acts 22: 3 is correct and is strictly interpreted, Paul did not spend much of his youth in Tarsus; sympathetic understanding of Greek thought and life, as distinct from familiarity with Greek idiom, he probably did acquire when conversion gave him a freedom he had not earlier possessed. The main part of his education was received in Jerusalem. There is no doubt that this gave him an excellent knowledge of Scripture and of the oral Torah which supplemented, interpreted, and applied the written Torah of the Old Testament. What Paul's original Jewish understanding of Torah was and how this was modified when he became a Christian will appear more fully as we study his thought. It is wise to proceed in such matters *a posteriori* rather than *a priori*. He is a rash man, whether Christian scholar or even Jew, who supposes that he understands first-century Judaism and first-century Jewish Christianity better than Paul did. It is unfortunate that what Paul thought of them comes out mainly in polemical passages; perhaps he was not altogether fair to them; but at least he knew them at first hand, and had, or supposed that he had, surpassed his contemporaries in his study of Torah and in zeal for the ancestral religion.

The Law was the gift of God, a gift of grace, to his people; it was the gift of him who had delivered them from their bondage in Egypt and undertaken to settle them in a land flowing with milk and honey. It was the foundation of a covenant that originated in a free act of election on God's part. The people had not chosen God; he had chosen them. But written into the covenant was the promise of obedience: 'All that the Lord hath spoken will we do, and be obedient' (Exod 24: 3, 7). The Law was not merely an indication of the means by which the covenant might be sustained, and repaired when broken; nor was it simply a badge by means of which the Jews might be distinguished from all other peoples. It was there to be obeyed; and in fact disobedience had broken the covenant, and prophets had seen that it needed not to be mended but replaced.

> I will make a new covenant with the house of Israel, and with the house of Judah: not according to the covenant that I made with their fathers in the day that I took them by the hand to bring them out of the land of Egypt; which my covenant they brake, although I was a husband unto them, saith the Lord. (Jer 31: 31f.)

God indeed had not cast off his people (Rom 11: 1, 2), and there was a constant endeavour to renew the covenant; but without obedience there was no renewal. This was a matter that had two aspects. On the one hand, there was a national hope that God, acting perhaps through a Messiah, would re-establish his kingdom, reigning triumphantly over a renewed people living henceforth in obedience to the Law—perhaps as re-interpreted by the Messiah. On the other hand, there was in the meantime a life to be lived by the individual Jew, who was called to direct his behaviour in accordance with the commandments delivered to him by Scripture and tradition. To the devout Jew, such a life was a privilege and a joy; and disobedience could be forgiven through repentance and the Day of Atonement. But obedience was what counted; on it the covenant depended, and it was universal obedience that (as many believed) could bring about its re-establishment.

So much for the background, the environment out of which Paul emerged to become the Christian thinker that he was. There was a point at which Paul the Jew became, without ceasing in his own understanding to be a Jew, a Christian. The point is traditionally referred to as his conversion. It is often said now that this is a misnomer;[2] the event was not a conversion for Paul did not take up a new religion with a different God. He continued to worship the God of the Old Testament; the event was not a conversion but a vocation. He was called to become a missionary of the Christian way of understanding the God and the religion of his fathers. This distinction is unreal; no one has ever made clearer than Paul himself did that to become a Christian is at the same time to receive a call to some kind of Christian service—for Paul, the call to missionary work among the Gentiles. Conversion is vocation. Both aspects of the one event are made explicit in Galatians 1. Conversion, a change of life, could hardly be clearer than in the comment Paul quotes from the churches of Judaea: 'he who once persecuted us is now preaching the faith he formerly harried' (1: 23). The moment of change is marked by the claim that 'God revealed his Son' (alive, therefore, not dead) 'to me; he did this' (and the link with the verse just quoted is immediately apparent) 'in order that I might preach him among the Gentiles' (1: 16).

As this verse shows, the essence of Paul's conversion lay in a revelation of Jesus Christ. With this the story of the conversion given three times in Acts (9: 1–19; 22: 1–21; 26: 2–18) is in sufficient agreement. Investigation of the historicity of the Acts story would be out of place here. Acts represents Paul as engaged on a mission of persecution; Paul confirms this (Gal 1: 13, 23; 1 Cor 15: 9; Phil 3: 6). The event is connected with Damascus; Paul confirms this (Gal 1: 17). Christ appears to Paul in a blaze of light; Paul has nothing to say about the attendant light, but we have just read his statement in Galatians that Christ appeared to him; cf. 1 Cor 9: 1;

15: 8. In a different way Philippians 3: 7–11 points to the centrality of the figure of the risen Christ. Festus rightly described Paul (Acts 25: 19) as concerned about someone called Jesus who was really dead but alleged by Paul to be alive.

Paul's conversion did not make a morally good man out of a morally bad man; he had not been a morally bad man. That it was not without influence on his way of living may appear in due course, but its primary effect was in his understanding of God and of his own relation with God. If Jesus was now alive, having been dead, it was because God had raised him from death. If God had raised him from death he must have been not a false prophet leading Israel astray but the bearer of the truth that God himself affirmed; the Messiah, perhaps, though Paul has little interest in Jesus as Davidic king, much in the fulfilment of prophecy and in the crucifixion and resurrection as the final suffering and vindication by which God's kingdom would be established. Negatively, Jesus was the end of the Law as the means by which man might be related to God; positively, he was the beginning of the realization of the eschatological hope of Israel. There was much in these propositions for a theologian to get his teeth into; we shall see in due course what Paul made of them.

Along with the theological task, and closely related to it, went the practical task of evangelism. If the benefits of the age to come were available, and available not through the practice of Judaism but by a relation with Jesus, crucified and risen, there was no reason why Gentiles should not be invited to share them. Jesus was less a Jewish Christ than a universal Lord and consequently willing to receive all. Hence Paul's life work as apostle of the Gentiles; not that he ever forgot the roots of theology in the Old Testament and Judaism, or lost his love for and obligation to his fellow Jews. This double loyalty introduced into his mission a difficult and often painful ambiguity.

To the Jews I became as a Jew, in order that I might win Jews; to those who were under the Law as if I were under the Law (though I am not myself under the Law), in order that I might win those who are under the Law; to those who were outside the Law I became as if I were outside the Law (though I am not free of legal obligation to God but under legal obligation to Christ), in order that I might win those who are outside the Law; to the weak I became weak, in order that I might win the weak. I have become all things to all men, in order that at all events I might save some.

11

But whatever I do, I do for the sake of the Gospel, that I too may have my share in it. (1 Cor 9: 20–23)

'As a Jew'; 'as if I were outside the Law': the language shows that he was in fact neither the one nor the other, and the awkward parentheses confirm it. This paradoxical apostolic existence was one aspect of the new creation that was involved in Paul's Christian faith (2 Cor 5: 17). It was to lead him from one problem to another. His thought may be best introduced by a glance at some of them.

The spread into the Gentile world of the originally Jewish Gospel of Jesus the Messiah was not planned and organized in advance. In the Acts of the Apostles Luke collected what information on the matter he could find, and it is not possible to set out a record of the development of Gentile Christianity in terms of an ordered chronology. Luke knew that one of the beginnings took place in Antioch (in Syria); lacking precise details, and the names of those concerned, he could only record it in the simplest way. Christians leaving Jerusalem on account of persecution found their way to the Syrian capital. Concerned to commend their faith they spoke of it at first only to Jews; some of them, however, of Cypriot and Cyrenean origin, began to speak also to non-Jews, and with considerable success. Report of this reached Jerusalem and the church there sent an inspector to see what was going on. This was Barnabas (a figure already familiar to the reader of Acts—see 4: 36, 37), himself a Cypriot Jew. Barnabas approved and joined in the work, which prospered further; Barnabas went off to Tarsus to look for Paul, evidently confident that Paul was one who would be willing to help and could do so effectively. Thus the story in Acts (11: 19–26); and there is no reason to doubt that Paul was involved in the foundation of a mixed, Jewish and Gentile, church in Antioch. He was a trusted member of it, chosen to be, with Barnabas, a bearer of its charitable assistance to the poor in Jerusalem (Acts 11: 30), and later, again with Barnabas, to be a missionary, commissioned to take the Gospel further still (Acts 13: 1–3). At this point in Acts there follows Paul's so-called First Missionary Journey, at the end of which the two missionaries report back to the church of which they are evidently considered agents (Acts 14: 26–28). We now encounter the problem of the Apostolic Council (Acts 15 and Gal 2), which has already been mentioned and will be considered again. It will be convenient here to move over from Acts to Galatians, our primary authority for the development of events in Antioch. At Galatians 2: 11, the Council over, we find Paul,

Barnabas and Peter in Antioch, participating in apparent harmony in the life of the mixed Antiochian church. All, Christians of Jewish race and Christians of other races, took part together in common meals; these were occasions of Christian fellowship and probably also provided the framework for what was subsequently to be known as the eucharist. Harmony was disturbed by the arrival of people who came from James, the brother of Jesus and now leader of the church in Jerusalem. These evidently spoke and acted with such vigour and authority that they frightened Peter, who withdrew from the united fellowship, drawing down upon himself Paul's energetic rebuke:

> When Cephas came to Antioch I withstood him to his face, for he was self-condemned . . . If you, Jew as you are, can live like a Gentile and not like a Jew, how can you compel Gentiles to live as Jews? (Gal 2: 11–14)

At this point the story ends. The modern reader would like to know what happened next. Did Peter accept the rebuke and return to his former ways? Did he succeed in bringing back Barnabas and the other Jewish Christians who had followed him into separation (Gal 2: 13)? Did the Gentile Christians accept some Jewish regulations in order to facilitate communion? Is this the point at which and the purpose for which the Apostolic Decree was formulated? It is clear that Paul did not retract; what did the church of Antioch make of him? He had been their apostle; does Galatians 1: 1 ('an apostle not from men or through man') indicate a change of status, a change in Paul's understanding of apostleship? We do not know the answers to these questions. If we may judge from silence both in Acts and in the epistles, Antioch ceased to be the base of Paul's missionary operations. This may have been because relations were broken off, or possibly for no other reason than that Paul's interests and activities were moving westwards and lines of communication with Antioch would have been inconveniently if not impossibly long. To the theological basis of the dispute in Antioch and Paul's application of it to the Galatian troubles we shall have to return. For a second introductory glimpse of his single-minded and by no means peaceful career we must travel west with him.

Corinth plays a prominent part in both Acts and the Epistles. According to Acts (18: 1) it was Paul's next base after his work in Athens, there that he fell in with Priscilla and Aquila, important in themselves and also (it seems) his first significant link with Rome.

They had left Rome among the Jews expelled by the edict of Claudius. It is no more than a guess, but not a bad one, that the expulsion had been caused by riots attending the first Christian preaching and the founding of the Christian church in Rome; certainly the two are introduced as from the beginning colleagues, not converts, of Paul. Paul's work in Corinth (as described in Acts) follows on a large scale a pattern that is found repeatedly in Acts. He begins in the synagogue, seeking every Sabbath to persuade both Jews and Greeks—the latter, one supposes, Gentiles who were allowed to be present in the synagogue without becoming proselytes —of the truth of the Gospel, 'testifying to the Jews that the Christ was Jesus' (Acts 18: 5). This was the all-important identification, the objective formulation of the Gospel. Some Jews believed, others did not, and reacted violently against Paul. Presumably the synagogue was closed to him, and he moved next door to the house of Titius Justus, with the words 'your blood be on your own head; I am clean. Henceforth I am going to the Gentiles' (18: 6–8). He had begun with the Jews; when they rejected him he turned to the Gentiles. It is however important to observe (as is clear in Acts and is confirmed in the letters to Corinth) that he had already, before the move to Titius Justus's establishment, been persuading Greeks as well as Jews, and that after it he continued to be concerned with Jews. The change, so far as there was one, was relative and at least in part a matter of opportunity. The closing of the synagogue meant that a new approach was necessary. Paul, encouraged by a vision of the Lord himself, remained eighteen months in Corinth—for him, a very long time (Acts 18: 9–11).

It was probably towards the close of this period that the appointment of a new Roman proconsul for the province of Achaea provided an opportunity for Paul's adversaries to move against him. The Jews brought Paul before Gallio on a charge (according to Acts) of notorious ambiguity: He was persuading men to worship God contrary to the law. What law? Did they allege that he was inducing his hearers to adopt a religion that was not recognized by Rome as legitimate and permissible? Or did they assert that his (Christian) version of Judaism was contrary to the true meaning and practice of the Law of Moses? It is impossible to be certain. Gallio (again according to Acts) had no intention of allowing his court to be turned into a religious tribunal and drove the accusers out.

At this point the Acts story of Paul in Corinth comes to an end; but it was by no means the end of Paul's relations with the Corinthian church. These can be reconstructed from the letters

Paul wrote to the church that he had founded. The reconstruction of Paul's correspondence with and visits to Corinth is a complicated matter which it is not necessary to pursue in detail here.[3] He wrote at least four letters and paid one or two visits, one of them a very painful one, which are not recorded in Acts. His experiences in Corinth drew from him, in 2 Corinthians, the most personal, moving, profound, and difficult letter in the whole corpus, a letter that reveals him as a man, an apostle, and a theological thinker at great depth. Inevitably it will be frequently used in this book. For the present we may take a brief glance at 1 Corinthians, which is mainly concerned with questions and problems that had arisen in the life of the Corinthian church. Some of them had been put to Paul in a letter the Corinthians had sent to him; of others he became aware through information that reached him by various channels, some reported by members of Chloe's household (1 Cor 1: 11), some possibly by Stephanas, Fortunatus, and Achaicus, who had visited Paul (16: 17). The church was, if not yet actually divided, in a process of division, a process that manifested itself partly in religious terms, as different coteries idolized different preachers (1: 12), partly in social terms, as rich and poor kept to themselves at the church's supper (11: 18–22). There was a bad case of sexual immorality, which had been treated as a matter of congratulation rather than of shame (5: 1–13) and a general laxness of moral standards (6: 12–20). Church members had gone to law with fellow Christians in secular courts (6: 1–11). The Corinthians sought advice with regard to marriage and singleness (7: 1–40) and with regard to the eating of meat that had been slaughtered in the course of heathen sacrifice (8: 1–13; 10: 1–11: 1). The practice of common worship generated problems too: how, if at all, might women take part? Were speaking with tongues and prophesying both indispensable, and which was to be preferred? (11: 2–16; 12: 1–31; 14: 1–40). There were problems regarding resurrection (15: 1–58). Treatment of these issues was enough to make a long letter, and Paul had words to add about his own and his colleagues' plans, and especially about the collection he was organizing for the benefit of Christians in Jerusalem (16: 1–12).

This long letter marks a stage in the development of Paul's ministry (and therefore also of his thought, which was constantly at work on practical problems) beyond that which had, as far as our evidence goes, been reached in his relations with Antioch, sketched above. At Antioch the difficulty arose out of the attachment of some Christians to the religion of Judaism in which they had been nurtured and of which they wished to preserve what Paul regarded as the wrong elements. In Corinth they were Gentile Christians, still in contact with their pagan past, who caused trouble. So far as this was simple party-spirit, litigiousness, a taste for the sins of the flesh, it was straightforward enough; dangerous enough, but to be countered with an equally straightforward Run from fornication! (1 Cor 6: 18), Run from idolatry! (10: 14). But it was more difficult than that; again religious issues were involved, and on more fronts than one. Behind the arguments on both food sacrificed to idols and resurrection it is possible to trace converging lines of religious thought, both of which provoked response from Paul. The former is the more complicated argument because two parties reached what Paul regarded as the correct answer, but reached it by the wrong methods and handled it in the wrong way. One group built on gnosis — religious knowledge. We know that there is only one god; the sacrifices are therefore offered to non-existent beings, so that the process of sacrifice leaves the meat untouched, unpolluted. It may therefore be eaten. Correct; but what of those Christians who lack your advanced religious knowledge? Another group built on sacraments. We have been baptized; we eat spiritual food and drink spiritual drink. No harm can touch us; we may do what we like, eat whatever we fancy. Do not be so confident; remember the Israelites of old. They had a baptism, they had spiritual food and drink; but they sinned and they perished. And neither of the two groups had learned that freedom is not Christian freedom if it is not directed by love. The gnostics were at work too on the spiritually offensive notion of the rising up of dead bodies. Paul answers them first (1 Cor 15: 1–34). There were others who were puzzled: 'How are the dead raised? With what kind of body do they come?' (15: 35). Paul answers them abruptly (15: 36), but not without sympathy.

Corinth as a Pauline centre follows Antioch chronologically and also points to a different set of contacts, contacts that resulted in a new set of problems, the problems of a church living in and coming to terms with a secular society. For a new Pauline centre we move on in time but hardly in context. Paul spent eighteen months in Corinth; he spent even longer (according to Acts 19: 8, 10; 20: 31) in Ephesus, which may probably be thought of as a fresh base of operations, succeeding Antioch. In Ephesus Paul was within reasonably easy reach of Corinth, also of the Macedonian churches, Philippi and Thessalonica for example, and there was a large and densely populated hinterland. According to Acts 19: 10, while Paul was in Ephesus 'all the inhabitants of (the Roman province of) Asia, both Jews and Greeks, heard the word of the Lord'. This does not mean that Paul himself travelled all over the province, though no doubt from time to time he moved outside the city walls. Acts 19: 22 records that he sent two of his assistants, Timothy and Erastus, to Macedonia, and there is in the epistles sufficient evidence to confirm missions of this kind. Colossians, whether written by Paul or not, attests the existence of Christians in Colossae and Laodicea who knew about Paul though they had not seen his face (2: 1), and at 1: 7 speaks of Epaphras, 'our dear fellow servant', through whom the Colossians learned to know the Gospel. He is described as 'on our behalf a faithful minister of Christ'; that is, he had visited Colossae as an evangelist working with Paul and under his direction. To go further and speak of Ephesus as a centre of Christian organization and administration would be to modernize and distort ancient history, but Acts contains further hints that point in that direction. On his last journey to Jerusalem, Paul passing by ship down the Aegean halts at Miletus, and from there summons the elders (presbyters) of the church in Ephesus, whom he addresses at length, recalling his work in the city. This suggests that there was a recognized and in some way distinctive body of church workers. It appears in the course of Paul's address that the elders are also called bishops (*episkopoi*). The churches of the first journey have a similar organization (14: 23), but it would be unwise to build much on these two passages in view of the fact that the word presbyter does not occur in any of the genuine letters; it probably reflects the period at which Acts was written rather than the period that it describes. It is however not wrong to think of Paul's Ephesian period as one in which the church was becoming something more than the memorial of a travelling evangelist.

If, once more, we may take at least a cue from Acts, we may say that, like Corinth, Ephesus gave the civil authority an opportunity of protecting Paul. Acts 19 describes a serious riot in which Paul was advised by the Asiarchs, who were his friends; the riot was finally quelled by the town clerk, who could not see that Paul and his colleagues had wronged anyone. Dealings with the authorities, however, cannot always have been peaceful. It was at this time that he wrote in 2 Corinthians 11: 23-26, '. . . in prisons more frequently, . . . three times I was beaten with rods [a Roman punishment], . . . in dangers in the city . . .'. Philippians and (if genuine) Colossians, if, as some think, they were written in Ephesus, bear witness to imprisonment there. More probably they were written from Rome; but 1 Corinthians 15: 32 ('If, humanly speaking, I fought with wild beasts in Ephesus') and 2 Corinthians 1: 8 ('Our affliction that happened in Asia'), though notoriously obscure in their precise reference, show clearly enough that the Ephesian period was marked by serious trouble. Like Paul's Corinthian ministry it was punctuated by migration from the synagogue to a secular building (Acts 19: 9), was successful enough to affect the economics of pagan religion (19: 23–27), and threatened the business of magic, for which Ephesus had a special reputation (19: 18, 19). Details apart there is no good reason to doubt the general tenor of these statements in Acts; they could have been made about Paul's work in other cities too.

If it was necessary for Paul to shorten his lines of communication by moving his base from Antioch to Ephesus, then it is clear that Ephesus, having served the provinces of Asia, Macedonia, Achaea, and doubtless others, would itself have to be superseded in the westward drive. It was Paul's intention to continue his mission as far as Spain, and for this destination Greece (including the Greek colonies east of the Aegean) was too remote; he must move on to Italy, and that meant Rome. The letter to the Romans expresses not only a long-felt desire to visit the city (1: 8–15), but the intention to visit it on the way to Spain, and the hope that the Roman Christians would help to send him on his way (15: 24, 28). Put like this, Paul's intention sets Rome alongside Antioch and Ephesus; but Rome differed radically from the other cities in that Paul could write to it; that is, there was already a church there which had never seen him and could not look upon him as its founding apostle. It is clear that Paul considered those to whom he wrote in Rome to be as fully Christian as his own converts; indeed he thanks God that their faith is spoken of throughout the world (Rom 1: 8). But he was not unaware that different preachers preached the Gospel in different ways, and one of his reasons for writing so fully to these Christians whom he did not know was probably to set out, with here and there a polemical touch, his own understanding of Christian truth, with the result that Romans, great as is the value of the other letters, is the classical exposition of Pauline theology. We shall turn to it again and again.

Paul hoped to include Rome in his missionary programme, to contribute something to the development of the church (Rom 1: 11f.) and then to move on to a new mission field in Spain (15: 24, 28). If Acts is to be followed, it did not turn out that way; Paul reached Rome and was welcomed by the local Christians, but he was a prisoner, on appeal to the Emperor's court. The story that takes Paul from Jerusalem to Rome occupies the last eight chapters of Acts and can here be given only in outline, and with little critical examination.

Romans itself tells of Paul's immediate intention, which he must fulfil before his westward move, to visit Jerusalem, taking with him the product of the collection for the poor which he had been making in his Gentile churches (Rom 15: 25-32). He was evidently somewhat doubtful of the welcome that he and his offering would receive, and it is surprising that Acts should barely refer to the collection (24: 17); not surprising that he should be received by the Jerusalem Christians with little warmth (21: 20-25). There was a report that Paul was teaching apostasy from Moses, and it was essential that he should perform some public act that would give the lie to the report. He was asked to join in and to pay for the ceremonial cleansing of a group of Jewish Christians. This he did, accompanying them in the Temple, but the plan was misjudged, for it led to the accusation that he had defiled the Temple by bringing Gentiles into it. The mob set upon him. At this point the Romans, concerned to keep order, became involved. Paul was rescued from lynching and allowed to speak to the crowd, but as soon as he mentioned his vocation to go to the Gentiles the uproar began again and Rome intervened once more. Paul's Roman citizenship (mentioned more than once in Acts, never in the epistles) saved him from examination by flogging, and there began a series of trials (though so formal a word is scarcely proper) in which the Jewish authorities, the Roman tribune (Claudius Lysias), the provincial governor Felix, his successor Festus, and King (Herod) Agrippa II all took part. The upshot was evident from the start. The Jews pressed for a sentence of death against the betrayer of their religion; the Romans could see nothing in the matter beyond a theological dispute in the interpretation of the Jewish religious law and the curious notion that a certain dead Jew, Jesus, was now alive. In the end, in order to escape Jewish plots and to ensure a fair trial, Paul exercised his right as a Roman citizen to appeal to the Emperor. The process of *provocatio* was not an appeal against verdict and sentence; this stage had not been reached. It meant a transference of the case to the higher court. Accordingly Acts concludes with the removal of Paul, under guard and in the exciting circumstances of a storm and shipwreck, from Palestine to Rome. Here he was not only met by Christians but conversed with Jews, and remained, still under guard but with a limited measure of freedom, for two years. At this point the story ends. The narrative in Acts, here briefly sketched, is like all ancient historical sources open to criticism; but when Acts closes there is not even anything to criticize.

Did Paul, released from captivity, continue his journey to Spain? Was he re-arrested and executed? Or did the two years of Acts 28: 30 end in his death? *1 Clement* (5: 7) claims that Paul went to the 'limit of the west' before he 'bore witness (*martyrēsas*) before the authorities'. This (given the intention clearly expressed in Romans) suggests that he travelled to Spain before dying as a martyr. The Pastoral Epistles, on the other hand, which speak of a 'first defence' in court (2 Tim 4: 16) and plainly suggest that death was near (4: 6–8), seem to imply a return to the east (1 Tim 1: 3; 2 Tim 1: 15, 18; 4: 13, 20; Titus 1: 5; 3: 12). Paul may have done both, he may have done neither; we do not know. Later tradition points out his prison and his place of martyrdom at Tre Fontane at Rome, and there is theological appropriateness if something less than historical conviction in the rough inscription on the fourth-century sepulchral slab in S. Paolo fuori le Mura: PAULO APOSTOLO MART.

A life of Paul has no necessary place in a discussion of the apostle as a Christian thinker, and all that has been offered here is a sequence of glimpses of the man in various settings, chosen because they represent some of the major stages of his career and included because he was not an abstract thinker, given to speculation about abstract truth. He was a preacher, missionary, and pastor; he was these things because of certain fundamental theological convictions which had been given to him, as he believed, by divine authority. The authority was conveyed along two channels, never, he believed, in contradiction but often in tension with each other. There was the authority of Scripture, that is, of what Christians call the Old Testament; and there was the authority of Jesus Christ, 'crucified, yea rather risen' (Rom 8: 34). The centrality of preaching in Paul's understanding of his vocation will repeatedly appear. It must already be apparent that, though he did not seek it, he was unable to avoid controversy. It was in controversy rather than in any other context that his theology was shaped and developed; and it is to his controversies that we must now turn.

Notes

1 See e.g. W. G. Kümmel, *Einleitung in das Neue Testament* (19th edn, 1978; ET: *Introduction to the New Testament*, 1975).

2 See K. Stendahl, *Paul Among Jews and Gentiles* (1977), pp. 7–23.

3 See C. K. Barrett, *1 Corinthians* (2nd edn, 1986), pp. 11–17; *2 Corinthians* (1973), pp. 11–25.

2

Paul's controversies

The first chapter will have made it clear that Paul was not the kind of theologian who can with any plausibility be alleged to have spent his time in peaceful meditation, insulated in his ivory tower from the tumult and conflict of the world. He worked at two jobs at once, working with his hands to make a living and at the same time occupied as preacher, pastor, and theologian — not three additional vocations but one, for his work as preacher and pastor was theologically determined and, in reverse, fertilized his theology. As a preacher he was despised, as a pastor he was flouted, and as a theologian he was constantly engaged in controversy with those who bitterly disagreed with him. Perhaps he was too disposed to see theological issues in blacks and whites; but truth was truth, and it had to be fought for; better a church in conflict than a church in error. And often it was in conflict — conflict with others, but sometimes, it seems, conflict within his own mind — that he found the truth, or came to see more in the truth he already knew, or discovered the way to express truth and apply it to the circumstances in which he lived.

Conflict was inevitable, for early Christianity was a diverse phenomenon. This too was inevitable. Jesus had left his followers with, in the ordinary sense of the terms, no dogmatics, no code of ethics, no church order, and no liturgy. True, he had had, even when he cried out on the cross that he could not understand what God was up to (Mark 15: 34), an unshakable conviction of the reality of God, a God who was understood not as the idea of the good or the ground of being but as the loving heavenly Father. True, even if he had

22

never taught anything by speech, his own way of living and his own way of dying would have communicated something of an ethical ideal. But he left in his remembered words what is virtually a contradiction or annihilation of every church order already known or to be generated after his death:

> You know that those who are supposed to rule over the nations lord it over them and their great ones exercise authority over them; but it is not like that among you. Whoever wishes to be great among you shall be your servant, and whoever wishes to be first among you shall be slave of all. (Mark 10: 43, 44)

And though there is no liturgy to match that of Temple and Synagogue, he did hope that they would remember him when they sat down to eat bread and drink wine.

Jesus died; and whatever he had said to them his disciples had not grasped the notion that a couple of days later he would be with them again. But he was; and, whatever the modern believer and unbeliever may make of the Easter stories, the disciples of Jesus were convinced that he was alive, not a surviving spirit or ghost, but a raised-up man. In the light of this conviction they found themselves obliged to improvise those things with which they had not been provided. The improvisations might not have to last long; one miracle may well be followed by another, and the Lord who had been raised from death would no doubt soon appear as Son of man with the clouds of heaven. Liturgy and church order hardly mattered, and dogmatics and ethics could for the most part be taken over and adapted from the Judaism in which the first disciples had grown up, though both found a new centre in the overwhelming experience of the resurrection appearances — how overwhelming, it requires a considerable exercise of the historical imagination to conceive. This could not be forgotten and it inevitably controlled the process of improvisation and extemporization that went on in the first months and years. *Control*, however, is perhaps too strong a word. The earliest disciples, though no doubt for the most part faithful Jews, were not trained and gifted theologians, and had no experience of critical thought, and there could be no serious Christian theology until someone with these qualifications appeared. He was not long in coming. Paul's conversion cannot be precisely dated, but there is no doubt that it took place little if any more than three years after the crucifixion. A profound critical mind was now at work on the Christian tradition, especially upon the basic fact of Christ crucified and risen.

There are in his writings traces of his work on unsatisfactory earlier attempts to express basic Christian truth. 'Unsatisfactory' is not necessarily a condemnatory term; the attempts were usually, probably always, well-meaning; they conveyed some part of the truth, but did so in an incomplete and therefore unbalanced way. A clear and illuminating example of Paul's critical work on earlier tradition is probably to be seen in the opening verses of Romans. In Romans 1: 3, 4, as they stand, Paul defines the Gospel of God as 'Good news about his Son, who in the sphere of the flesh was born of the family of David, in the sphere of the Holy Spirit was appointed Son of God in power after his resurrection from the dead'. This calls to mind immediately the parallelism of clauses that is the commonest poetical form in the Old Testament:

Who in the sphere of the flesh . . .
    in the sphere of the Holy Spirit . . .

But it is a rather clumsy unbalanced parallelism; the second clause has too many members. It has however another feature, not apparent in my translation, that recalls the Old Testament, the Hebrew in which it was written, and the Aramaic that tended to replace Hebrew in common use. 'The Holy Spirit' is literally 'the Spirit of holiness'; 'of holiness' serves the purpose of an adjective, so that 'Holy Spirit' is not an incorrect rendering, but Paul never uses this form elsewhere in his extant writings. It was however the common way of referring to the Holy Spirit in Hebrew and Aramaic literature. It seems plausible to suggest that there was once a very early – Hebrew or Aramaic – Christian formula that spoke of Christ in the two parallel statements

In the sphere of the flesh he was born of the family of David;
In the sphere of the Holy Spirit he was appointed Son of God.

The two propositions were bound together by the fundamental conviction, after his resurrection from the dead. Paul had no great interest in the family of David (in only one other place – Romans 15: 12 – does he mention the matter and that in an Old Testament quotation that refers not to David but to his father Jesse), but the word Christ (Messiah) implies it and Paul would certainly not have denied the Davidic descent of Jesus; and he would only have applauded the reference to the resurrection. But *appointed* was wrong. A Son of God, a divine being, does not come into being in

24

or about the year AD 30; he must be, Paul knew, pre-existent (Gal 4: 4). The formula, however, which Paul probably wished to use in the opening lines of Romans partly because it would introduce him suitably as a genuine Christian to his unknown correspondents in Rome, could be saved by a small addition. Damage to the metre was a small price to pay for mending the sense, and Paul adds *in power*. This suggests a contrast, historically and theologically correct, between the frail, vulnerable, and eventually destroyed human life of Jesus of Nazareth, and the victorious glory of the risen Lord. There is no hint of controversy here; a stroke of the pen puts the matter right.

It was not always so simple. Improvisations in theology and practice did not always follow the same lines, and once a line of thought or behaviour had become established it generated a life of its own. A formula could be put right by a couple of words; people could not be corrected so easily, and in the New Testament divergent strands of doctrine and behaviour can be discerned. It has, for example, been rightly pointed out that Acts contains more than one Christology.[1] Up to a point different ways of apprehending Christian truth can live at peace with one another, each recognizing others as valid though partial statements of the faith, Christians picking out their own points for emphasis without denying that others have a right to other emphases. This however is not the only impression given by the Pauline letters. There were some interpretations of the Gospel, other than his own, that Paul could live with; there were others that he could view only as destructive of the Gospel and therefore of his work in the interests of the Gospel. The exponents of such views were in fact out to destroy Paul's work, and in the cause of truth he made it his business to destroy theirs. The bitter conflicts that resulted have often been passed over, but they have been recognized by the greatest of Pauline scholars, of whom it will suffice to quote J. B. Lightfoot. Of the apostolic age in general he writes:

> However great may be the theological differences and religious animosities of our own time [he was writing in 1865], they are far surpassed in magnitude by the distractions of an age which, closing our eyes to facts, we are apt to invest with ideal excellence. In the early Church was fulfilled, in its inward dissensions no less than in its outward sufferings, the Master's sad warning that He came 'not to send peace on earth, but a sword.' (*The Epistle to the Galatians*, p. 374)

25

Of Paul more particularly, he writes 'The systematic hatred of St Paul is an important fact, which we are too apt to overlook, but without which the whole history of the Apostolic ages will be misread and misunderstood' (p. 311). There is no word of exaggeration in this; what needs to be added is that without this element of controversy Paul would not have been the theologian that he was; his mind became even sharper than the sharpest words he used in reply to those who attacked him and his message.

CONTROVERSY IN GALATIA

The classical example of Pauline controversy is found in the Epistle to the Galatians. Paul could recall his first visit to the area and the extraordinary reception the Galatians had given him. He was a sick man; he would not have been surprised had they spat on him; instead 'you received me as an angel of God, as if I were Christ Jesus . . . if it had been possible you would have plucked out your eyes and given them to me' (4: 14, 15). But that attitude had gone, and Paul could only say 'I can't think what to do with you' (4: 20). There were new missionaries who were corrupting the Gospel and thereby destroying the church, whose only foundation was the creative message God had given in Christ. These missionaries were (that is, they claimed to be) Christians, and to be preaching the Gospel (1: 7-9). But it was a different Gospel from the one Paul preached, and, since there was only one Gospel, that meant that theirs was no Gospel at all; they were perverting the Gospel of Christ. They did not reject Christ; had they done so Paul would have found the situation easier to deal with. They regarded Paul's message of Christ only as inadequate. We can probably reconstruct their message from Galatians 5: 2, which presupposes the claim 'If you are not circumcised, that is, if you do not become proper proselytes to Judaism, Christ, mere faith in Christ, will do you no good'. Something like this is presupposed by what is clearly a rejoinder: 'Look! this is what I, Paul, say to you: If you *are* circumcised Christ will do you no good'. If you try to add something to Christ you will lose Christ. This inference is confirmed by another allusive passage. It was claimed that the Gentile Galatians had made a good beginning by accepting Christ; they were now on the right road to Judaism; it remained for them to complete the process by entering fully, by way of circumcision, into the Jewish religion. Paul replies:

This is all I want to learn from you: did you receive the Spirit as the result of doing works in obedience to the Law or by hearing [the Gospel] in faith? Are you so senseless? Having begun with the Spirit are you finishing with the flesh? (3: 2, 3)

Paul replies to his opponents, who are clearly winning the ear and the heart of his Galatian Christians, with direct negatives of this kind, and with aspersions (whether or not these were wholly justified we cannot tell) on their motives and sincerity.

It is those who wish to make a fair show in the flesh who are trying to compel you to be circumcised; and they only do it in order not to be persecuted for the cross of Christ. For not even do those who are circumcised keep the Law, but they wish you to be circumcised that they may glory in your flesh. (6: 12, 13)

According to this, the circumcisers have a double motive. Jewish authorities will persecute those who, like Paul (cf. 1 Cor 2: 2), preach only Christ crucified; one may escape this persecution by adding the requirement of circumcision, that is, of proselytization. But also to insist on circumcision gives those who require it a sense of power over their converts; they have something, a visible mark in your flesh, over which they can boast and congratulate themselves. Fortunately (for hard words, even Paul's, do not constitute adequate rebuttal) Paul supports his position on both historical and theological grounds, and his argument has the additional value of permitting us, within limits, to reconstitute theirs.

Paul sets out the history first, in Galatians 1 and 2, and in this we may follow him. The remainder of the first chapter is an elaboration of its first verse: 'Paul, an apostle not from men or through man, but through Jesus Christ, and God the Father who raised him from the dead'. This probably reflects the fact (see above) that Paul was no longer what he had at first been, an apostle, an accredited representative, of the church in Antioch. This relation probably ended with the dispute of Galatians 2: 11; but the severance was not the end of Paul's apostleship, an office, or function, given to Paul by no human authority but by Christ himself, in a calling described in terms used in the Old Testament for the vocation of prophets (Gal 1: 15f.; cf. e.g. Isa 49: 1; Jer 1: 4–10). This vocation accompanied, or resulted in, a complete change in his life, as has been mentioned above. What is to be noted now is that this new vocation gave him a new form of authority, at once more powerful and more vulnerable. It was more powerful because it came directly from God and was itself a part of the Gospel Paul was commissioned to preach; and it was vulnerable because there was no means of proving that it existed at all. Not only indeed was there no means of proving it; it was manifested in what must have seemed, and to many did seem, a contradiction of itself. It was manifested most fully in Paul's weakness — a fact that will become clearer when we turn to the Corinthian epistles.

Already before the break with Antioch Paul had become aware of a radical divergence between himself and those who claimed (probably with a greater show of authority, because they were connected with Jerusalem, the original centre of the Christian faith) to represent the true Christian Gospel. The divergence was so sharp that it would have brought to nothing the work Paul had already done; there was a danger that he might be running or have run in vain (Gal 2: 2). Accordingly he (accompanied by Barnabas, the Christian Jew, and Titus, the Christian Gentile) went up to Jerusalem to thrash the matter out. There it became clear that Paul had to deal with two distinguishable groups. First were the *false brothers* (Gal 2: 4, 5), for whom Paul has no good word. They sneaked in as spies, trying to find out what they could about the freedom which for Paul was the mark of the Gospel, not in order that they might share it and disseminate it in the Gentile world, but in order to put an end to it; 'that they might enslave us'. They would have had Titus circumcised; but Paul would have none of that (Gal 2: 3); not for a moment did he give way to their demands but maintained the truth of the Gospel (Gal 2: 5).[2] For these false brothers, though (as the word *brother* shows) they desired to be recognized as Christians, Christianity was essentially Judaism and its basis was the Law, including circumcision, on which stress was inevitably laid if only because it constituted the way into Jewish life.

Had this been the only group he had to deal with in Jerusalem Paul's task would have been stern enough, but it would also have been simple. They said no to him, and he said no to them. But they were not the leading figures in the Jerusalem church. There were others who were spoken of, and liked to speak of themselves, as pillars, the base on which the people of God, compared to a building, rested. These were Peter (whose Aramaic name Cephas is also used), James (presumably the brother of Jesus), and John (presumably one of the sons of Zebedee). Paul makes it clear that he did not consider that they had any special authority (Gal 2: 6), but as a matter of policy he laid before them the Gospel that he preached among the Gentiles (Gal 2: 2). They 'added nothing to him' (2: 6) — which may mean either that they added no fresh propositions to the content of his message or that they conferred no additional authority upon him, or possibly both — but recognized that he had been entrusted with the Gospel for the uncircumcised as Peter with that for the circumcised (2: 7), and this not simply as a human arrangement but as a gift of divine grace (2: 9). On the strength of this recognition the Pillars gave to Paul and Barnabas the right hand of fellowship; that is, they shook hands on the agreement that 'we [Paul and his partners] should go to the Gentiles, they to the circumcision', that is, to the Jews. There was no other requirement (such as, that Gentile converts should be circumcised), but the Jewish apostles hoped that Paul and his colleagues would remember the poor (in the Jerusalem church). Paul needed no persuading to do this.

This probably appeared to Paul a satisfactory arrangement. He had got what he wanted; he could continue his mission, and on the old lines. If he thought in this way he had not considered fully what had, and especially what had not, been said. The Pillars had conceded that Paul had been entrusted with 'the Gospel of the uncircumcision' — a message for Gentiles, as Peter had been entrusted with 'that of the circumcision' — a message for Jews; that he who had created for Peter an apostolate to the circumcision had given Paul a mission (it may not be accidental that the word 'apostolate' — *apostolē* — is not used) to the Gentiles. But the two Gospels and the two missions are not related to each other; and Paul in Galatians (1: 6, 7) has already made it clear that he knows only one Gospel. And was Peter never to preach to and convert a Gentile? Paul never to exercise a mission to Jews? A great deal had been left unsaid, not necessarily out of malice or guile, but with divisive results, which inevitably, and surely foreseeably, manifested themselves as soon as the scene shifted from Jerusalem (where the church must have been nearly 100 per cent Jewish) to Antioch, where the church was mixed. Paul was there, Peter was there, and all went well. Jewish Christians and Gentile Christians joined together in the Christian fellowship meal. This happy state was interrupted when messengers arrived from James. Paul does not tell us what they said, but the essence of it is clear from its effect. Not only Peter but Paul's colleague Barnabas (who knew what had been said in Jerusalem) and the other Jewish Christians withdrew and separated themselves from their uncircumcised non-Jewish Christian brothers. The messengers must have said something like

'At Jerusalem we agreed that Paul might take his Gospel to the Gentiles and that Gentile believers might be recognized as Christians. We did not say that uncircumcised Gentile believers might, on the strength of their faith in Christ, be admitted to fellowship with Jews. The old distinction is still valid and must be strictly enforced.' Paul says (Gal 2: 12) that Peter acted as he did because he was afraid of 'the circumcision party' (*those of the circumcision*). This must mean that James's group were insisting upon circumcision as the means of entry into the people of God; and this insistence is what makes the story Paul tells relevant to the situation in Galatia. What is not clear is precisely how those who infiltrated the Galatian churches and there demanded the circumcision of those who had already become Christians were related to the false brothers, to the Pillars, to Peter (evidently a somewhat mobile figure), and to James. We must put up with our ignorance, and it is no severe hardship in our present inquiry, for we know something of the arguments they used in support of their requirements, and have Paul's theological response.

Inevitably the argument was conducted on the basis of Scripture (that is, of course, the Old Testament) and it supplies the background of Galatians 3 and 4, where Paul wrestles with a number of Old Testament passages which it is unlikely that he would have chosen for himself but was obliged to deal with because they had been used by his opponents.

They began with Abraham. It was to Abraham that the promises were made, and to his family, with him that God entered into covenant. The people of God were thus constituted by the descendants of Abraham, joined by any willing to assimilate themselves to the family by the sign of the covenant, circumcision. This argument Paul seems to dispose of in his first four verses (3: 6–9); in fact Abraham, a key figure, will return, but the beginning is radical. Making the assumption (of which we shall hear again) that man, to be saved, must be righteous before God, must have righteousness, Paul turns to Genesis 15: 6: Abraham believed God, and it was counted to him as righteousness. So (Paul argues) the essential thing in Abraham was believing, trusting, faith; it is therefore (not those sprung from his body but) those who depend on faith who are, in the theological sense, sons of Abraham. Moreover, God said to Abraham (Gen 12: 3; 18: 18) 'In thee shall all the nations (or Gentiles; *ethnē*) be blessed'. This shows that it was from the beginning God's intention to include the Gentiles in the blessing prepared for Abraham, his chosen one.

30

To this Pauline exegesis it was possible for the circumcision party to reply: Abraham is only part of the story, and Abraham must be interpreted in terms of the rest. The great figure of Abraham is followed by an even greater, Moses, the giver of the Law, and the promise to Abraham is to be understood in the light of the Law. Consideration of this theme falls into two paragraphs.

No doubt it was Paul's opponents who first quoted Deuteronomy 27: 26 (Gal 3: 10): 'Cursed is everyone who does not abide in all the things that are written in the Law, so as to do them'. The inference is clear: You, Paul, and your party, do not conform to the legal requirement of circumcision (and doubtless many other requirements too); you are under a curse. The logic of Paul's reply runs as follows. What does abiding in the things written in the Law mean? Just listening to them? Certainly not; Law is concerned with doing, hence that other text in the Law (Lev 18: 5), 'He who has done them shall live by them'. So if we are to have life, which all desire, we must, if we depend on Law, do the things it prescribes. But Scripture itself (Hab 2: 4) declares that this is not the way to life: 'He who is righteous by faith [which is quite different from doing] shall live'. The way to life is the righteousness which is God's gift to faith. This shows that in fact no one (not even the most observant Jew) does abide in all the things written in the Law. The effect of the Law therefore is a universal curse on all mankind. A grim conclusion! But the Law itself points outside itself to the way of hope. Accursed is every one who hangs on a tree (Deut 21: 23; Gal 3: 13). This is the crucified Christ; he has absorbed our curse and freed us from it. This is how the blessing of Abraham comes in Christ Jesus to the Gentiles (Gal 3: 14).

This brings us back to Abraham and the second argument. It seems (if we may argue back from Paul's reply to the case that he was rejecting) that the Galatian Judaizers took the view that the terms of the covenant made by God with Abraham had now, since the time and through the work of Moses, been modified. To Abraham God had made a gracious promise and the only response he looked for was faith; but the Law marks a new stage in the development of God's dealings with his people. Not faith alone, but concrete and detailed obedience to specific commandments, such as those relating to circumcision and the festivals in the national calendar, was required, and membership of the people of God, who alone might hope to receive the promised blessing, was conditional upon such obedience. Whether all first-century Jews took this view is a question too wide to be discussed here; it is probable that many

31

of them did, and as good as certain that it was maintained in Galatia. If it was not so there is little point in Galatians 3: 15–20. The Greek word for covenant (*diathēkē*) also means 'testament', and Paul plays on the ambiguity. God made a covenant (*diathēkē*) with Abraham; but when a human being makes a testament (*diathēkē*) and it is duly ratified, no one can annul it or make any addition to it. Correspondingly the covenant of promise ratified by God to Abraham cannot be annulled and the promise made void by the Law, which was given 430 years after Abraham's time. The Law, whatever its purpose may have been, could not change the covenant of grace, promise, and faith. In reaching this conclusion however Paul has left a loophole in his argument. He was well aware of it; probably he had used the argument in oral debate and his opponent would not be slow to point out the flaw. Paul's answer is ready. 'You say, Paul, that no one can vary the terms of a will or add a codicil to it, but there is one person who can — the testator himself. This is what we are saying: God himself varied the terms of the Abrahamic covenant when he enacted the Mosaic.' Paul replies: 'The very fact that the covenant was made through Moses disproves your case. Moses was there to act as a mediator. But a mediator is not needed when two individuals (as God and Abraham) are dealing with each other; Moses the mediator was needed to establish relations between on the one hand the Israelites and on the other not God (who is one) but the angels, who are the true givers of the Law. Thus the Law, if not actually contrary to the promises, is inferior to them and cannot annul them.' This leaves us with the question what in fact the Law was intended to do, and to this we shall have to return. There is however another point that must be mentioned now though to this also we shall have to come back. Paul picks up the formulation of the promise in Genesis 13: 15; 17: 8; 24: 7. In its characteristic form it is made 'to thee and to thy seed'. The word 'seed' (*sperma*) is indeed normally a collective noun, but it is used rather than a plural (such as children) that might have been used, and Paul fastens on the singular number: 'It does not say *seeds* as with reference to many, but with reference to one: *and to thy seed*' (Gal 3: 16). He adds immediately 'That one seed is Christ'. This is a curious argument, or seems so in the twentieth century, but it is not unintelligible. 'Seed of Abraham' is a term of which God supplies the meaning. In the first generation, the seed of Abraham was Isaac, not Ishmael or any other of the sons of Abraham's body; in the next generation the seed was Jacob, and Esau his twin was rejected. The fulfilment of the covenant of grace and promise was in Christ.

32

Hence (and it is here that Paul's argument becomes fully relevant) membership of the people of God is defined in terms of being in Christ, not of being circumcised.

We return to the argument of the Galatian circumcisers with one more Old Testament passage, again relating to Abraham. Abraham had (in accordance with law current in his day) a concubine as well as a wife: a free woman and a servant, Sarah and Hagar. Sarah's son was Isaac, and from him (no doubt it was argued) the Israelites are descended; they, as they observe the Law, are the heirs of the promise. And they did not forget that the story ended (Gen 21: 10) with the command 'Cast out the slave woman and her son, for the son of the slave shall not inherit with the son of the free woman' (Gal 4: 30). It was by an elaborate exegetical device (which I have described in detail elsewhere[3]) that Paul was able to reverse the argument, showing that the law-keeping Christians were the slaves, while the converts of his law-free Gospel were the free people of God, the children not of the earthly Jerusalem but of the heavenly Jerusalem.

It is possible thus to get a glimpse of the way in which Paul's opponents in Jerusalem understood Judaism, and the way in which they developed their case. The heart of Judaism was the Law, and the Law was a matter not of faith but of doing things (Gal 3: 12), such as, in the first instance, of carrying out the initial requirement of circumcision. Whatever may have been true in the time of Abraham, since Moses the covenant was a covenant of law. There is no need here to develop at length the view that Paul set over against this Judaizing understanding of the Law and of the calling of Israel; this will appear below. It may be said that he had a new understanding of Israel and its place in the purpose of God, a new exegesis of the Old Testament, a new covenant, and a new people, in which there could be neither Jew nor Greek, bond nor free, male nor female (3: 28). All was focused upon the one central figure of Christ.

CONTROVERSY IN CORINTH

On the surface the position in Corinth seems very different from that in Galatia; under the surface they have much in common. The practical problems that make up the agenda of 1 Corinthians have already been mentioned; they will appear again when it is time to consider Paul's ethical teaching in detail but they are not controversy in the sense in which the term is used in this chapter. There are hints of it in 1 Corinthians. Presumably those who said 'I am of Paul', 'I am of Apollos', 'I am of Cephas', 'I am of Christ' (1 Cor 1: 12) did not agree with one another in all respects and there were divergent views on such matters as marriage, the place and role of women in the church, the eating of meat sacrificed to idols, and speaking with tongues. These Paul could deal with, not without difficulty but not without effect, in the exercise of his pastoral ministry in the local community. Their importance (for our present interest) is that they could be used to provide a foothold for those who came into Corinth from without, bringing their controversial programme with them. In 2 Corinthians a number of anonymous figures appear. It is evident that an unfortunate event—which for lack of evidence we cannot describe—happened on a visit by Paul which is not recorded in Acts. It was so unpleasant that Paul changed his plans, deciding that he would not come to Corinth again 'in sorrow' (2 Cor 2: 1) and inviting thereby the complaint that he was fickle in his relations with the church (1: 17). There was someone who had caused sorrow (2: 5)—not, Paul insists, to himself but in some measure to the whole church. It is often thought that this person, the one who did wrong (7: 12),[4] was a Corinthian, but it is more probable that he came from elsewhere. 'You—Corinthians—showed that you were innocent in the matter' (7: 11); their fault had been only that they had not more vigorously taken Paul's part. This event, Paul might hope, he had put behind him. Perhaps he had; we cannot with confidence identify this wrongdoer with others who are to be noted.

The epistle as it stands in the New Testament takes a turn between chapters 9 and 10, perhaps because the last four chapters (10–13) were written a little later than 1–9. It is immediately clear that bad opinions of Paul are current. 'When he is absent he is bold enough, but when present he is mean-spirited' (10: 1). It may be—one cannot be absolutely confident—that these opinions are to be associated with one particular person. 'If anyone is confident that he belongs to Christ, let him take account of this, that as he belongs to Christ so also do we' (10: 7). 'Anyone'—'he'—'him'—'he': these may be pure generalizations, but they may refer to a person not named but clearly to be recognized. 'His letters are weighty and strong, but his bodily presence is feeble and his speech to be despised' (10: 10). This opinion is introduced by a word (*phēsin*) whose normal meaning is *he says*, though it could be taken to mean *people say, it is said*. There is similar evidence in 11: 4: 'If he who comes preaches

another Jesus, whom we did not preach, or you receive a different
Spirit, which you did not [at first] receive, or a different Gospel,
which you did not [at first] accept, you put up with him all right'.
The verse is sometimes understood as if it said 'If anyone comes
and preaches . . .', but it does not say this. There is a clear reference
to 'the one who comes' (*ho erchomenos*), and we must suppose that
the Corinthians knew very well who was meant, though we do not.
If however there lurks behind 2 Corinthians a particular person he
was not alone but (presumably) the ringleader of a group. A very
obscure passage (obscure mainly because allusive, and we do not
know the allusions) at the end of 2 Corinthians 10 (10: 12-16) refers
in the plural to persons who do what Paul will not do, commending
themselves and comparing themselves with themselves (and thus to
their own advantage), boasting in a foolish and unmeasured way of
what lies outside their province. Analysis of the situation is complicated by the fact that Paul appears to refer to two groups. In
11: 13-15 he refers to men of whom no good can be said. They are
false apostles, servants of Satan;[5] they disguise themselves as
servants of righteousness, but it is a disguise comparable with
Satan's camouflage as an angel of light. Thus they are *deceitful
workmen*. Traces of them are to be seen elsewhere in 2 Corinthians
10 - 13, but it is hard to think that they are referred to in 11: 22-29.
Here we have men who are Jews (*Hebrews, Israelites, seed of
Abraham*), but also *servants of Christ*, a status Paul does not deny
them; he adds, recognizing his own folly in doing so, that he is even
more a servant of Christ than they, but this is certainly not a denial.
The same persons cannot be servants of Satan and servants of
Christ. Again, there are those whom Paul describes (11: 5; 12: 11)
as *super-apostles* (*hyperlian apostoloi*); these cannot be equated
with the *false apostles*. Moreover, Paul compares himself with
them; in no way did he, in his Corinthian mission, come short
of them. It is surely inconceivable that he should say 'I reckon I
am just about as good as the servants of the Devil'. The existence
of these two groups reminds the reader of Galatians. In that epistle
there were those whom Paul calls not false apostles but *false
brothers*; the difference is not great. And there are those whom
Paul calls not super-apostles but *pillars*; again the difference is
not great. False brothers and false apostles he can have no dealings
with; of super-apostles and pillars he speaks with nothing worse
than irony. God is no respecter of persons, even of theirs (Gal 2: 6);
I am at least as good as they are (2 Cor 11: 5; 12: 11), better indeed
in the sense that I have suffered more (2 Cor 11: 23-33). The

parallels do not prove identity, but at least they suggest similarity and relation.

It is probably a correct observation that Paul was obliged to fight the intruders at Corinth with one hand tied behind his back. They came bearing letters of commendation (2 Cor 3: 1; cf. 4: 2; 5: 12; 6: 4; 10: 12, 18; 12: 11, for the theme of commendation); from whom? In all probability from Jerusalem. To say this is not to say that James and others in the Jerusalem church approved of all that their protégés were doing; it must have been very difficult, was probably impossible, to control them at a distance. But if they could use the great names of the mother church Paul must have felt that there were limits (even if he exceeded them in 2 Corinthians 11: 13-15) to what he could do and say without breaking off relations with men who had given him a measure of approval in Jerusalem (Gal 2: 6-10). He is prepared to claim equality with them, and claims to exceed them in what he has endured for Christ, but as far as they themselves are concerned he will go no further.

If the Corinthian intruders came bearing commendatory letters from the Jerusalem church, they must have been Judaizers. This, it is often said, they cannot have been, because in the Corinthian letters we read nothing of a demand for circumcision. This lay at the heart of the Judaizing mission in Galatia, and it is natural to take it as the hallmark of any Judaizing movement. This however is not necessarily true, and it seems to have been one of the marks of the anti-Pauline mission in Corinth that it was quick to adopt any methods that would make it attractive to the Corinthian constituency. It is clear that those who caused the trouble were, or at least claimed to be, Christians. From 2 Corinthians 11: 4 we see that they preached a Gospel, but it was not what Paul recognized as the Gospel; in their Gospel they proclaimed Jesus, but it was 'another Jesus', that is, they interpreted Jesus in a way different from Paul's way. The reader of 2 Corinthians is reminded of 5: 16. There was a time when Paul knew, interpreted, Jesus *according to the flesh* (*kata sarka*); he now understood him so no longer; but he is (one may suppose) aware of those who do still understand him according to the flesh. It is not a fleshly, truly human, Christ that Paul repudiates but a human, man-centred, way of understanding him, and (though we cannot know this for certain) the man-centred interpretation of Jesus would be one that saw him as no more than a Messiah whose work and benefits were man-centred. As a result of hearing and receiving this Gospel, which was no Gospel, the Corinthians had received a different Spirit. The meaning of this is probably that the visitors encouraged the natural Corinthian predilection for such spiritual gifts as speaking with tongues, seeing in these the authentic marks of the Spirit of God, whereas Paul looked for these on the lines of Galatians 5: 22, 23. The theme which more than any other runs through 2 Corinthians 10 – 13 is boasting (*kauchasthai*). It appears at once (10: 13–16) that the difference between Paul and his adversaries is that they boast and he does not; he could, for the very existence of a church in Corinth was his work not theirs; but they will pick up another man's work, invade his territory, compare themselves with themselves, and find plenty to boast about. They transgress the rule that Paul quotes from Scripture (10: 17; Jer 9: 22, 23): he that boasts (*or* glories), let him boast (glory) in the Lord. What matters is not to commend oneself but to be commended by the Lord (10: 18).

In 2 Corinthians 11 Paul tries a new line of thought. Boasting is foolish; but let us try a little folly. With passionate and biting irony, which sometimes cuts like a knife and sometimes breaks down into the non-ironical outcry of a man goaded beyond literary form so as to expose his own heart, Paul enters upon the forbidden territory of comparison and boasting. 'Put up with a little folly on my part; you put up with it readily enough from others. If the intruder who seduces you from loyalty to Christ preaches to you another Christ, you put up with him; why not with me? You should do so, for I do not need to compare myself with him; I don't think I come short of the super-apostles in Jerusalem. I may not be good at speech, but I know the truth, and however bad the teaching method was I did communicate that to you. Yes, I know, I did it for nothing; you didn't have to pay; gifts from other churches kept me so that I could give you the impression that I was a poor teacher who knew that his lessons were not worth paying for. Well, that – giving the Gospel away for nothing – is what I boast about, and no one shall stop me. What's that? It shows I don't love you? God knows the truth about that. Let your boastful friends prove their apostleship by my kind of behaviour.'

At this point the irony stops, or takes a different form, nearer to direct attack, 'I know they think of themselves as servants of righteousness, offering you the righteousness of the Law. That means nothing. We know that Satan can disguise himself as an angel of light; small wonder if his servants too are good at disguise.'

'Let us get back to the business of playing the fool. I too will boast of very human qualifications. Take the men in Jerusalem. Whatever they are, I am. Whatever they have done, I have done more.

Whatever they have suffered, I have suffered more. And that indeed is the point. If I am to boast I shall boast not of my strength but of my weakness. Take another field of religious life: visions and divine revelations. I have things here that I could tell, if it were legitimate for a man to tell what he had seen in Paradise, in the third heaven. That I am not allowed to do; more than that, so great was the exaltation I experienced that God in his goodness gave me, to compensate for it, to prevent any sinful boasting, a thorn in my flesh, a messenger of Satan sent to beat me. I asked God to take it away, asked him three times; and he answered, My grace is enough for you; for power comes to perfection in weakness.'

So much for folly; the Corinthians had asked for it, and got it. In the rest of the epistle Paul turns to straightforward self-defence — and attack. Two historical inferences may be drawn with some confidence. Those who were actually in Corinth associated themselves — perhaps more closely than the truth would warrant — with the Jerusalem apostles, and used this association as a means of impressing the Corinthians, whom they ordered about (11: 20) and made to pay for the privilege of being their disciples. They must have been Jews, and taught a way of righteousness, which since it was (one may infer from 5: 16; 11: 4) not found in Christ was no doubt found in the Law. The argument that since they did not (so far as our texts go) insist on circumcision they cannot have been Judaizers is fallacious; Peter did not insist on circumcision but could (on occasion if not always) behave as a Judaizer (Gal 2: 11, 14). Secondly, they were clever enough to adapt themselves to the criteria which (as 1 Corinthians shows plainly enough) the church at Corinth would naturally use in the assessment of apostolic messengers. They were fine, inspired, speakers (10: 10; 11: 6; cf. e.g. 1 Cor 1: 5), they performed signs, portents, and mighty works (2 Cor 12: 12 — for himself, Paul adds 'in all endurance'), they bore commendatory letters (3: 1, and all the references to commendation), they saw visions (which the Corinthians, eager to enjoy spiritual gifts, must have admired), they expected to be paid for their services, and they imposed themselves as superior persons on their inferiors (11: 20). A picture emerges of the situation in which Paul had to fight these servants of Satan in order to rescue the sycophantic Corinthians from their grasp. Through the conflict (as in Galatia) his thought was fixed on the figure of the crucified Christ. 'We are weak in him, but we shall live with him' (13: 4).[6]

CONTROVERSY IN PHILIPPI

Galatians and 2 Corinthians are the most notable but not the only epistles of conflict, though no other calls for such detailed treatment. There is however more controversial material in Philippians than is sometimes noticed. It is not necessary here to discuss the question where and when the epistle was written. Some think that it was written from prison in the Ephesian period. That Acts does not mention an imprisonment in Ephesus is no proof that one (or, as some think, two) did not take place. The very fact that Philippians does allude to controversy may count as an argument for dating it with Galatians and the Corinthian letters. Another view is that the letter was written during Paul's imprisonment in Caesarea (see Acts 23: 31 – 26: 32). This is not impossible, but there is little positively to be said for this location, and the 'two years' of Acts 24: 27 may refer not to Paul's imprisonment (giving him plenty of time for letter-writing) but to Felix's tenure of office. The traditional view, which has perhaps most to be said for it, is that Philippians was written from Rome, during the two-year imprisonment of Acts 28: 30, or possibly in a later imprisonment. Whatever the place of origin, it was marked by trouble for Paul. He was in prison—the opinion that he had been in prison but had recently been released is not very probable. This was not in itself a matter of controversy, but there were those who thought to add to Paul's unhappiness by taking the opportunity to further their own understanding of Christian truth, which differed from his. It will be remembered that Paul was not the founder of Roman Christianity; others had been there before and were now making the most of their chance to build up their cause while Paul was safely out of the way. It is at first sight surprising that Paul takes this so calmly, and can even rejoice in what is going on (Phil 1: 18), but the reason for this is clear. As always, Paul is fundamentally concerned with preaching, the public representation of the Gospel. For him, this meant proclaiming Christ; and this his rivals (as they saw themselves, though he refuses to describe them so) were doing. Whatever their motive (Phil 1: 15, 17), they were preaching Christ. Of course it was better that Christ should be preached out of love for Christ's prisoner (Phil 1: 16), but better also that he should be preached out of malice than not at all. Perhaps this should be called rivalry (cf. Phil 1: 15, envy and strife; 17, sharp practice) rather than controversy. On the hypothesis that the letter

39

was written from Rome we shall meet the matter again when we consider Romans.

A certain amount of disharmony at Philippi itself, important in view of the Christological passage (Phil 2: 5–11) it evoked, is not controversy; but controversy arises in strength in chapter 3. It looks as if the letter is ended at 3: 1a; on second thoughts Paul decides that it will be wise to repeat things that he had said before: 'To go on writing the same things is no burden to me, and for you it is a means of safety'. Another view is that two letters have been joined together at this point; it makes no difference to the present argument. There is no doubt that those whom Paul has in mind here were Judaizers. He calls them *dogs*, in the Old Testament a general term of abuse, which Paul may be turning against those who were using it of others; they were *workers*, a word that Paul used of his adversaries in 2 Corinthians 11: 13 (there they are deceitful, here *evil*); the most revealing word is the third Paul uses, probably inventing it for the purpose. It is not *circumcision* (*peritomē*), but a play on the word, in the AV, *concision* (*katatomē*). They may be called *mutilationists*, though this word fails to give the appropriate connection with *circumcision* in the next verse. We are the circumcision (Phil 3: 3); it is clear that Paul is saying, in effect: These Judaizers prowl round my churches like scavenging dogs, pretending to be Christian workers, but in fact the opposite; they wish to have Gentile believers circumcised, arguing that circumcision is the only way into the people of God. But what they call circumcision is mere mutilation of the flesh; true circumcision is circumcision of the heart (Rom 2: 29; cf. Deut 10: 16; 30: 6; Jer 4: 4), and this is what we represent. It means that we worship not in terms of external rites and ordinances but by the Spirit of God, that our boasting is in Christ Jesus alone (cf. 2 Cor 10: 17; also 1 Cor 1: 31), and not in any human qualification. That Judaizing propagandists are in mind is confirmed by the human qualifications in which Paul himself could once have confidence but had confidence no longer. He had been circumcised on the eighth day (that is, as the child of a Jewish family, not a proselyte), he came of the race of Israel, of the tribe of Benjamin, he was a Hebrew born of Hebrews (Phil 3: 5; cf. 2 Cor 11: 22). Not content with these advantages he had become a Pharisee, observing the whole Law, and in his zeal for authentic Judaism had persecuted the church. The legal righteousness he had thus acquired had been flawless. His use of the word *righteousness*, recalling Galatians and the Galatian controversy, is significant; so in a different way is his digression from the Philippian controversy to describe his conversion, which had meant the reversal of the values of his earlier life. What had been credit in his account he now reckoned debit; it stood on the opposite side of the balance sheet, and the only ground of confidence was Christ:

> that I may gain Christ and be found in him, not having my own righteousness, which comes from the Law, but that which comes through faith in Christ, the righteousness that comes from God on the basis of faith; to know him and the power of his resurrection and participation in his sufferings, made to share the image of his death, if by any means I may attain to the resurrection of the dead. (Phil 3: 8–11)

The theme of controversy is dropped, but returns in verse 18 as the negative counterpart to the exhortation that the Philippians should follow good examples. There are bad ones. Again Judaizers appear to be in mind. They are numerous, they move Paul to tears as he thinks of the peril in which his Philippians, subject to such pressure, stand; they are enemies of the cross of Christ. Compare Galatians 5: 11; 6: 12; such men do not, as Paul does, regard the cross as the central divine act of salvation; they repudiate it because they know that not to do so would bring persecution. 'Their end is perdition' (3: 19) stresses the seriousness of their error; 'whose god is their belly and whose glory is in their shame' may mean simply that they are gluttons and dissolute, though we have no reason for thinking that they were and it is perhaps more probable that Paul is referring to their adherence to food laws and insistence on circumcision, an operation on the male pudendum. Again, 'they set their mind on earthly things' may mean not that they are worldly but that the provisions of the Law to which they require obedience belong to this world.

CONTROVERSY IN ROME

Philippians 3 does not add much to what we know from the other epistles about Paul's adversaries. It is important because it indicates that they were active in Macedonia as well as in Galatia and Achaea. 'They' is a comprehensive term and the anti-Pauline agitation took different forms in different places; always, however, it had a Judaizing element. This points the student on to Romans, where

41

clearly the problem of Judaism and Jewish Christianity is in mind; much of the language of Galatians reappears, though the thought is in some respects developed. Is there a sense in which Romans, addressed to a church of which Paul had no first-hand knowledge, may be regarded as a controversial epistle? The very fact that Paul wrote the epistle indicates that he was aware of a mission other than his own that had reached the capital of the Empire before him. He may exaggerate when he writes that the faith of the Roman Christians was proclaimed throughout the world (Rom 1: 8), but chapter 16 shows (unless, as some think, the chapter was originally addressed not to Rome but to Ephesus—not a probable view) that he was acquainted with quite a number of them. He hoped to visit Rome and prepared for his visit by stating at considerable length and depth his understanding of the Gospel. The fact that he had (we may suppose) little precise knowledge of the form Christianity had taken in Rome may be responsible for the great length of the letter; he must cover a good deal of ground in order to make sure of touching on every relevant point. The question of God's righteousness in relation to the Law and to the Christian, the core of his Gospel (Rom 1: 16, 17), is the main theme; towards the close of the epistle (14: 1 – 15: 13) the practical application of this in a divided community comes to the surface. Did Paul know that the question was being debated in Rome, or did he infer that what had happened in Corinth might happen anywhere? It is impossible to be confident about this. More difficult is the treatment (in Romans 9 – 11) of the relation of the Jewish people, the Israel of God's election, to the Gospel and the church. There are marks of real controversy here, for it seems almost certain that Paul had been accused of heartlessly neglecting his own people in favour of the Gentiles. It was disgraceful that he, who could describe himself as a Hebrew son of Hebrew parents (Phil 3: 5; cf. 2 Cor 11: 22), should think of himself, and act, as an apostle for Gentiles (Rom 11: 13), and Paul twice in these chapters (9: 1–5; 10: 1) asserts his devotion to his people, his readiness even to be separated by a curse from Christ if that would benefit them. Behind his emotional language there appears to lie (it may also lie behind Gal 2: 9) a difference of opinion over the way in which the mission should be conducted. There were, it seems, those who said: 'It is necessary first of all to win the allegiance of the Jewish people. Let us convince them that Jesus is the Messiah for whom they hoped. Then, when they have accepted him, it will be possible to go out in irresistible strength and win the Gentile world for the same truth.' It was a practical application of what Paul himself was ready to affirm as a theological principle: To the Jew first, and also to the Greek (e.g. Rom 1: 16). But this kind of argument, or attack, from strength was at a deeper level inconsistent with Paul's Gospel. The Gospel could be accepted only in a situation of unbelief and guilt. This meant that the Gentiles could accept it at once; when they had accepted it the Jews would see their disobedience and accept it too. 'A partial hardening has fallen upon Israel, and will remain until the full number of the Gentiles has come in; when this is done, all Israel will be saved' (Rom 11: 25, 26).

In this part of the epistle controversy is real; elsewhere it has from time to time (in comparison with Galatians, 2 Corinthians, and Philippians) a slightly academic flavour, which is due to the fact that Paul, unaware of precisely what vein of Christianity is current at Rome, has to write to some extent in abstract terms and has to cast his net widely in order to make sure of catching whatever fish may be about. The Marcionite Prologue to Romans (these early prologues are found in some Latin manuscripts) runs:

> Romans live in the parts of Italy. These were got at in advance by false apostles and brought into the Law and the prophets under the name of our Lord Jesus Christ. The apostle calls them back to the true Gospel faith, writing to them from Corinth.

This puts the matter too strongly; it was because Paul did not know precisely by whom the Roman Christians had been got at (*praeventi*) that he wrote as he did. Experience had made him ready to meet trouble, even to expect it; but he did not go out of his way to create it.

THEMES OF CONTROVERSY

As we have seen, it was not necessary to invent causes of controversy; they were unavoidable. Perhaps there were more occasions when what Paul encountered was not wilful perversity but well-intentioned muddle-headedness than he was prepared to allow. But he had the gift of penetrating sight that enabled him to see through a mist of pious language down into the corrupt source and on into the calamitous consequence of notions and modes of expression that would satisfy the majority. The result was a lifetime of conflict.

Without debate he would have found life strange; perhaps dull. It was however because he was a theologian, as most of his contemporaries were not, that he was obliged to fight; in turn, the fighting made him the kind of theologian that he was, and gave his letters the combative air that most of them have. He did not develop all theological themes with equal intensity, or equally far; it was controversy that determined the selection — that, certainly, rather than any desire to evolve a well-balanced and comprehensive system. Our next task is to note some of the lines of controversial development; when in the next chapter we take a more systematic, thematic, view there will be some overlapping and consequent repetition, but not much.

If the first controversial theme is headed Christology the designation may be misleading. There is nothing like the *homoousios-homoiousios* conflicts of later centuries. Paul did not lay down a precise statement of the union of God and man in the one Lord Jesus Christ. In fact, the controversy lay at a deeper level. I have pointed out that the root of the Galatian controversy is to be seen in Galatians 5: 2: 'If you think that you must add something, such as circumcision, to what you already have in Christ, then Christ himself will do you no good'. The theme recurs. In the face of Corinthian thirst for wisdom Paul declares that he had nothing to preach but Christ, Christ crucified (1 Cor 2: 2); this follows aptly on the claim (1: 30) that Christ 'as God's gift became wisdom for us, and sanctification and righteousness and redemption too'. It was 'another Jesus' whom the intruder in Corinth preached (2 Cor 11: 4), and 'other', though capable of various elucidation, meant primarily a Jesus who needed to be supplemented, whether by legal observance, gnosis, or spiritual experiences. *Solus Christus*, Christ alone, is the primary motto of Paul's theology, and most of the errors against which he fights can be regarded as in some form or other qualifications of that *solus*. It is probably clearest in Paul's treatment of the demand in Galatia (and Philippi) for the circumcision of Gentile converts. If God has declared his unconditional acceptance of mankind, including the Gentile world, in Christ, to impose a further demand is to cast doubt on God's veracity. It is not that the Law is a bad thing, or failed to serve a useful purpose in God's plan. Paul repeatedly asserts that it is good — holy, righteous, good, spiritual (Rom 7: 12, 14). It is not contrary to God's promises (Gal 3: 21); all it lacked was the power to give life — indeed, a fairly considerable disadvantage. It was the advantage and privilege of the Jew (Rom 3: 1, 2; 9: 4, 5), and precisely because it was so it created a distinction between Jew and Gentile. But the disadvantage and the distinction are overcome in Christ, who is the end of the Law, with a view to conferring righteousness on all who believe (Rom 10: 4). However the word *end* is interpreted (see below) it is on Paul's principles clear that to say 'we had better make believers in Christ more certain of righteousness and salvation by returning to the Law' is intolerable.

It was no different if some other supplement was advocated, even though the supplement were spiritual experiences truly generated by the Holy Spirit. For the function of the Holy Spirit is not to comfort the Christian and exalt his ego with pleasing forms of ecstasy but to bear witness that Jesus is Lord (1 Cor 12: 3). This may indeed be done in inspired speech, even, though obscurely and inadequately, in speaking with tongues, but it is also and especially done in human life that is emptied of human egocentricity; for the fruit of the Spirit described in Galatians 5: 22f. would serve (as does the description of love in 1 Corinthians 13) as a portrait of Jesus Christ. The clearest witness to the lordship of Jesus Christ consists in human life in which his image is reproduced. When glossolalia occurs, it is clear enough that the speaker himself is not lord; that is, his conscious and rational faculties are under the control of another. But, since no one understands what he says (1 Cor 14: 2), it is not known who this Other is. Prophecy, articulate confession of Jesus in explicit terms, is a clearer and superior witness (1 Cor 14: 3-5). Experiences of supernatural exaltation were of no consequence; better to boast of weakness in which the weakness of the Crucified was manifest (2 Cor 12: 1-10).

Wisdom (*sophia*) was a term that gave Paul some difficulty. It is clear from 1 Corinthians that it was regarded by some as a suitable supplement to or substitute for Paul's *solus Christus*. Understood in this sense, it was to be rejected. Paul would have none of it in his preaching (1 Cor 2: 4f.); human wisdom was a completely inadequate means of approach to God (1 Cor 1: 20f.). Yet there was also a good wisdom, God's wisdom which confounds human wisdom (1 Cor 1: 21), wisdom which we speak among those who are capable of understanding it (1 Cor 2: 6). It is clear however what this wisdom is; it is nothing other than the word of the cross, Christ the power of God and the wisdom of God (1 Cor 1: 24), though perhaps (in view of the 'among the mature' of 2: 6) Paul implies the word of the cross reflected on under the guidance of the Spirit. This is true wisdom. A term related to wisdom (*sophia*) is knowledge (*gnōsis*). Paul's use of the Greek word shows that it is on the way to the technical sense of *gnōsis*, though the developed Christian (or semi-Christian) gnosticism of the second century still lies in the distance. *Gnōsis*, knowledge, is good; but it is an inadequate guide to life, it is at best partial, and it is no substitute for and a dangerous addition to the Gospel of Christ alone. Thus it is a valid piece of Christian *gnōsis* that 'for us there is one God, the Father, from whom come all things and to whom our being leads, and one Lord Jesus Christ, through whom all things, including ourselves, come into being' (1 Cor 8: 6). Paul is in agreement with those who profess this knowledge, and draws with them the conclusion that an idol has no real existence, so that the offering of meat to that which does not exist does not make the meat religiously unfit to eat. But 'it is not everyone who has this knowledge' (8: 7), and love, which is a higher consideration than knowledge, demands that they be considered. Knowledge, even of what is true, can be dangerously misleading.

> We know that 'we all have knowledge'. Knowledge puffs up, but love builds up. If anyone thinks he has achieved some piece of knowledge, he has not yet attained the knowledge that he ought to have; but if anyone loves God, he has been known by God. (8: 1–3)

Paul points here to the only way in which he thinks that the concept of knowledge can be satisfactorily used. It is not (as a gnostic would say) a matter of man's knowledge of God; what matters is God's knowledge of man. Thus in Galatians 4: 8, 9 Paul corrects himself:

> Then indeed when you did not know God you were enslaved to beings which by nature are not gods; but now that you have come to know God, or rather, have been known by God, how is it that you are returning to the feeble and poverty-stricken elements?[7]

The same contrast appears in 1 Corinthians 13: 12: 'Then I shall know even as also I have been known'. Full knowledge of God belongs to the future; it is enough for the present that God knows me.

Faced with controversy on various sides, and with churches full of moral and other problems, Paul perceived that the first essential was the centrality of Christ. How this developed in terms of more formal Christology, in (for example) the use of such terms as Christ, Lord, Son of God, must be considered later.

The central controversial theme of Christology has, as we

have seen, a number of controversial corollaries. Of these the most important in any account of Paul may be headed by the word 'justification'. This theme is so important that, like Christology, it must be discussed systematically below. It arises out of Christology – Christocentricity – when this is considered in the light of belief (deeply rooted in the Old Testament) in a righteous God, one of whose functions is to judge the whole human race, and that without respect of persons. How can man receive acquittal – justification – in the court of this Judge? To this question, as to other theological questions, Paul has one answer: Christ. And if other answers are given they must be resisted.

Paul can view the error (as it must seem to him) of his own people in regard to God's righteousness only with sorrow; he views with anger the attempt of some, professing to be Christians, to foist the error upon those who under his guidance have heard and accepted the truth. It is not that the Old Testament account of the calling of Israel by God is false; it is true, and Paul wrestles with the problem of the continuing role of Israel – if there is one – in the purpose of God. It is not that they have not devoted themselves to the service of God; they have done so with passion. They have a zeal for God; alas that it is uninstructed and mistaken (Rom 10: 2). They have misunderstood the central elements in their own vocation. It is not that God has withheld from them the most precious gifts: they have the sonship, the glory, the covenants, the law-giving, the Temple worship, the promises, the fathers, the Christ himself (Rom 10: 4, 5). It is not that Paul himself does not love them with self-sacrificing and prayerful concern (Rom 9: 1-3; 10: 1). All the components of a true understanding of the matter are present, but they are disordered. At the root of the disordering is a misunderstanding of the Law; this too will be discussed below.

If the Old Testament itself is true, there is no possibility of true life except in relation to the one true God. This requires, for the disobedient creature, reconciliation; and reconciliation, sharpened in the light of judgement, becomes justification. The doctrinal problem arises out of the fact that man is unjustifiable; he is the ungodly one (the *asebēs*), whom (the Old Testament declares) human judges must never acquit, and God will never acquit (Exod 23: 7; Isa 5: 23). It is not merely that Paul can paint a lurid picture of contemporary society (Rom 1: 24–31) and compile (or borrow) a cento of Old Testament passages which bring a charge against the whole human race (Rom 3: 10–18 – there is not even one righteous person). Those who are most assiduous in doing 'works of the Law'

47

(for the interpretation of this phrase see below) condemn themselves by the fact that they are using the instrument of their condemnation to establish their own position before God. Ignorant of (or misunderstanding) God's righteousness and seeking to establish their own righteousness (a righteousness based on Law, that is, on works done in obedience to the Law: Philippians 3: 9) they did not submit themselves to God's righteousness (Rom 10: 3). It is in this sense, not in that of discovering hidden peccadillos in apparently virtuous and pious men, that all have sinned, and lack the glory of God (Rom 3: 23). The answer to this situation is that God does justify, acquit, the ungodly, and that without sacrificing his own character as an upright judge. How this is done may be considered below, though to say that it takes place through the death and resurrection of Jesus is only another way of saying that controversy about justification is an immediate corollary of controversy about Christology. Indeed it proves to be the major cutting edge of Paul's controversial writing, in Romans, Galatians, and Philippians, and less clearly in the Corinthian letters too. Thus Paul can declare that he has nothing on his conscience, but that does not justify him (1 Cor 4: 4); he performs the good work of a Christian preacher, but may nevertheless prove to be rejected at God's judgement; there is a different turn of phrase in the controversial chapter 10 of 2 Corinthians (10: 18: 'It is not the man who commends himself who is approved (in the judgement), but he whom the Lord commends'), but the righteousness terminology is present with force if with less than perfect clarity in 5: 21 ('Him who knew no sin he made sin on our behalf, that we might become God's righteousness in him'). The essence of Paul's Christological position is given vividly in his adaptation of Deuteronomy 30: 12, 13, 14):

Say not in thy heart, Who shall ascend into heaven? That is, to bring Christ down; or, Who shall descend into the abyss? That is, to bring Christ up from the dead. No: what does it say? The word is near thee, in thy mouth and in thy heart. (Rom 10: 6–8)

There is no need (as there is no possibility) to fetch Christ into the human scene; he has come, an act of God's own initiative, without which salvation would not exist. Justification is a particular expression of the same divine spontaneity, and means that the gracious God is prepared to deal with man not as he ought to be but as he is. Deny this, as to Paul his Judaizing opponents appeared to do, and all possibility of salvation is excluded.

48

Christology and justification point to a third controversial theme which lies under rather than on the surface of the letters. The coming of Christ is not an event that has somehow to be hurried along; it has already happened. Yet it has not finally happened; he has come, and he will come. In 1 Corinthians 15, for example, Paul can use the simple chronological terms of the apocalypses:

Each one will be brought to life in his own rank: Christ himself as the firstfruits, then, at his coming, those who belong to Christ. Then comes the End, when he hands over the kingdom to him who is God and Father, when he shall have brought to nought every Ruler and every Authority and Power. For Christ must continue to reign in his kingdom until he shall have set all his enemies under his feet. Death is the last enemy to be brought to nought. (15: 23–26)

1 Thessalonians is even more explicitly chronological in its mode of expression.

We, the living, who are left till the coming of the Lord, shall in no way anticipate those who have fallen asleep. For the Lord himself shall come down from heaven with a shout of command, at the archangel's voice and God's trumpet, and the dead in Christ shall rise up first, then we, the living, who are left behind, shall along with them be caught up in the clouds to meet the Lord in the air; and so we shall be always with the Lord. (4: 15–17)

Thus the Lord has come, and the Lord will come. There is a similar duality in the theme of justification. This implies judgement, and in the judgement, contrary to human expectation, a favourable verdict is pronounced; this is justification. But it is not the end of judgement, for Paul believes that there will be judgement in the future. 'We shall all stand before the judgement seat of God' (Rom 14: 10) 'We must all appear before the judgement seat of Christ in order that each one may receive recompense for the things he has done by means of his body' (2 Cor 5: 10). 'You are storing up for yourself wrath which will break forth in the day of wrath, the day when God's just judgement is revealed' (Rom 2: 5). Judgement has taken place, and the day of judgement is still to come.

It is perhaps not surprising that Paul's paradoxical eschatology (to which we shall return) was sometimes misunderstood. It would be historically misleading to build on the reference, in 2 Tim 2: 17,

18, to Hymenaeus and Philetus, who taught that the resurrection had already happened, but they appear to have had predecessors. Paul writes ironically to Corinth:

> Already you have reached satiety; already you have become rich; apart from us you have come to your kingdom. Yes, and I wish you had come to your kingdom, that we too might be crowned with you. (1 Cor 4: 8)

As a mere apostle he is all too well aware that he is not yet living in heaven (4: 9–13). It may be that some of those who in 1 Corinthians 15 are said to have denied the resurrection did so because they believed that they had already been so transformed, so spiritualized, that death was impossible, or at least unreal, so that there was no need to think of a future resurrection, and indeed no place for one. This kind of belief could, and did, lead to moral indifferentism. Since we have already been justified we may do what we like. The question was a serious one, which Paul found himself obliged to ask. 'Are we to go on in sin in order that there may be yet more grace? . . . Are we to sin because we are not under the reign of Law but under the reign of grace?' (Rom 6: 1, 15). The answer to these questions is not simply that there remains a future judgement, which Paul himself must await with fear; the present tense of salvation has to be emphasized in appropriate terms.

> How shall we, men who died to sin, go on living in it? . . . Consider that you yourselves are dead to sin, but alive to God in Christ Jesus . . . Do not offer your members to sin, as weapons in the service of unrighteousness, but offer yourselves to God as dead men brought to life, and offer him your members as weapons in the service of righteousness. For sin shall not dominate over you; for you are not under the reign of Law, but under the reign of grace. (Rom 6: 2, 11, 13, 14)

It was necessary to resist both those who supposed that the whole of the eschatological future had been already realized, and those who supposed that none of it had.

This has a further connection with Paul's understanding of Christ. For him it was in Christ that the eschatology was realized; this was in fact the origin of the phrase 'in Christ' which he uses frequently and in many different connections. It is probable (the matter cannot be discussed here) that the earliest Christian understanding of the death and resurrection of Jesus was cast in terms of the Jewish belief in the 'travail pains of the Messiah'—the time of (at least relatively) innocent suffering of the people of God which they must endure before they could experience the bliss of the promised good time to come—the kingdom of God. Only Jesus could suffer innocently; only he passed through death and resurrection. He died and rose on behalf of the people. This thought Paul developed into suffering that was not only endured on behalf of others but was such that others might by faith enter into it and share it. *In Christ* they died, and *in Christ* they were raised up. They thus entered by faith into an anticipation of the age to come, and Paul could urge them to become the new creation that by faith they already were. The Christological and eschatological themes interlock.

Paul never shrank from controversy; yet he could also be surprisingly tolerant. In Romans 14 and 15 the discussion of the views of 'strong' and 'weak' Christians touches matters that are of central importance to Paul's theology; there is no doubt that he is one of the 'strong' or that if the 'weak' are right Paul's theology is destroyed. Yet he refuses to lay down the law or to deny the right of the 'weak' to a place in the people of God. 'Let each one be fully convinced in his own mind' (14: 5). It is more important that each Christian should think matters through, reach his own conclusion, and at the same time recognize the right of his fellow Christian to reach a different conclusion, than that there should be an artificial uniformity, and Paul has no intention of imposing his own view on others. In Philippians 3 he concludes a fundamental statement of his own Christian conviction by commending his opinion. 'So let those of us who are mature think in this way. And if in any way you think differently, this too will God reveal to you. Only we must stand by that conclusion that we have already reached' (3: 15, 16). That is: I am sure that mine is a correct, mature, Christian view, and I believe that, in God's time, you will in the end share it. But what matters is that you honestly maintain and live by the position you have at present reached. It is in the same vein that he refuses to be a dictator.

> What is Apollos? and what is Paul? Servants, through whom you became believers, and each one simply performed the service the Lord gave him to do. I planted, Apollos watered the plants; it was not we, however, but God who made them grow. (1 Cor 3: 5, 6)
> We are not lords over your faith, but we work together with you for your joy. (2 Cor 1: 24)

It is not ourselves that we proclaim, but Christ Jesus as Lord, and ourselves as your slaves for Jesus' sake. (4: 5)

This is an aspect of Paul that is often overlooked.

The last quotation provides a clue to the apparent contrast between the Paul who fights resolutely for what he conceives to be truth, and the Paul who is meek in dealing with his own converts — his own children (Gal 4: 19; 1 Cor 4: 15). His primary concern is with proclamation, preaching. It is of fundamental importance that this should be correct. It is repeatedly the point at which controversy focuses.

I marvel that you are so quickly moving away from him who called you in the grace of Christ to a different Gospel; it is not a second Gospel, only there are some who are disturbing you and wish to pervert the [one] Gospel of Christ. But even if we or an angel from heaven should preach to you a Gospel different from that which we preached to you, let him be anathema. As we have said before, so now I say again: if anyone preaches to you a Gospel different from that which you received, let him be anathema. (Gal 1: 6–9)

There is a similar passage in 2 Corinthians.

I am afraid lest, as the snake in his craftiness deceived Eve, your minds should be corrupted from the sincerity of their attachment to Christ. For if your visitor proclaims another Jesus, whom we did not proclaim, or you receive a different Spirit, which you did not receive, or a different Gospel, which you did not accept, then you put up with him all right! (11: 3, 4)

We have noticed above what at first sight seems a different attitude in Philippians. In the place where Paul is writing there are those who preach Christ out of envy and contention. They know that Paul is in prison and unable to continue his own preaching ministry, and they think that by preaching, adding to the number of their own disciples and perhaps to their own reputation, they will add affliction to Paul's bonds — he will be hurt by their success, with no opportunity of response. They are mistaken; he rejoices in their work and its success. 'What then? It only means that in every place, with deceitful motive or honest, Christ is being preached; and in that I rejoice and will go on rejoicing' (Phil 1: 17, 18). Their intentions may be dishonourable and hurtful, but what of that? They are preaching Christ; the content of their preaching if not its motivation is sound; that is sufficient. Paul does not ask, he does not himself propound, a Christological orthodoxy; what matters is the centrality and sufficiency of Christ. This controversial theme has already been noted; it has its sharpest edge in the context of preaching. This is not only for the obvious reason, that the hearer must be presented with truth, not with falsehood, not only because Paul had found that in fact the foolishness and weakness of the crucified Christ whom he preached proved to be the power and wisdom of God by which human life was redeemed and renewed. It was because the preached word was itself part of the Gospel, so that it was in the proclaimed Gospel that the righteousness of God was revealed (Rom 1: 17) and the power of God operated with the result of salvation (1: 16). This was because in the preaching Christ himself was heard. 'How are they to call upon one in whom they have not believed? How are they to believe in one whom [not *of whom*] they have not heard?' (Rom 10: 14). But Christ will only be heard if Christ is preached.

Two further points may be briefly made before we leave the theme of Paul's controversies and the way in which theology grew out of them. There was a content of preaching that must be determined by the Gospel, understood as concentrated upon its central figure; but there was also a strategy of preaching, and the strategy had, in Paul's view, to be determined not by considerations of expediency but by the Gospel itself. It cannot be proved but it seems probable that in this respect also Paul ran into controversy. This matter has been dealt with above. They were theological considerations that dictated that the Gentiles must be evangelized first, though in the end all Israel would be saved.

Paul was caught in a paradox here, for he himself uses the formula, 'The Jew first and also the Greek' (Rom 1: 16; 2: 9, 10). In Acts, this proposition takes the form of missionary tactics. When Paul set about work in a fresh town he habitually begins in the synagogue, moving out of it only when compelled to do so by the opposition that he encounters. On these occasions he makes the opposition and the consequent move the occasion and justification for turning to a Gentile audience (Acts 13: 46; 18: 6; 28: 25–28). There is no reason to doubt that this sometimes happened; the synagogue would provide Paul with a ready-made audience, and it might well have seemed foolish not to use it. But this was tactics, not strategy, and for him (Luke was less of a theologian, more of a historian) 'Jew first, then Gentile' was a theological proposition rather than a programme. The story began with the Jews, even though God was equally God of the Gentiles (Rom 3: 29).

Finally we may recall the moral problems that Paul encountered in his churches. These are not matter of controversy as the themes that have been discussed in this chapter; rather the pastoral concerns that Paul was bound to meet in his care for the churches that his preaching brought into being—especially, one is inclined to say, the church at Corinth, but that may be simply because we have the evidence for Corinth and not for the other churches. Here too, however, was a factor that contributed greatly to the development of Paul's theology. The immaturity of the Corinthian Christians (1 Cor 3: 1–4) led him into deeper levels of mature reflection. Their problems in regard to sex and marriage, and over food sacrificed to idols, led him to think out the meaning of Christian freedom (1 Corinthians 9); their childish love of noisy speaking with tongues led him to picture Christian love (1 Corinthians 13). These matters have already been mentioned and will arise again below, but it would be wrong not to note them here. The controversial, polemical nature of Paul's theology will also find further assessment.

Notes

1 C. F. D. Moule in L. E. Keck and J. L. Martyn (eds), *Studies in Luke-Acts* (1968), pp. 159–85.

2 There is an important variant in the text here; I follow what seems to me to be almost certainly the correct reading. See C. K. Barrett, *Freedom and Obligation* (1985), pp. 11, 112.

3 In J. Friedrich, W. Pöhlmann and P. Stuhlmacher (eds), *Rechtfertigung* (1976), pp. 1–16.

4 See C. K. Barrett, '*Ho adikēsas* (2 Cor 7: 12)' in O. Böcher and K. Haacker (eds), *Verborum Veritas* (1970), pp. 149–57.

5 See C. K. Barrett, '*Pseudapostoloi* (2 Cor. 11: 13)' in A. Descamps and A. de Halleux (eds), *Mélanges Bibliques en hommage au R.P. Béda Rigaux* (1970), pp. 377–96.

6 On the conflict over apostleship in 2 Corinthians see E. Käsemann, 'Die Legitimät des Apostels', *Zeitschrift für die neutestamentliche Wissenschaft* 41 (1942), pp. 33–71 (reprinted separately 1956).

7 On these elements see pp. 57–9.

3

Paul's theology

It is important to begin the study of Paul's thought by relating it to the often contentious circumstances of his life. To fail to do this would give his theology a static quality that it did not possess. It was related in a living way to the disputes in which he found himself obliged to engage, and, of equal or even greater importance, to the work of preaching and pastoral care, which he always understood as his primary vocation. This does not mean that it is possible (except at one or two points) to trace lines of development in his thinking. This has been attempted (notably by C. H. Dodd[1]), but without success. The attempt, for example, to trace development in his eschatological thinking from a strictly futuristic view in the earliest letters to one in which he saw eschatological conditions as already realized in the present, founders on the recurrence in what is probably the latest of his letters of the old futuristic view: Philippians 3: 20, 21, 'Our home state is in heaven, whence we expect as Saviour the Lord Jesus Christ, who will transform our humble bodies and make them like his glorious body' (cf. 1 Cor 15: 23, 51–58; 1 Thess 4: 15–17). Paul reacted to circumstances as they arose, and if the same circumstances returned at the end of his life he would react to them in much the same way as at the beginning. Moreover, it is probably true that the major developments in his thought had taken place before the earliest of his extant letters. He found, as many people do, that pointing out error helped him to find truth.

The occasional treatment of Paul's thought is not only allowable, convenient, and interesting; it is essential. But it must be supplemented by thematic treatment. It is probably better to say thematic than systematic. Whether Paul can properly be described as a systematic theologian is a question often answered in the negative. To a great extent the matter turns upon the definition of the terms used. Beyond the occasionalism of Paul's theology there is a real unity; he reacts to circumstances spontaneously but he does not react at random; he reacts in accordance with principles, seldom stated as such but detectable. He does so moreover in the light of what he knew of his environment—of a profound knowledge of Judaism and at least a smattering of Greek culture. To do this is the task of the systematic theologian,[2] who does not need to qualify for the title by writing a large textbook of systematic theology but by his grasp of Christian principles and his ability to think them through and express them in terms of his own environment. It might be said that New Testament theology is the systematic theology of the first century, and this is pre-eminently true of Pauline theology. Paul is early enough to lay the classical foundation of Christian principle, but also mature enough to be no haphazard improviser.

A thematic approach is called for, in order to supplement the controversial, but it must be carried out with care, and must be presented in dynamic rather than conventional and therefore static terms. Variety, mobility, spontaneity are so characteristic of Paul as to constitute part of the substance of his thought, and to omit them would be to misrepresent the subject. And the material must be presented with continual, though not always explicit, reference to the preaching that was always Paul's main concern.

THE REIGN OF EVIL

Nothing more self-evident, and nothing more profound, can be said about Paul's theology than that it was a theology of salvation. Those who are Christians may be defined as 'the saved' (1 Cor 1: 18), or perhaps rather as 'those who are in process of being saved', for Paul uses a continuous present participle, and salvation in its fullness and finality still lies in the future. Now is salvation nearer to us, as we march onward through time, than when we first became believers (Rom 13: 11). The verb *to save* regularly appears in the future tense or the subjunctive mood, with an element of contingency, or at least of futurity. Finality is sure, yet it is uncertain, for Paul himself, having preached to others, may in the end turn out to be rejected (1 Cor 9: 27). This does not, however, call in question the fact that for Paul the central theme of theology is salvation.

A theology of salvation presupposes a world disordered, a situation from which man needs to be delivered. It is here that Paul's theology, and any discussion of it, must begin. This does not mean that Paul's thinking starts at this point; he worked back from the fact and the ground of salvation to the circumstances from which humanity must be delivered. Religions of salvation were not scarce in Paul's environment, and their presuppositions were not unfamiliar. Some of Paul's contemporaries thought of a world that had been wrong from the start, that was wrong in itself and could only cease to be wrong by ceasing to be itself. Creation was an unfortunate error that had to be undone; salvation could be thought of as de-creation. The empirical universe could be thought of as an unhappy mixture of spirit (which was good and immortal) and matter (which was evil and subject to death). Salvation consisted in the resolution of this radical dualism. The mixture had to be sorted out, and spirit freed from matter. This was the basic proposition which the various gnostic myths expressed in an endless series of mythological fantasies — fantasies indeed, but not fantasies that can be regarded as objects of scorn, for they were the products of sensitive minds burdened by the world's evil, which they took as seriously as it deserved to be taken. Yet this was a view that no orthodox Jew, adhering to the Old Testament, could hold; Paul did not hold it. Yet his view of the world was in some respects akin to this astrological, gnostic view that he was bound to reject. The fundamental difference was, indeed, absolute. The world was not made wrong, it had gone wrong. It had gone wrong because, though made by the good God, it had escaped from his dominion and come under that of evil powers; at this point the resemblance between Paul and his gnostic contemporaries was absolute.

Gilbert Murray wrote (*Five Stages of Greek Religion*, pp. 144, 146) that

> Astrology fell upon the Hellenistic mind as a new disease falls upon some remote island people . . . In all the religious systems of antiquity, if I mistake not, the Seven Planets play some lordly or terrifying part.

These seven heavenly bodies, whose regular and predictable movements created a strong impression of destiny and determinism, had each of them its own sphere (or hemisphere) in which it moved.

These seven spheres formed an impenetrable barrier between the material world of bondage to destiny and to the heavenly powers and the upper world of spirit, freedom, life, and God. The astrologers might, for a suitable fee, inform the inquirer about his destiny. For escape from it, one might look to the mysteries for sacramental agencies, or to gnosis, which was in essence (though capable of great refinement) the secret of how to get out, to escape from the material world and enter the spiritual. Paul looked elsewhere, but in part retained the same framework of thought.

To examine further both the parallel and the contrast we may turn to a passage of central importance, Galatians 3: 23 – 4: 11. The whole section is worthy of outline consideration because it begins explicitly in the time before the coming of faith (3: 23). Whether *faith* here means *the* (Christian) faith (*fides quae*) or faith as trust (*fides qua*), and the matter is disputed, man is imprisoned. At first his imprisonment is described as under the Law of Moses; there will be more to say about this at a later point. This servitude is ended when men become sons of God in Christ (3: 26). This however is essentially (at any rate, is most simply) an account of Jews who become Christians; but Paul is writing to Gentiles. Recognizing that what he has written does not quite suit the circumstances with which he is dealing, in 4: 1 he changes the metaphor. Even an heir, while under age and still an infant at law, is kept under the rule of stewards and governors. Similarly, until the appointed moment when God sent forth his Son (4: 4), we were enslaved under the cosmic elements. Who, or what, these elements were is brought out in 4: 8–11 (looked at from another angle on p. 46). The Galatians were in danger of falling back into the bondage from which they had been liberated by Christ. They were going back to the feeble and poverty-stricken elements, to be enslaved all over again. This earlier state of theirs was one of slavery to things which by nature are not gods (4: 8). These are the elements, beings regarded by some as gods, though in the proper sense they are not god. Paul does not say that they do not exist, only that they are 'no-gods'; not exactly 'anti-gods' but not to be described by the word 'God' as a Jew would understand it. They are the heavenly powers; planets, perhaps, or powers represented by the planets, or inhabiting the planets. The unredeemed human race is in bondage to them in a servitude which is somehow related to man's servitude to the Law; when the Galatians turn to the Law they are returning to the elements.

The word *elements (stoicheia)* recurs elsewhere, but especially in Colossians. Other words are used; there is a notable collection of them in Romans 8: 38, 39, where the whole context is full of astrological and related terms.

> I am confident that neither death nor life, neither angels nor their princes, neither things present nor things to come, nor spiritual powers, whether above or below the level of the earth, nor any other created thing, shall be able to separate us from the love of God which is in Christ Jesus our Lord.

These powers are all inimical to man and constitute a potential threat to his relation with the loving God. If they were friendly and helpful Paul's shout of triumph would have an empty ring. This is true even of angels, who, in Paul's usage, are more often bad than good. In view of the Old Testament expression 'the angel of the Lord' this is a surprising fact; but at 8: 38, 1 Corinthians 6: 3; 2 Corinthians 12: 7, and perhaps 1 Corinthians 11: 10, angels are bad and constitute a threat. At 2 Corinthians 11: 14 what appears to be a good angel may turn out to be Satan in disguise. At Galatians 1: 8 the possibility is considered that an angel may preach a false Gospel. At 1 Corinthians 4: 9; 13: 1 the angels are neutral. At Galatians 4: 14 and perhaps at 1 Corinthians 11: 10 angels are good. Angels and other cosmic powers are at war with Christ, notwithstanding the check they have received in his crucifixion and resurrection and the fact that their ultimate defeat is certain (1 Cor 15: 24, 25). Paul and his readers live between these two decisive points, which define the conflict in which they find themselves. They do more than this; they make possible a combination of astrology and gnosis with another element in Paul's background, apocalyptic Judaism. Here too, religious man knows that he stands between a past when evil entered the world and a future in which it will be finally overthrown. Apocalyptic (itself not without a mystical element) provides a strict historical framework for what without it can become a timeless and therefore hopeless mysticism. Astrology and the reality of the present conflict with evil prevent apocalypticism from developing into a supine waiting for something good to turn up.

This analysis of a world and life under the dominion of evil, in dire need of salvation, calls for further consideration. The tyranny under which man lives is internal as well as external. He is not simply an unfortunate sufferer under the malign influence of the planets. A new word is needed to define his situation—sin.

This word itself is not easy to define. One might do worse than invert our proposition and say that sin is the inward correlative of the external tyranny, the subjection to astrological and demonic forces under which man lives. He is not simply, as some Jews tended to think of him, the unfortunate victim of oppression, the deprived heir of an Adam who had lost his wisdom, beauty, strength, and freedom; nor is he the unlucky product of a gnostic mythical 'accident' (as in the Hermetic tractate *Poimandres*, where heavenly man, leaning out of heaven to enjoy his own reflection in the watery deep, leaned too far, fell out of heaven, and found himself in the embrace of the — female — Nature), out of which a mixture of spirit and matter, good and evil, was generated. He is himself a guilty rebel against his Creator, condemned to perish by his own most grievous fault. How far he was himself responsible for this fault, how far he inherited it, how far he acquired it from his environment, are questions that must be deferred (and probably never answered in terms of simple proportion).

It is however worth while to point out that we meet here for the first time one of the most important hermeneutical and theological problems in the Pauline literature, a question which in different forms will recur from time to time. How far is the inward bondage of man to sin simply a demythologized way of expressing the outward bondage of man to the elements of the cosmos? Are the two capable of being equated without remainder? That they are related is, or will become, clear; are they, though cast in different terms, identical? If they are, then we may, if we wish, give up the elements at once, and most modern theologians would be glad to see them go. They are an embarrassment; we do not think in terms of such beings. The consequence of their dismissal would be that Pauline theology could virtually be rewritten on the basis of existentialism; theology would become anthropology. There is some truth in this view, some measure of equivalence as well as parallelism between the two forms of bondage. Man's rebellion is man's way to his own loss of cosmic privilege and of life itself: by man came death. There will be (though this assumes ground not yet covered) a corresponding parallel and equivalence in the sphere of redemption, for salvation will consist in an existential renewal or reorientation of man's life: by man came also the resurrection of the dead. Some truth: but is this the whole truth? Or does there remain an objective, external element in man's bondage, and hence in his liberation also? *Christus extra nos, Christus pro nobis*, as well as *Christus in nobis*? For the present the question must remain a question, but it is one that cannot be ignored.

Paul's commonest word for *sin (hamartia*, with a number of cognates) has as its basic meaning failure to hit a target, to reach a goal one aims at, but Paul's use is complicated by the fact that his word is used in the Septuagint (abbreviated LXX; the oldest Greek version of the Old Testament) to represent a number of Hebrew words, which bring into the Greek word a number of additional meanings. One (*ḥaṭaʾ*) means much the same as the Greek word, to do the wrong thing (e.g. 1 Kings 8: 46). Another (*ʿawon*) adds the notion of guilt (e.g. Numbers 5: 15; the memorial sacrifice not only reminds me that I have done something I ought not to have done; it brings to mind a relation with God that I have disturbed and that must now be put right by the prescribed means). A third (*peshaʿ*) is often used in secular, military contexts, and means rebellion (e.g. Psalm 19: 14, 'I shall no longer be in rebellion against God'). One cannot simply assume that these meanings will appear in Paul's use of his word; they are however demonstrably present. Thus 1 Kings 8: 46 has a close parallel in Romans 3: 23; guilt can be seen in 8: 3; and for rebellion 1 Corinthians 8: 12 is a clear and striking example — if you rebel against and injure your fellow Christian you are rebelling against and injuring Christ.

We may advance by seizing a nettle firmly. A verse often found difficult, Romans 14: 23, claims that everything that is not of faith is sin. If this meant (as readers sometimes think) that everything that is not consciously religious is sinful it would indeed be a most objectionable proposition. But this is not what Paul means. If for the moment we may assume (see below) that faith is the true relation of man to God, then anything that is outside this true relation, anything, that is, that is wrongly related to God, is sin. That is, sin is primarily a relational rather than an ethical word, and nothing if not (in the strictest sense) theological. Of course, to be wrongly related to God will have ethical consequences; this follows from the nature of God; but in the first instance sin is defined not in relation to an ethical system but in relation to God. This fundamental truth is best examined in the early chapters of Romans.

In the latter half of the first chapter (1: 18–32) the sin of the Gentile world is traced back to its idolatry, its rejection of the true God, so that sin immediately appears as a false, negative relation with God. The very existence of creation exterior to himself, the existence of objects for which he was in no sense responsible — sun, moon, earth, and so on — should have convinced man of an eternal power, a divinity (1: 20), a power not his own, not human, conceivably demonic but in fact (as a reader of the Old Testament did not need to be told) divine. This is 'that which can be known of God' (1: 19) — not the whole truth about God but the fact of the 'not-I' with which I am confronted in the universe. What does man do in the presence of this divinity? The correct response is to be inferred from 1: 21: he should glorify God and give thanks to him. But this verse contains a negative; this is precisely what man will not do. Instead of believing gratitude he gives God a rebuff. Why? because to recognize such an eternal power and divinity — such a 'not-I' — would mean recognizing a master; and this is what man is unwilling to do. There are allusions in this paragraph that show that Paul has in the back of his mind the story of creation and the fall in Genesis 1 - 3. What has happened is the perversion of an element in God's good creation. The human creatures were intended to have dominion over the rest of creation (Gen 1: 28; cf. Ps 8: 6); but their lust for dominion was unbridled. Having tasted the sweets of authority man sought more, and to make himself free even of God by depressing God to his own level — or lower. He changed the truth of God into a lie (1: 25) and rejected all the intimations of God that came to him from a world still unfallen. He preferred to worship human and animal images which could never be his lord (1: 22, 23); they were and must remain under his control. This (Paul's conclusion echoes the Wisdom of Solomon, which also sees the root of evil in idolatry, but on a deeper level) is the origin of man's disorder. His wisdom becomes folly (1: 21, 22) and he plunges into moral wickedness, and that by God's decree (1: 24, 26, 28: God handed them over). Immediately we meet the words 'lust,' 'uncleanness'; for Paul, sexual — and especially homosexual — sin is the most blatant of all sins because it is the clearest example of man's self-assertion, the ultimate case of arrogating to oneself a right that one does not possess. It is bad enough when I make an illicit claim on another person's property; worse when I make such a claim on another person's person.

The theme that runs through the second chapter of Romans is set by the apparently paradoxical statement of the first verse: 'You who judge do the same things'. Unless Paul has taken to writing nonsense this cannot mean that all, including those who take the moral high ground and condemn their neighbours, are equally guilty of the sins described in 1: 28-31, any more than keeping the ordinances of the Law in 2: 26 can mean that Gentiles observe the Sabbath and abstain from pork. It is in the act of judging that the self-appointed judge becomes guilty of the sins of his sinful neighbour. In simple terms it means that the human judge, religious Jew or Gentile moral philosopher, dispossesses God, putting himself in his place; instead of giving glory to God he gives it to himself. Morally he may be upright, but sin, as we have seen, is a matter of relation, and his relation with God is one of pride rather than faith. He is not prepared to wait for God and accept his assessment (2: 7, 8); and this is to rebel against him.

Chapter 3 contains the joint indictment of Jew and Greek (3: 9), with a detailed demonstration of the point out of the Old Testament (3: 10–18). This is important because it shows that for Paul the charge of universal sinfulness is not a matter of observation (which could be mistaken and must certainly be incomplete – perhaps a perfectly good man will turn up some day), but of the word of God. This provides another aspect of the quasi-philosophical (but really exegetical – it turns on Genesis 1 – 3) argument of chapter 1. The argument does not amount (and is not claimed by Paul to amount) to coercive proof; he uses the Old Testament (and some other sources too) as language quarries. Finally in this chapter we may note once more 3: 23, containing the absolute statement, 'All have sinned', which Paul now regards as sufficiently grounded. This statement however is set in a paragraph which constitutes a positive statement of the Gospel and must for the present be deferred.

In chapter 1 Paul makes allusive use of the figure of Adam and of the narrative of Genesis 1 – 3. In chapter 5 his use of this Old Testament material becomes explicit. The paragraph 5: 12–21 takes up again but in somewhat less analytical terms the themes of chapters 1 and 2. New terminology is introduced which requires attention. There are three words that mean, roughly, sin: the one that we have already encountered (*hamartia*), occurring now in verses 12, 13, 20, 21; and two, both of which can be rendered *transgression* (*parabasis*, in verse 14; *paraptōma*, in verses 15, 16, 17, 18, 20). The essence of the matter is that sin is an almost abstract term, used in a non-ethical sense to describe a negative or perverted relation between man and God. It is incapable of being measured or even observed unless a further factor, law, is introduced into the situation (verse 13). It is law that turns sin into concrete acts of transgression. So it was with Adam, who received the simplest of commands – 'Thou shalt not eat of it'; and so it is with the rest of mankind: all sinned (verse 12). It wanted only law to turn universal sin into universal transgression and so far as law was not universal, or might have seemed not to be universal, some might seem to have escaped, so that Paul makes a special point in verse 14. What Adam's sin was is given fundamental definition by its contrast with the *act of grace* (verse 16) and the *obedience* (verse 19) of Christ, who humbled himself in obedient trust before God. Grace is condescending, outgoing, giving, non-acquisitive love. This is contrasted with, and illuminates, the acquisitiveness of Genesis 3, and of all human life since. This is not simply greed, but man's desire to secure himself, even vis-à-vis God, and Adam's transgression is either plain disobedience or, more subtly, obedience rendered with a view to gaining control over the person obeyed.

It is worth while to spare a glance ahead into chapter 6; see especially verses 6, 12, 14, 17, 19, 20. Sin once admitted into human nature proceeds to reign as a king or a lord, and correspondingly makes men its slaves; this is the ethical consequence of the essentially non-ethical, relational nature of sin.

Summarizing so far we may say:

1. Sin is connected with Adam; *'adam* is a Hebrew word that means *man, humanity*. That is, sin is co-extensive with the human race and proper to the being of man as such, not an accident, which any given man may or may not incur, but a definition of human nature — at least a partial and provisional definition. The ultimate definition of human nature, for Paul, is Christ, but this is a proposition we have not yet reached.

2. Sin is connected with idolatry, the most primitive of all sins. It is essentially a theological (rather than a moral) concept, a relation (or lack of relation) with God. It exists wherever God is dispossessed of his place and his right. In this sense Jews as well as Gentiles may be idolaters. The root of idolatry (to press still further back) is pride, for the only way in which man can put himself on a level with his God, the being whom he worships, is by denying the true God and putting a no-god in his place. This makes him an idolater.

3. The consequence of sin is death. The more man seeks life in and for himself the more he turns his back on God, who is life. Again the story of Adam (*man*) is in mind. By rebelling, seeking life by illicit means, Adam condemned himself to death. This man, collectively, continues to do.

4. It follows that sin, like death, is a matter that concerns the whole person, not part of him. It is a definition of human existence in this age.

The last observation will lead to a further step in our discussion. We must consider Paul's account of human nature. Does examination of the terms he uses to describe the human person bear out the view that sin is a feature and function of man as a whole, or does it (as is sometimes maintained) suggest that there is one element in man (*flesh, sarx*) that is inherently sinful and infects the rest? If this is so it would bring Paul fully within the gnostic world-view.

A number of the words Paul uses in his description of human nature can be quickly dismissed because it is clear at once that they signify what is neither inherently good nor inherently evil; they can go either way. One example is the *heart*, one of Paul's most frequently used terms. He uses it in substantially the same way as the Old Testament; it is the seat of thought, will, and affection — a very comprehensive word. It may be evil; so for example at Romans 1: 21, 24. It may be good. This use is more common (for example Rom. 2: 29; 10: 1, 10; 2 Cor 1: 22), but that is probably because Paul uses the word most often when speaking of Christians.

A word of similar ambiguity is *mind*; in this Paul differs from most of his contemporaries, for whom mind was undoubtedly a higher, or the highest, part of human nature. A saying attributed to Apollonius of Tyana (Eusebius, *Praeparatio Evangelica* 4. 13) gives an inquirer the advice 'Let him ask good things from the noblest of the things that are through the noblest of the things within us; this is mind'. There may be some resemblance to this view in Romans 11: 34, and 1 Corinthians 2: 16, but the resemblance here is misleading because Paul is quoting Isaiah 40: 13, where a Hebrew word, usually translated *spirit*, is exceptionally rendered *mind*. When Paul adds 'We have the mind of Christ', he means 'We have the spirit of Christ'. Compare 1 Corinthians 7: 40. Mind certainly is a reasoning faculty (Rom 14: 5; 1 Cor 14: 14, 15, 19; Phil 4: 7), but this does not make it in Paul's view good. At Romans 1: 28 it is the reverse of good: God handed them over to an unfit mind. The treatment of sin in this paragraph has a strongly intellectual element. Idolatry means the denial of a potential knowledge of God. When this denial takes place moral depravity follows, and in the end man loses the capacity to make moral distinctions. His mind (here not far removed from conscience) ceases to function. At 12: 2 it is stated that the mind can be and implied that it ought to be renewed; left to itself it is the reprobate mind of 1: 28. From passages such as these (and others could be added) it is clear that the mind is not in itself a 'higher' side of human nature over against a 'lower' side (such as flesh might be thought to be). It may in fact be dominated by flesh. Like heart, but with a markedly more intellectual emphasis, it is an aspect of the whole person.

A word difficult to assess is *spirit*—difficult not least because it is hard to tell when Paul is speaking of the human spirit (which he does only infrequently) and when of the Holy Spirit of God (which he does much oftener). It is seldom that the latter possibility can be ruled out completely and this means that spirit (though it has its own importance) is not an important anthropological term, or perhaps rather that it is one which it is difficult to use with confidence. It is however important that spirit in man corresponds with spirit in God as a self-cognitive element: 1 Corinthians 2: 11. This does not amount to any kind of *analogia entis* between man and God. Like most people in antiquity Paul probably did think of spirit as a kind of very rarified substance, but he certainly did not think that because it was rarified and relatively immaterial it was necessarily good. This is shown by such passages as Romans 8: 15; 11: 8, and 1 Corinthians 2: 12.

It is particularly difficult at 1 Corinthians 14: 14 (cf. 32) to settle whether Paul is speaking of God or man. *My* spirit may be (a) part of my psychological make-up; (b) the spiritual gift entrusted to me, or the spiritual agency that effected it; or (c) the Holy Spirit as given to me. No solution of the problem is entirely satisfactory because Paul appears to be combining three thoughts in one phrase (one of his habits): (a) it is no less than the Holy Spirit of God that inspires Christian worship; (b) the work of the Spirit is crystallized in a special gift; (c) the gift is given in such personal form to *me* that I can think of it as mine (just as in Romans 12: 2 you may think of the renewed mind as your mind).

Another notable and difficult passage is 2 Corinthians 7: 1, 'Let us cleanse ourselves from every defilement of flesh and spirit'. The whole passage (6: 14 – 7:1) raises difficult problems. It has often been held to interrupt the sequence of thought and therefore to be an interpolation in Paul's text. As such it has been taken to be a wandering piece of a lost letter of Paul's to Corinth; more recently it has been held to be theologically akin to the writings discovered at Qumran (the Dead Sea Scrolls) and thus a foreign body in the Pauline corpus. Part of the argument for the latter view is that the notion of the cleansing of defilement of flesh and spirit is one that Paul could not have entertained. Briefly, the argument is that neither flesh nor spirit can be cleansed. Flesh cannot be cleansed because it is intrinsically evil and thus beyond cleansing; spirit cannot be cleansed because it is the Spirit of God and therefore always and necessarily good and by definition beyond the need and possibility of cleansing. This is logic-chopping. It is more plausible that Paul is speaking here in a popular way of total cleansing, cleansing in every respect and in every part, as he does at 1 Corinthians 7: 34. We shall come back to Qumran, in relation to flesh and to other matters, later.

Soul may serve as a representative—and suitably vague—rendering of a Greek word (*psychē*) which Paul uses in a variety of senses, as the Old Testament does a corresponding Hebrew noun. Sometimes it is simply *life*, as at Romans 11 :3, 'They seek my life' (cf. Rom 16: 4; Phil 2: 30). The same meaning appears in the Old Testament quotation (Gen 2: 7) at 1 Corinthians 15: 45, The first Adam became a living soul; this simply points to the difference between Adam as a moving, speaking being and the pile of dust out of which he was made. Paul is still following a common Hebrew use when he writes *every soul* for all representatives of the human race (Rom 2: 9; 13: 1). 1 Thessalonians 5: 23 seems at first sight to stand alone with a tripartite division of human nature: body, soul, spirit. But soul and body belong together and mean a living body, not a dead one.

Body may seem to be approaching *flesh*, for a body is made of flesh; but the word has both good and bad—and indifferent—senses. A body of some kind is the indispensable agent or instrument of the human ego. This is made very clear in 1 Corinthians 15: 35-49. The Christian hope for the future is that the whole person will be raised up and at the same time transformed. The present body is a body animated by soul, the future body will be a body animated by spirit, God's Spirit. But there will always be a body of some kind. So at Philippians 3: 21 there will be a transformed body; so also in 2 Corinthians 5: 1-4, where what we hope to avoid is (in Paul's image) nakedness, bodiless existence. Even for a short time this would be a horrifying experience.

A particularly interesting and instructive passage, especially in that it leads on to consideration of the word *flesh*, is 1 Corinthians 6: 12-20. Paul is qualifying the Corinthian proposition (which is essentially true), 'All things are permitted me'. He goes on to quote what is probably a further Corinthian argument: Food is for the belly and the belly is for food; both will in due course perish, so that what I put in my stomach has no religious or theological significance. This is an argument that Paul can and does accept. It appears later in the epistle (see pp. 139, 140) that he sees no harm in eating food that has been sacrificed to idols (except when it offends a weaker Christian conscience; to eat is then an offence against love, but that does not mean that there is anything essentially evil in the food itself). Verse 13b implies (but does not state — Paul found it too objectionable) that the Corinthian argument continued: As with the satisfaction of hunger, so with the satisfaction of sexual desire. Means are provided for this end. The body is framed for that use which is expressed in fornication — coition with a prostitute, and fornication exists for the release of the body's energy: the body is for fornication and fornication is for the body. The sexual organs and their action like the alimentary organs will perish, and have no permanent religious significance. Paul in reply distinguishes between the stomach and (what he means by) the body. Unlike eating, sexual intercourse is an act of the whole person, and though the stomach and its contents will perish God will raise up the body. It follows that sexual morality is not a matter of indifference. The body, though after death it will (as we have seen) be transformed, is the continuous organ by which the continuity of personality is expressed in this age and in the age to come.

Paul continues. Verse 15 is for Christians a self-evident truth, if indeed fornication means robbing Christ of his members (the word serves as a differentiated equivalent for body) and giving them to a harlot. To join oneself to a harlot is in fact to become one body with her (6: 16); this is supported by reference to Genesis 2: 24, where however the word is not 'body' but 'flesh'. This difference serves a useful purpose, for it enables Paul to make the contrasting statement that he who joins himself to the Lord becomes one spirit with him. This provides us with an important indicator of the decision under which the body stands. In itself it is neutral. It is intended for the Lord (6: 13), and if joined to him becomes one spirit with him, because he is spirit; his is a spiritual body. But it is also possible for the body to be devoted to fornication, to be joined to a harlot; in this case it becomes one flesh with the harlot — not because she is a human being made of a substance called 'flesh' but because the act takes place in the realm of flesh, in the sense in which we shall find the word to be understood.

Other passages also bring out the ambiguous position of the body, as the instrument of the ego. Romans 6 is a clear example. At verse 6 (. . . that the body of sin might be done away), the body has passed under the dominion of sin; it now belongs to and is characterized by sin. But at verse 12 ('Let not sin reign in your mortal body') it is clear that though Christians still have mortal bodies (that is, bodies doomed to death) sin must not be allowed to reign in them. The matter is repeated and clarified in verses 13 and 19, where (as in 1 Corinthians 6: 19) the body is (a) differentiated into members, and (b) identified with the self. The parallels are important:

Do not continue to present your members
. . . present yourselves
As . . . you presented your members
So . . . present your members

The same verb (to present, or offer) occurs at Romans 12: 1. And at Romans 7: 24 Paul asks, 'Who will rescue me from this body of death?' A body subject to sin is inevitably a body subject to death; the pay of sin is death (Rom 6: 23).

The members, that is, the body, may be offered to sin, or to God. Sin may, and does, reign in the body, though it should not do so. There is a body that has come under the dominion of sin, and is therefore a body under sentence of death. The sin-dominated body must die, or, as otherwise put, the body, the members, must be recovered from the rule of sin and presented to God.

Body is man at the crossroads; but so is *mind*; so is man however you look at him. Body and mind may turn in the direction of God, or of sin. Romans 12: 1 is of fundamental importance here; so, in a different way, is 1 Corinthians 9: 27, which does not mean that the body is an enemy; it is a servant, and must be beaten out of servitude to sin and presented to Christ.

The anthropological term that is of fundamental importance for the understanding of Paul's conception of evil is *flesh*. It is understandable but unfortunate that most modern translations of the New Testament avoid this word, paraphrasing with greater or less success. It is understandable that they should do this, for the English word suggests a material substance of which animal bodies are made, and though Paul occasionally uses the word in this sense it is not his most characteristic and important use. What this use is is difficult to define, and there is perhaps no single word, or two- or three-word phrase, that will give it in English. Paul's Greek word (*sarx*) also means the physical substance that the English *flesh* means. Further meanings his readers could determine only by attending to what he said about it; and there is no reason why English readers should not put themselves to the same trouble. They will in the end get a much more satisfactory notion of Paul's meaning than can be won from most modern paraphrases.

Paul can and does use the word flesh in its simplest physiological sense. Such uses are not in themselves of great interest for the student of his thought except in that they have a way of pointing beyond themselves. It was an infirmity of the flesh that led to Paul's first preaching in Galatia (Gal 4: 13, 14). Circumcision takes place in the flesh (Rom 2: 28; Gal 6: 13). Flesh is mortal (2 Cor 4: 11). It belongs to humanity, not to God; hence the danger that it may point away from God and toward man. An Old Testament passage that is often cited, and sometimes misunderstood, in discussions of Paul's use of flesh is Isaiah 31: 3: 'The Egyptians are men and not God, and their horses are flesh and not spirit'. No one can reasonably blame the Egyptians for being men or their horses for being flesh, and the prophet does not do so. But he does blame men who put their confidence in men and flesh rather than in God and spirit. Paul also uses several times the phrase *according to the flesh*. This too is sometimes neutral, but even so leaves the impression that a judgement according to the flesh leaves unsaid something that is necessary if the whole truth is to be expressed. For example, it is true that there exists an Israel according to the flesh (Rom 9: 3; 1 Cor 10: 18; cf. Rom 4: 1; Gal 4: 23, 29; also Rom 9: 8; 11: 14). Not only is this the fact; it was the will of God that there should be an Israel in history, along with Egypt and Babylon. But Israel according to the flesh has never fully achieved the divine purpose for Israel, and one looks for a fulfilment of what the nation could only suggest. Similarly it is true that there is a Messiah according to the flesh. As such, he is a Jew, descended from David (Rom 1: 3; 9: 3); and some would be content with such a Messiah. But for Paul, as these passages show, this was not enough. *According to the flesh* suggests a human standard of judgement; not necessarily false in itself and within its own limits, but inadequate and therefore possibly misleading. Thus 1 Corinthians 1: 26, 27: there are in the Corinthian church not many who are wise according to the flesh, that is, when judged by human standards of wisdom; but it is a different kind of wisdom that 'we speak among the mature' (2: 6, 13–16); 2 Corinthians 1: 17 (where Paul distinguishes between plans made on the basis of purely human considerations and those made on a different basis). These passages lead to a correct understanding of 2 Corinthians 5: 16, where the phrase is not adjectival but adverbial, and describes not two different kinds of Christ — an earthly-historical and a heavenly-spiritual — but two different ways of knowing, of estimating. One is the natural human estimate of Christ, based, like men's estimates of their fellows, on purely human, external standards and presuppositions. This is the view according to the flesh, and it provides an important pointer to the meaning (in Paul's use) of *flesh*. It leads to weighing up a situation but leaving God out of account.

Perhaps the most important passage for understanding Paul's use of *flesh* is Galatians 5: 13–24, in which he makes a double contrast of flesh with love and flesh with spirit. Of these the former appears immediately in verse 13: 'Do not use your Christian freedom as a jumping-off ground for flesh but—do the opposite: through love serve one another'. Love (as the quotation of Leviticus 19: 18 shows) is what God desires in human relations. Verse 15 jumps back to the other side, describing the extreme consequence of life directed by flesh; it leads to mutual destruction, the end of human society. Verse 16 is important in the introduction of two new words. One is *desire*; not lusts in the obviously evil sense of the word, but desire. The love that God requires can be somewhat clumsily but not badly described as non-self-centred existence; the desire of the flesh is the opposite of this, self-centred existence, existence determined by desire—what I desire (for myself). Desire is not necessarily lustful desire (though of course it may be). It may also be religious desire; this, as we shall see, is the fundamental point that lies behind Paul's discussion of faith and works. The other word introduced in verse 16 is *Spirit*. Flesh stands over against love; it also stands over against Spirit. 'Walk by the Spirit and you will not fulfil the desire of the flesh.' To walk—to live—by the Spirit is to lead not only a non-self-centred existence but what is in fact the only practical alternative to this, God-centred existence. Flesh means that I desire things (not for God or for my neighbour but) for myself. Hence the stark opposition of verse 17. Flesh and spirit are contraries not because they are higher and lower parts of human nature but because they denote respectively life as directed by and for self and life directed by and for God.

The 'works of the flesh' follow (vv. 19–21). The important thing to note is that they are not all 'carnal', but they are all egocentric. Some indeed are carnal—fornication, wantonness, drunkenness. It is here that egocentricity is easiest to see; in idolatry, envy, party-spirit it is more subtle.

Correspondingly the 'fruit of the Spirit' (vv. 22f.) is non-egocentric existence, of which the first example is inevitably love, non-acquisitive, giving, self-giving love. It is hardly too much to say that the remaining examples can all be regarded as special cases of love.

And those (Paul winds up the paragraph in verse 24) who belong to Christ have crucified the flesh with its passions and desires. They have shared the death to sin that Christ died (Rom 6: 10). This allusion in fact evokes the whole of Romans 6: the Christian life means the end of self-centred existence, the progressive detaching of the members from the service of sin and their presentation to God in the service of righteousness.

Another passage of great importance for the study of Paul's use of *flesh* is Romans 7: 17 – 8: 13. Here it must suffice to pick out three or four verses which take up the points already noticed in relation to Christ. We shall shortly be discussing Paul's view of the Law; here (8: 3) he declares that, though good, it is ineffective because of the flesh. Flesh is here a force that operates in a direction contrary to the true intention of the Law, which is to secure man's obedience to God. Clearly this does not mean flesh as material, or even flesh as 'man's unspiritual nature'; it means human life resolved upon its own will rather than upon God's. This is further emphasized by the expression 'sin's flesh' (better than 'sinful flesh') and especially by the statement that the Son of God came 'in the likeness of sin's flesh'. The word *likeness* does not imply any unreality in the human nature of Christ; Paul is emphasizing at once his identity with and his difference from the human race. The incarnation meant that Christ shared in existence that was normally anthropocentric. His condemnation of sin in the flesh—the only place where there was any point in condemning it—means that he lived a theocentric existence in anthropocentric circumstances. Paul goes on (8: 4) to show that the result of Christ's living a God-centred life while in the likeness of sin's flesh (real material flesh but not under the domination of sin) is that that which the Law righteously requires, namely God-centred existence, might be fulfilled in us, in that we live not according to the flesh but according to the Spirit. The righteous requirement of the Law is fulfilled only when this new existence is lived. Paul proceeds to a fundamental definition of what is meant by this (8: 5). The alternative to 'minding the things of the flesh' is not 'minding the things of the higher life' but 'minding the things of the Spirit (of God)'. Once more, *flesh* is anthropocentric life, *Spirit* is God-centred life.

If by the word *flesh* Paul did not normally mean what the word in ordinary use did mean—the soft constituent of the physical human frame—why did he use it in the way he did? There is a Jewish word that offers parallels to Paul's use of 'flesh'. Its roots can be found as far back as Sirach (see 15: 14), but it developed in rabbinic

72

Judaism to mean the inclination that pushes man in the direction of sin. The word is *yetzer*, used for example by Ben Zoma (in the second century) in Aboth 4: 1: 'Who is mighty? He that subdues his *yetzer*, as it is written, He that is slow to anger is better than the mighty, and he that ruleth his spirit than he that taketh a city' (Prov 16: 32). Later a distinction was made between the evil *yetzer* and the good *yetzer* that inclined man towards virtue. But whereas Sirach puts the *yetzer* into Greek as *counsel (diaboulion)*, Paul uses *flesh*; perhaps because there was an exegetical tradition that pointed this way. Philo (a contemporary of Paul's) interprets Gen 6: 3 in his tractate *De Gigantibus* 29–31:

> The chief cause of ignorance is the flesh, and the tie which binds us so closely to the flesh. Moses himself affirms this when he says that *because they are flesh* the divine spirit cannot abide . . . But nothing thwarts its [Wisdom's] growth so much as our fleshly nature . . . Souls that are free from flesh and body spend their days in the theatre of the universe and with a joy that none can hinder see and hear things divine . . . But those which bear the burden of the flesh cannot look up to the heavens.

Philo is concerned about the material nature of flesh, as Paul is not; but some resemblance remains. There are parallels of a sort in the Qumran MSS too.[3] More important than the source of Paul's terminology is the use that he made of it; and here one further observation will provide a transition to the next theme.

There is an important parallel in Paul's usage between the *cosmos* and the *flesh*. It is instructive to recall the argument of Galatians 3 and 4. Man's past (and in Galatia it threatened to be his future too) was slavery under the cosmic elements. From this bondage the Law was unable to liberate man because, given 430 years after the promise and administered by angels (3: 19), it belonged within the framework of bondage and thus could not break out and inaugurate the life of the age to come; it was not able to give life (3: 21). Some new power was needed to do this. This is parallel to what Paul says in other terms in Romans 8: 3. Here the powerlessness of the Law is caused through the flesh. The Law is a good law, but it belongs within the fleshly and cosmic framework, and there is no liberation till God sent his Son 'in the likeness of sin's flesh and to deal with sin', and thus condemned sin in the flesh. Neither the flesh nor the cosmos is evil in itself: it is not evil because it is material; but each tends to make itself self-sufficient and independent of God, and this is evil.

This invites us to a final summary of Paul's account of the world under the power of evil; it will effect a transition to the next theme.

1. Independently of man, and objectively, the universe is perverted because it has come to be under the wrong direction: under the wrong rulers. It is in bondage to corruption (Rom 8: 21); the elements of the cosmos (Gal 4: 3) and other powers (or the same powers under other names) have seized control. The enemy is at large and the war is not yet over (1 Cor 15: 24, 25). Man is subject to death; even Christians continue to be threatened by the evil powers (Rom 8: 38, 39). Since one of the evil personified powers is sin, this is not far from . . .

2. . . . the fact that inwardly man is himself perverted. The disorder is anthropological as well as cosmic, and the essence of it is that man lives within the closed circle of his own existence, seeking to control his own affairs in his own interests. Turning away from God and manufacturing deities according to his own choice he falls into foolishness and immoral behaviour. As a result he abuses even good gifts of God, such as the Law (as we shall shortly see).

The anthropological analysis is in the main Paul's. His contemporaries saw some of the consequences of Adam's fall—his loss of power, privilege, immortality, his falling under the dominion of forces he should have controlled. On the whole, this was man's misfortune. But gnostic astrologers and apocalyptists viewed man as the unfortunate prisoner in a hostile world, waiting for someone to deliver him. Paul shared the apocalyptic world-view, and he was capable of borrowing at least the language of astrology, but he does not allow the apocalyptic picture to dissolve in myth or mysticism. He insists on its existential character, yet at the same time he proclaims an objective cosmic redemption as well as an existential conversion.

LAW AND COVENANT

There is then something wrong with the cosmos, and with its inhabitants. It was made good by a good God, who made it with good will; that is, with the intention of being on good terms with the human race. He has not changed his mind about this, and it may therefore be presumed that he will take steps to set right what has gone wrong. This however is a complicated process, which may be expected to operate on two levels. There is a cosmic failure to put right, and there are individual human beings, each of whom pursues his own course through life, a course that proceeds with no uniformity but in fits and starts. So much is generalization, arising out of inference from Paul's account of what is wrong. It is necessary now to look at his account of how things have been, are being, and will be put right.

The process begins with a false start; though Paul himself would have rejected the expression. God does not make false starts. Fault lay on the human side. What God offered was mistaken, wrongly understood, misused. This refers to God's Law and his covenant with his people; these are central concepts in Paul's own theological thinking; they are central concepts in Judaism. They have evoked much discussion, which in recent years has become sharp; there is, notwithstanding disagreements, a clearer and more profound understanding of the subject than in the past. To follow out the controversies, outline the various opinions held on controversial topics, is beyond the limits of this small book. Some of the most important and readily accessible analyses are referred to in the Bibliography. In these pages I shall be concerned with sources (though I shall not always be able to quote them) rather than with 'secondary' literature, even when it is of primary importance.

Here is the first part of the problem. The sources for our knowledge of Judaism in what may be broadly called the Pauline period are immense, and not particularly easy of access. There are constant problems of date and consequently of relevance. It is necessary to begin with Scripture, not only because the Old Testament as a whole is certainly older than the period with which we are dealing but because all Jews regarded it as authoritative. They might differ sharply in their understanding of Scripture and in the methods by which they reached their understanding of it, but they all took it to be true and the foundation of their religion. Problems arise at once. The Old Testament (nearly all of it) was written in Hebrew; many Jews read it as a Hebrew text. Not all; some Jews, living in a Greek environment, were more familiar with Greek than with Hebrew, and they read their Bible in Greek. This meant the translation known as the Septuagint (LXX). It is important that this represents from time to time a different text from that known in the Hebrew manuscripts. It is perhaps even more important that words that may, in different languages, mean more or less the same thing nevertheless have different overtones and may thus suggest different meanings to those who read the one language or the other. There is a point here that is not always observed. Students of the Old Testament, noting that Hebrew word A is represented by Greek word B, are apt to say 'When in the LXX we read B we must remember that it is not used as (say) Aristotle would define it; it is filled not with its own Greek overtones but with the Hebrew overtones of A'. This may be fair enough in the study of the Old Testament for its own sake. But it must be remembered that the LXX came into being not for the benefit of scholars who delight to compare Hebrew and Greek semantics but for Jews who knew Greek but not Hebrew, and when they read in their Bible (for example) the Greek word *nomos (law)* understood it as a Greek word and did not import into it all the connotations of the Hebrew word (*torah*) that it translated.

Greek is not the only language that must be considered. The extent to which Hebrew continued to be in everyday use is a disputed question, but it was certainly replaced to some extent by a cognate Semitic language, Aramaic, and Aramaic translations of the Bible, called Targums, came into existence. Problems of dating here are severe; and the Targums are both more important and more difficult to use because they are often explanatory paraphrases rather than precise translations.

The Greek and Aramaic Bibles may be taken as pointers to the diverse character of Judaism in the ancient world, though this is a proposition that calls for immediate qualification, since it is now universally recognized that the old analysis into Palestinian and Hellenistic Judaism is a misleading over-simplification. Greek-speaking and Semitic-speaking is a more objective distinction, but even this must be used with caution. Many Jews could speak, or at least understand, Hebrew, Aramaic, and Greek. In Paul's time Palestine had been for a century or more part of the Hellenistic world, and Hellenistic modes of thought as well as the Greek language, had penetrated Jewish thought, often by unnoticed channels and with unobserved results. It is only to a limited extent that two bodies of literature, Greek and Semitic, can be distinguished. The LXX itself must stand out as the most important memorial of Greek-speaking Judaism, though its Greek is less pure, more tainted (as a purist would say) with Semitic idiom, than the work of the outstanding Jewish writers of Greek. These were Philo, the Alexandrian philosopher, and Josephus the historian, both men of the first century, Philo an almost exact contemporary of Paul, Josephus a little younger. Philo had absorbed a good deal of Greek philosophy but remained a propagandist for and expositor of the biblical faith; Josephus when he deals with Old Testament history is a sort of Targumist; elsewhere he shares the methods and the ideals of Hellenistic historiographers. There were others who wrote in Greek, including poets and dramatists; but there are other books which we know in Greek though they were originally written in Hebrew or Aramaic. Such for example were some of the apocalypses which are known to us as Greek literature but for other purposes have to be classified elsewhere, and belong with the other great wing of Jewish literature, written in Hebrew or Aramaic. The great body of rabbinic literature belongs to this field, and includes scriptural commentary and developments of the Law on various lines, sometimes edificatory, sometimes purely legal. Here, since all the texts were written down much later than the New Testament period, the problem is to know which parts of the literature contain traditions old enough to provide trustworthy illumination for Paul's thought. Older, undoubtedly old enough to be relevant, is the Qumran literature, the so-called Dead Sea Scrolls, which contain biblical commentary, regulations for the community, and apocalyptic, almost all of it material from which history can at least be inferred.

So much it has been necessary to review in the briefest of sketches if Paul's understanding of the Law is to be grasped, and grasped in the light of current discussion. Closely related to the Law is the notion of the covenant, and a term that has deservedly achieved considerable prominence in recent exposition of Judaism is 'covenantal nomism' (*nomism* being derived from the Greek *nomos*, law). The phase was coined by E. P. Sanders, and he should be allowed to say for himself what he means by it.

(1) God has chosen Israel and (2) given the law. The law implies both (3) God's promise to maintain the election and (4) the requirement to obey. (5) God rewards obedience and punishes transgression. (6) The law provides for means of atonement, and atonement results in (7) maintenance or re-establishment of the covenantal relationship. (8) All those who are maintained in the covenant by obedience, atonement and God's mercy belong to the group which will be saved. An important interpretation of the first and last points is that election and ultimately salvation are

77

considered to be by God's mercy rather than human achievement. (*Paul and Palestinian Judaism*, p. 422)

This summary of the principles of Judaism constitutes a problem as soon as we turn to Paul. It presents so favourable a picture, especially when to it is added the fact that it was possible for one who was not a Jew to become – religiously though not racially – a Jew by the process of proselytization. He must be circumcised and baptized; as long as the Temple stood he must offer sacrifice; and of course henceforth he must observe the Law, with its requirements and its privileges. What more could be required? Yet Paul speaks (and a discussion of his understanding of the Law may well begin from this point) of 'that which the Law could not do', 'that which was impossible to the Law' (Rom 8: 3). This impossibility God achieved when he sent his Son (ibid.). Virtually the same point is made in Galatians 2: 21: 'I do not make void the grace of God, for if righteousness comes through law, Christ died for nothing'. For Paul this is evidently the ultimate *reductio ad absurdum*; it is unthinkable that Christ died needlessly or in vain; therefore righteousness does not come through the Law. The positive side of these statements – the way in which the mission of the Son achieved what the Law could not do, the way in which the death of Christ made righteousness possible – must be discussed later, though it will not be possible to keep it out entirely at this point because positive and negative are closely bound up together: it is Christ (not the difficulty or inconvenience of keeping it) who is the end of the Law (Rom 10: 4). It will be well also to avoid generalization and to keep as close as possible to the Pauline texts, bearing in mind Paul's own claim (which receives some support – which it does not need – from Acts) that he had shown unparalleled enthusiasm and ability in the practice (which must have included the study) of Judaism (Gal 1: 14). He is a bold man who supposes that he understands first-century Judaism better than Paul did, and the more clearly it is recognized that Judaism, for all its diversity, cannot be split up into Palestinian and Hellenistic wings, the less legitimate is it to dismiss Paul as a Hellenistic Jew who failed to distinguish Greek *nomos* from Hebrew *torah*. The association, in the Hebrew Bible no less than in the Greek, of Torah with words such as commandments, precepts, judgements, is significant.

The first thing however to be said about the Law, in Paul's understanding of it, is that it is a good gift of the gracious God. It is his speech to men, spiritual (Rom 7: 14), that is, not concerned only with matters of religion, but inspired by the Spirit of God. Because it comes from God it is holy, righteous, and good (Rom 7: 12); it could be nothing else. It is marked by glory (2 Cor 3: 7, 9, 11). It is not to be blamed for the fact that when it is read a veil lies on men's hearts (2 Cor 3: 14, 15), or for the fact that it is not as good and glorious as the Gospel (2 Cor 3: 10). It commands what is right, though it lacks the power to give life (Gal 3: 21). If it is weak this is not so much on its own account as through the flesh (Rom 8: 3). It performs useful functions. It generates its own kind of righteousness, which is not to be despised (Phil 3: 6, 9). It provides the basis for Christian argument (1 Cor 9: 8, 9), since it truly is God's word. It gives supreme guidance for the Christian life – the law of love is written in the Old Testament (Rom 13: 8–10 and Gal 5: 14, quoting Lev 19: 18). This indeed is the true understanding of the Law; it arises out of God's love for his people (Rom 9: 4) and commands them to love one another, as they must still do. This is why the Law bears witness to righteousness, faith, and salvation (Rom 3: 21; 10: 6–8).

So the Law is a good gift of the good God to men – his word, which never changes, for it is always his will that men should love one another and live in trustful obedience to him. Jesus also finds the Law summed up in the command of love, and affirms it (Mark 12: 29–31). But Paul perceives, as the gospels do, that in achieving this aim the Law can get in its own way. It produces wrath (Rom 4: 15). It is a ministry of death (2 Cor 3: 7; Rom 7: 7–11). It was responsible for 'passions of sins' (Rom 7: 5); Paul had had to die to the Law, through the Law (Gal 2: 19); Christians in general have been put to death to the Law, been discharged from the Law (Rom 7: 4, 6), not that he or they might live lawless lives but that they might live to God. Paul was unable to avoid the (to a Jew) horrifying question 'Is the Law sin?' (Rom 7: 7).

In the light of evidence we have already seen, Paul is bound to answer, and does answer, 'Certainly not'. But the question is important and unescapable, and we must go on to ask: If the Law is not to be identified with sin, how is it related to sin? What has happened to it since God gave it? How does it come to have the effects observed?

To some extent these questions have already been dealt with, in the discussion of the controversies that lie behind Galatians. If the favourable account of 'covenantal nomism' that has been quoted above is taken to be the understanding of the Law in which Paul was brought up, and that which was held by his Jewish contemporaries and by the Judaizing Christians, it is difficult to understand the ferocity with which the conflict was waged—the threat to Paul's life that is implied in 2 Corinthians 11:26 (where 'perils among false brothers' forms a climax to a series that contains several examples of danger of death) and his own bitter rejoinder in Galatians 5:12. Paul may have misjudged those who wished to impose the Law on Gentile converts, but their existence is attested by Acts (15:1, 5) as well as in the epistles, and unless Paul misrepresents them they did maintain a form of religion that required works done in obedience to the given Law—and how could they be blamed, when the Law was made up of so many precepts and prohibitions? The main point of contention lies in the relation between covenant and Law, and it is necessary only to recall what has already been pointed out. It is to Paul essential to begin the story with Abraham. God's covenant with Abraham was indeed a matter of free grace expressed in an act of election, to which the only possible response was the obedience of faith—not the obedience of works done in the observance of specific commands, for there were none, but the obedience expressed in the trusting acceptance of a call to expect no security except the security of the promise. It is hard to make sense of Galatians 3 if Paul's opponents, who threatened the existence of his churches, did not say—or, to beg no questions, if Paul did not believe that they said—'True; that was the covenant with Abraham; this has now been supplemented, or replaced, by the covenant under Moses, and of this obedience is an explicit and essential element'. It originated in an act of saving grace, by which God constituted a people rescued from slavery, but its origins include also the words of acceptance, 'If you will obey my voice and keep my covenant, you shall be my own possession among all peoples . . . All that the Lord has spoken we will do' (Exod 19:5, 8). And what should this mean if not being circumcised, observing the Sabbath, keeping the food laws, and so on, as well as abstaining from idolatry, murder, adultery, stealing? Hence Paul's argument that the first covenant could not be varied; he insists on going behind Moses to Abraham.

But there is more to say about the Law, both positively and negatively, than this; we have not yet got to the bottom of the paradox of a Law which is the word of God—always a gracious as well as a righteous God—and the instrument of death.

First and most simply, the Law is not kept, and when not kept it makes sin—in itself, as we have seen, a pre-moral relation—observable in moral evil, and thus constitutes man's accusation. This is worked out in a somewhat complicated argument in

Galatians 3: 10–14, which we unravelled above, and stated in bald terms in Romans 3. First comes (3: 10–18) a catena of Old Testament quotations, which amount to the accusation that there is not a single righteous person to be found: crude perhaps but it is important to Paul that the analysis of human nature and society that he gives in Romans 1 and 2 should be seen to be not the result of his personal observation, certainly limited and possibly misleading, but the judgement of God pronounced in his word. This leads to the general statement of Romans 3: 19: what the Law says (and it has just pronounced a verdict of condemnation) it says to those who stand under its authority in order that every mouth may be stopped and the whole world come under God's judgement. Israel who have the Law have it both as privilege and as threat not simply on their own behalf but on behalf of mankind as a whole. The existence of the Law is made effective through Israel for the whole human race. And this is proved by Galatians 3, where the argument proves that the Law can be shown to demonstrate its own failure, failure to produce human beings who are rightly related to God.

Secondly, the Law actually provokes sin. This is obscurely stated in Galatians 3: 19, which must be interpreted in the light of Romans 5: 20: the Law crept into its subordinate place (it was indeed *added* but not with the effect or intention of destroying the Abrahamic covenant) in order that sin might abound. We turn back to Romans 7, where Paul asserts more emphatically than elsewhere that the Law in itself is good. Yet its effects are sinful, because when it is applied to one who is already sold as a slave under the power of sin (7: 14) it passes itself under the power of sin, which uses it to bring sin to life where previously sin had been dead (7: 9). It is not the Law's fault; the Law forbids desire, yet its effect is to kindle in me every kind of desire (7: 7, 8). So the commandment that was intended to keep me alive — to keep me, as some would say, within the covenant — killed me. That sin can do this with so good a thing as the Law proves how very sinful sin is (7: 13); but it does it.

How does the Law encourage sin? The question is often answered in psychological terms: forbidden fruit is always sweet; it is fun to break the rules. There is superficial truth in this, but Paul goes deeper. He uses the tenth commandment, 'Thou shalt not covet', but when he quotes it he omits the objects of the verb which are liberally supplied in the Old Testament: 'thy neighbour's house', 'thy neighbour's wife', and so on. Before the commandment reaches these, coveting, desiring for oneself, is already wrong, as wilful self-aggrandizement; and the Law is there as a thing to be attained.

Man takes up the command to act as lord over all creation (Gen 1: 28; 2: 19; cf. Ps 8: 6), and takes it too far. He will be lord not over creation only but over the Creator too.

Thirdly, it is very difficult (perhaps not in the end impossible) to have a law without legalism, and legalism in religion is sin because it magnifies the human ego. This is perhaps only another way of expressing the second point. Paul insists, quoting the Law itself, that the principle of the Law is *doing*, it is a matter of *works* (Gal 3: 12, quoting Lev 18: 5; cf. Deut 17: 26 in Gal 3: 10). Paul had done works and counted them credits in his account with God (Phil 3: 7, 8); when he became a Christian he changed his credits into debits: he had got his accounts wrong. What mattered now was to be found in Christ and to have a righteousness that came not out of the Law but through faith in Christ. This puts the matter on a personal level—not surprisingly in so personal a letter as Philippians. Paul puts the same matter on a broader basis in the least personal of his letters—Romans. In Paul's view his own people had misunderstood their vocation and the Law which gave substance to it; these they had misunderstood because they had misunderstood God. This misunderstanding—perhaps for the present we should be content to say, this alleged misunderstanding—determines Paul's relation with his own people as well as with the Law. This fact is not always recognized and when it is not recognized there is inevitable failure to grasp Paul's attitude, and sometimes the allegation that he did not know, perhaps because he was at heart a Hellenist rather than a Jew, what the Law was and how one should respond to it. It is of course open to anyone to reply that it was Paul who was mistaken; those whom he accused of error were right. But at least he knew what he was doing and put his finger on the spot. They, the Israelites, have a zeal for God, but it is an uninformed zeal (Rom 10: 2), and leads them in the same direction that Paul's pre-Christian zeal had led him. He had been zealous beyond most for the ancestral traditions (Gal 1: 14) and his zeal had led him into resistance to the Christian movement, even into persecution of Christians. There were others who had been led to the same error (1 Thess 2: 15, 16), but more important was the injury they did to themselves. In his discussion of the matter in Romans Paul does not complain of persecution but makes two related points. The Jews' zeal for God was not 'according to knowledge'; this was shown by the fact that they did not recognize, did not know God's righteousness, and seeking to establish their own righteousness did not subject themselves to God's righteousness (10: 3). The positive theme of God's righteousness must be discussed later; if we turn back we find (9: 31, 32) the corresponding statement: Israel pursuing a law of righteousness did not attain to the Law; Why? because Israel sought it not on the basis of faith but as if it were to be had on the basis of works. Thus—in Paul's view—his contemporaries were seeking to establish a righteousness of their own (as Paul himself had done, Phil 3: 6, 9) by doing works required by the Law; he does not say that they were seeking to establish their own identity by emphasizing those practices that were peculiar to Jews and not shared by their Gentile neighbours. Paul may have misunderstood them, but this is what he says.

Thus law turns to legalism, and is held to modify, not to support, the covenant of grace into which God entered with the father of the race. The Law of Moses is the peculiar privilege of the Jew (Rom 3: 2; 9: 4), but it is a dangerous privilege, and accuses not only the Jew but the whole human race. And paradoxically, as the Jew with the books of Moses in his hand can get the Law wrong, so the Gentile, who has never heard of Moses, can get the Law right. Circumcision is profitable if you practise the Law; that is, if you understand the Law rightly and offer to God the believing obedience that is its true requirement. If you do not do this, your circumcision is reversed; you have the outward sign but you have denied its meaning. The converse is true; if an uncircumcised man observes the things that the Law truly requires, will not his uncircumcision count as circumcision? In fact uncircumcision which keeps the Law will judge you, who with all your observance of its letter, including the command of circumcision, are a transgressor of the Law (Rom 2: 25-27). This is important for its own sake in proving that God shows no favouritism (2: 11), but even more important as showing what Paul understands by the keeping of the Law. By definition the uncircumcised man is not observing the detailed precepts of the Law, even one of the most fundamental of them. His observance of the Law is different from this; the righteous requirements (*dikaiōmata*) of the Law that he fulfils describe a relation with God. Paul makes some attempt to define this, drawing upon Stoic and similar notions of natural law and conscience, at least to the extent of borrowing some of their terminology. But his natural law is not Stoic in its requirements, and he knows that a 'good conscience' is not a ground of justification (1 Cor 4: 4). The story of Abraham is used to show that faith antedates law, and at the same time to show the true meaning of circumcision. In Romans 4 Paul begins by showing that Abraham was accepted by the gracious God in a relation which on Abraham's side included nothing but a believing acceptance of what God offered and a believing obedience that was prepared to trust God to give life even in circumstances that spoke of nothing but death. Abraham believed God and this was counted to him as righteousness: so Paul in Romans 4: 3 (as also in Gal 3: 6) quotes Genesis 15: 6. He goes on to ask in what circumstances this new relation was brought into being: was Abraham circumcised or uncircumcised? This is an easy question; in the Old Testament Abraham's circumcision does not take place till Genesis 17. It is clear therefore that Abraham had the faith that constitutes a right relation with God not only before Moses, the human architect of the Law, was born, but before the introduction of the basic condition of Jewishness, circumcision. This leaves the question, which Paul cannot ignore, 'Why then was circumcision introduced?' What purpose does it serve? The answer (Rom 4: 11) is that circumcision as a physical operation in the flesh has its value not in itself but in that of which it is a sign, something other than itself to which it points. It is a seal of the righteousness of faith, a righteousness that Abraham already had when still uncircumcised. This makes Abraham a universal and archetypal Christian figure. He is the ancestor, the father, of Gentile Christians, uncircumcised but believing and therefore accepted as God's children; and he is the father of Jewish Christians who are not only circumcised but follow in the footsteps of believing Abraham, sharing the faith he had while still uncircumcised.

A universal and archetypal Christian figure when he lived so many years before Christ? Yes, because his faith is of precisely the same pattern as Christian faith. He believed in a God who raises the dead and calls into being things that do not exist. Paul quotes Genesis 17: 3 (there are similar statements elsewhere in Genesis): 'God appointed Abraham a father of many nations'. This quotation serves a double purpose. It indicates that it was from the beginning God's intention to include Gentiles in his plan of salvation, for *nations* (*ethnē*) could equally be translated Gentiles – we may recall Paul's use in Galatians 3: 8 of Genesis 12: 3, where the same word is used. But it also made a special promise to the childless Abraham: he would have innumerable descendants. It was unthinkable: he was 100 years old, his wife was 90. There could not be one child, let alone a multitude of descendants. But Abraham recognized the promise as the word of God, and not even death could prevent God from keeping his promise and fulfilling his word. The faith that gave Abraham righteousness was the confidence that God would keep his word, bringing life out of death. And all this was written, Paul concludes (Rom 4: 23–25), not for Abraham's benefit only but for ours too, who believe in him who raised up Jesus from the dead; he was handed over to death for our sins, and raised up for our justifying. Abraham too believed in a God who raises the dead.

The Law is not contrary to God's promises (Gal 3: 21), but the relation between them, the relation between Law and Gospel, is not easy to state. There are two ways in which it may be considered. In the first, they are successive historical elements in God's dealing with his people. The Law followed the promise made to Abraham, and the Gospel of Christ crucified and risen followed the Law. The Law could not alter the terms of the promise (though it seems that many thought that it could), and it could not be allowed to interpret, which could only mean to misinterpret, the Gospel. It had a temporary and provisional role; this is borne out by the plain statement that Christ is the end of the Law (Rom 10: 4); not a negative but a fulfilling end, for the Law bears witness to the Gospel (Rom 3: 21) if it is rightly understood, and if it is interpreted by the Gospel. But 'the end of the Law' is heard again in other terms; in the repeated *abolition* (*katargeisthai*) of 2 Corinthians 3 (vv. 7, 11, 13); in the temporal clauses in Galatians 3 and 4 ('until the seed should come'; 'before faith came'; 'up to the time of Christ'; 'now faith has come we are no longer . . .'; 'such time as . . .'; 'until the time appointed'; 'when we were infants'; 'but when the fullness of time came . . .'); in the 'discharge' of Romans 7: 6; in the 'death' of Galatians 2: 19. The Law indicated the way in which the children of God must walk, and is given with authority to Christians: every commandment there is (but not such commands as for example the food laws) is summed up in the one word 'Thou shalt love thy neighbour as thyself' (Rom 13: 9; Gal 5: 14). To possess such laws, and still more to be given through them the knowledge of a holy, righteous, forgiving God, was the greatest privilege any nation had ever had.

So much for history—and of course Paul took the Old Testament stories of Abraham and Moses at their face value. In addition to representing different stages in the history of God's dealing with his special people, and through them with the world, they represent also different ways in which man can understand his own existence and his relation with his Maker. These too can be set out in chronological, that is, in biographical, form. 'I was alive apart from the Law once, but when the commandment came sin sprang to life and I died' (Rom 7: 9, 10). This is the first act of the story. Many commentators have connected it with the event at which a boy becomes *Bar mitzwah*, fully responsible before the Law and obliged to render an obedience that must have been taxing even when it was given with gratitude and love. It is not clear however that there is so much autobiography in Romans 7, and it would be an exceptional 13-year-old who could see through the happiness of the Bar-mitzwah celebrations to the accusation of a law that ruled not only one's diet but the deepest levels of life. It is in fact probable that Paul was aware of the first act only when he had passed through the second. Here we do find autobiography. 'I through the Law died to Law that I might live to God' (Gal 2: 19). Before he could say this, Paul would have said 'I live to the Law that I may live to God; I live to God by living in obedience to the Law'. It was not the discovery that the Law was too hard to keep, that he could not and did not love his neighbour as himself, that led to death; it was rather the discovery of a new positive factor. 'I have been crucified with Christ; I no longer live, Christ lives in me. The life I now live in the flesh I live by faith in the Son of God who loved me and gave himself for me' (Gal 2: 19, 20). Paul had been well content with the Law (Gal 1: 13, 14; Phil 3: 4b–6). It was the intervention of Christ that gave him new insight into the Law, a new way of understanding it. It has in recent years been argued that our understanding of Paul has been distorted by the fact that his theology has been approached by way of the experience of Luther and others like him. Such men apprehended the Gospel through 'the introspective conscience of the West'—an experience that was foreign to Paul. There is an element of truth in this, a measure of difference between Paul and Luther, but it is not the difference that some have found. Paul too had an introspective conscience; no man has had a livelier conscience than the man who wrote Romans 7. But whereas Luther approached the Gospel by way of the Christian tradition, which told him that, if he was a Christian, he would have peace with God—which he had not— Paul learned the Gospel by a different route, and for him the sting of conscience came at a different stage. Luther's *Anfechtungen*, of course, continued after his discovery of the Gospel; it was at this stage that his experience converged with Paul's.

The Law may prepare the way for the Gospel: I find that its requirements are a debt too great for me to pay, and I come to God for mercy. But it is at least equally possible that I may boast of the Law and of my achievements in obeying it. In each case, the Law is misunderstood, for the response the Law seeks is faith. But law, so often misunderstood, comes to stand for a way of conceiving man's relation with God, and it is one in which man easily settles down, whether in contentment or despair. After considering negative aspects of Paul's thought we must at this point begin to deal with the positive.

GRACE AND RIGHTEOUSNESS

How is the new understanding, which leads to new existence, to be achieved? So far as it is true that law stands for a settled way of conceiving man's relation with God it is clear that no change is likely to come from the human side. The confident and self-satisfied Paul of Philippians 3 is likely to remain as he is, confident and self-satisfied; the despairing author of 4 Ezra—despairing if not of himself at least of the majority of his fellow human beings—will remain in despair. The bliss of the world to come is for few (4 Ezra 8: 1-3). Law is in essence religion, and religion is a specific way of dealing with the supernatural. It may leave man confident that the supernatural is being kept firmly in its place, that God—personifying the supernatural—is being properly handled by the appropriate procedures and will do no harm or even make impossible demands; or it may and sometimes does evoke the terrible thought that there is beyond this an unseen world that may some day break out in uncontrollable fury. Law has the effect of channelling the rewards and the terrors, but it does not mean that they cease to exist. Only something from outside the system will change it. To study in Paul's thought this element that enters from without means consideration based on the words grace (*charis*) and righteousness (*dikaiosyně*).

Grace is a word with a long history in the Greek language and with a variety of interrelated meanings. Its primary meaning is that which in English has grown into the longer compounds: gracefulness, graciousness; grace in these senses; charm, attractiveness. A second meaning is that which can be understood as a response to the first, a feeling of favour, of good will, towards the person, or thing, manifesting charm; it need not, however, be so understood, but may be spontaneous, arising simply within the person who experiences it. A third meaning is a concrete expression of the second: a gift, or act of favour. And a fourth completes the circle, for the word may mean gratitude, the thankfulness of the person receiving the gift or favour.[4] It is characteristic of biblical usage, and certainly of Paul's, that though the first meaning occurs occasionally in non-theological contexts, the theological use is virtually confined to the second, third, and fourth. The favour of God is not grounded in some human attractiveness but is generated out of God's own being.

Paul's Greek word appears in the LXX as the rendering of a Hebrew word (*ḥen*) which also means charm, and favour; so, to take the first example in the Old Testament, Noah found favour (*ḥen, charis*) with, in the sight of, God. In the later books of the LXX Paul's Greek word sometimes translates a different Hebrew word (*ḥesed*), which is more often translated into Greek as *mercy* (*eleos*). This equivalence was developing in the New Testament period and is evidently important as part of the New Testament background; it must however be handled with the same care that was required by the Greek and Hebrew words for law. It is generally recognized that in the Old Testament itself the word *ḥesed* is not exactly the 'loving-kindness' of the older translations but means rather loyal faithfulness to a covenant relationship. 'To do mercy' is not to act mercifully, but to prove loyal. It would however be quite wrong to import this meaning into the LXX as a Greek book, or into Paul. By *charis* and *eleos* Paul means *charis* and *eleos*, grace and mercy. Moreover, in late Hebrew (and in Aramaic and Syriac) the root *ḥesed* came to mean kindness. It must suffice here to quote the most famous of rabbinic utterances (Aboth 1: 2, ascribed to R. Simeon the Just, *c.* 200 BC): 'By three things is the world sustained, by the Law, by the Temple service, and by deeds of loving-kindness [literally, by the doing of kindnesses]'. It is clear that the kindnesses are actions that go beyond law and liturgy in pure goodness.

Thus for Paul *charis* turns out to be almost the opposite of the covenant love which we have come to recognize as a meaning of *ḥesed* in the Old Testament. It is not a love that God is almost obliged to entertain for those who, on their side, keep their part of the covenant; it is love for the undeserving, indeed for the covenant-breakers, the more than legal goodness of the 'deeds of love' of Aboth 1: 2. This can be brought out by viewing grace in relation to law and in relation to sin.

Galatians 2: 21 ('I do not make void the grace of God; for if righteousness comes through the Law, then Christ died for nothing') formed part of our study of the Law; it is equally important in the study of grace. It appears at once that Law is contrasted with grace as a means of obtaining righteousness; and that the death of Jesus has something to do with grace—there is no need at the moment to attempt to make the relation between them more precise. It follows that to seek righteousness through the Law is to annul grace and to treat the death of Christ as of no effect. All the main points are made in this verse, though they are not expanded.

The fundamental contrast is made in Romans 6: 14f. Christians are not under law but under grace. It is manifest from the chapter as a whole that Paul does not mean by this that Christians are not under obligation to be obedient to God. Their obedience is constantly emphasized. What is meant is that their relation to God is determined not in terms of their observance (however satisfactory) of a law (however excellent) but in terms of God's grace, which means an extra-legal attitude to them, based upon the eternal will of God and independent of human virtue or other achievement (it is interesting to note 2 Corinthians 1: 12, where grace is contrasted with wisdom). Romans 6 further makes clear that though verbally Paul contrasts grace and law the real contrast is between grace and what Paul calls *works*, that is, the mistaken notion that works done in obedience to specific precepts are an adequate response to law, sufficient to secure and maintain God's favour and a satisfactory relation with him. The Law itself is, as we have seen, a gracious gift of God to his people; but if they (as a whole—doubtless exceptions could be found) had not misunderstood it in terms of works rather than faith, Paul had misjudged them. The relation between grace and works is made explicit in Romans 11: 5f. It is virtually a matter of definition that a remnant that has come into being on the basis of election and grace has not come into being on the basis of works; otherwise grace would no longer be grace—words would have lost their meaning.

Three further passages in Romans will make the matter clearer still. In Romans 4: 4 *according to grace* is contrasted with *according to debt*. A workman is paid as a matter of right and due; grace denotes an *ex gratia* payment made to one who, having done no work, has earned no pay and deserves nothing. The same point appears at 6: 23: sin pays a wage to those who serve it; they get what they deserve—death. God on the other hand gives away to those who do not deserve it eternal life as a gift of grace (*charisma*, an actualization or crystallization of grace; see below). The third Romans passage is 5: 14–21, considered above from a negative point of view. In 5: 18f. Paul brings out the parallelism implied by 'the type of the Man to Come' (5: 14). The *act of transgression*, the *disobedience*, of the bad Adam are balanced by the *act of righteousness*, the *obedience*, of the good Adam. But in verses 15,

16, 17 Paul makes a contrast; this is between Adam's self-seeking act in claiming life for himself, and the generous self-giving act of God in Christ, described as *grace, act of grace, gift*. Grace means outgoing, non-self-seeking, 'unmotivated' love, which does not require merit in the person loved.

Law and Gospel are closer to each other than is sometimes supposed. Each springs out of an act of grace in which God freely approaches his people, giving them the opportunity to respond. But the detailed preceptual character of law invited a response in *works*: sometimes it led to refusal to do the works required, to disobedience; sometimes to self-satisfaction (like Paul's) in the amassing of credits by obedience; sometimes to the despair of finding that one could not add together the fragments of obedience to make an obedient whole. The Law has grace at its heart because it comes from a gracious God; but it is grace in a wrapping — a wrapping not without important uses — that can easily conceal the contents.

Grace is the negative counterpart of what we have seen sin to be. Sin is existence centred upon itself; grace means that God's existence is not centred upon itself but is outgoing love, the love which the Law itself commands (Lev 19: 18). Thus it follows, in a passage considered above (Rom 6: 14, 15), that to be no longer under law but under grace is to be liberated from the dominion of sin. Superficially the opposite might appear to be true: since we are no longer under the Law that forbids sin let us do exactly as we please and sin as much as we like! But this, as Paul shows, is to misconceive grace: to be directed by grace, to stand in grace (Rom 5: 2; cf. Gal 5: 4), cannot result in sin. Grace is not merely intrinsically opposite to sin; it engages in conflict with sin. This is stated explicitly in Romans 5: 20, 21, and, in a different way, in Romans 3: 24. It is grace that is active in justification and redemption. 'The *charis* of God is the grace of the Judge, who "justifies" the guilty.'[5] This stresses the fact that grace is action rather than attitude, and there are many passages in the epistles where it is represented in this light (e.g. Rom 11: 5; 1 Cor 15: 10; 2 Cor 6: 1; Gal 1: 6, 15; 2: 21; Phil 1: 7). A special form of action is giving, and grace (see above) sometimes refers to a specific gift. Paul several times refers to 'the grace that was given me', often with reference to God's equipping him for his mission to the Gentiles: Romans 12: 3 and 15: 15; 1 Corinthians 3: 10; Galatians 2: 9; also Romans 1: 5, where *grace* may refer to what God gives to all, apostleship to his special gift to Paul. Alternatively, Paul may in this verse be using two words to express a single idea, *the grace of apostleship*, the gracious gift that fits him to be an apostle. Others too however receive appropriate gifts. The expression Paul has used of himself he uses with reference to all at Romans 12: 6, where *the grace that was given to us* is differentiated into a number of gifts, *charismata*, specific actualizations of grace.

Other words are associated with grace and call for mention here. We have seen that *mercy* (*eleos*) is a common rendering of the Old Testament *ḥesed*; with the cognate verb, *to have mercy* (*eleein*), it occurs a number of times in Romans 9 - 11. It is not as a result of human merit but purely of divine mercy that men — first Israel, then the church — are elected by God. This occurs especially in 9: 6–18, 23, and in the summary of the whole in 11: 30–32. It will be sufficient here to take notice of the last verse, which sums up the whole argument. 'God has shut up all men to disobedience, in order that he may deal with all men in mercy.' Mercy is the only basis on which God will deal with his creatures. It is because of this that as the Gentile world was disobedient in the past, so Israel must be disobedient now. Only the rebellious and disobedient can know that they are the undeserving objects of the mercy of God, whom they can never put in their debt. It follows that even the hardening of Pharaoh's heart may serve a purpose directed by mercy, though it is only in the eschatological future that this will be seen.

Love (noun and verb, *agapē* and *agapan*) occur less frequently than might be expected. They occur in Romans 9, but in quotations (9: 13, 25), which shows that the word was not Paul's own choice; it was given him by his source. The word does however occur in very important passages, such as 1 Thessalonians 1: 4; Romans 8: 35, 39. Specially important are Romans 5: 8 (connected with the death of Jesus, and with sin); 2 Corinthians 5: 14 (love determines the direction of the Christian life).

Grace, mercy, love constitute the motive that has led God now to do that which the Law, weak through the flesh, could not do. This is a paradox, though not one that seems to have worried Paul. The Law was a mark of grace; yet it needed grace to overcome it. This, of course, was because it had been seized and overcome by sin, and become sin's law (Rom 7: 23; 8: 2).

Also connected with the theme of law is the second word, or group of words: righteousness and its cognates. 'If righteousness comes through law, then Christ died for nothing' (Gal 2: 21); but presumably then some did think — or, to be cautious, Paul thought that they thought — that righteousness came that way. Indeed he had believed that he had a righteousness of his own, which came from the Law (Phil 3: 9; cf. 6). As a Christian he thought otherwise; but the presupposition that righteousness was a commodity a man must have he never abandoned. The question therefore what he meant by righteousness is unavoidable, and of central importance.

The group of words with which we are concerned consists of the adjective *dikaios*, righteous, and its cognates. The primary setting and meaning of these words is forensic. This means that, like the words for sin, their logically fundamental sense is not moral, or rather is premoral. They belong to the law court and in any given case they are given their precise sense by the verdict of the presiding judge. Naturally this gives them, in ordinary usage, at least moral overtones. This is because all courts profess to put into effect the moral standards of the community to which they belong. The moral standards may not be high; the claim to practise them may be made by the court with cynical deceitfulness; but the claim is made. The moral overtones, together with the underlying fundamental sense, are given (for the Greek world) in a well-known discussion by Aristotle. Thus 'that which is righteous (or just, *dikaion*) is that which is in accordance with the law, and is fair' (*Nicomachean Ethics* 1129a(2)). It is of course assumed here that there is a relation between that which the law prescribes and that which is fair, equitable. The point comes out clearly when Aristotle contrasts righteousness with a non-forensic concept, gentleness, kindness, considerateness (*epieikeia*): 'That which is kindly is righteous (just, *dikaion*), not simply in accordance with the law, but a correction of that which is legally righteous' (*Nicomachean Ethics* 1137ab(14)). That which is righteous (*dikaion*) keeps the law and may in consequence take the opportunity of working to rule; if it is commanded to go one mile it will feel no obligation to go a second. This is what that which is kindly will do. Righteous (*dikaios*) describes the person (or thing — such as a measuring vessel) that satisfies the judge because it is in accordance with the laws. If the laws are, and are interpreted as being, moral, the person (or thing) will be morally as well as legally correct.

The Hebrew Bible contains words that correspond to Paul's Greek words. It is enough here to say that there is one that means *righteous* (in the sense of that which satisfies and is approved by the appropriate court) and one that means the opposite — unrighteous (in the sense of that which fails to satisfy and is condemned by the appropriate court). Like the Greek words they are, as I have emphasized, in the first instance forensic terms, and as such they are pre-moral rather than moral. In the Greek Old Testament the positive term is rendered by Paul's word (*dikaios*); it begins with the objective 'right in the judgement of the court', but shades into the meaning 'good', 'upright', because courts and laws, especially in the Old Testament, are, at least in theory, supposed to count *right* that which is morally good and upright. The negative Hebrew word has several Greek equivalents; these between them show a moralizing and a pietizing tendency at work interpreting the basic forensic sense. The latter tendency arises because Old Testament law is not only civil and moral but also religious, so that the man who does not meet its requirements is not showing the right attitude to God; he is 'ungodly', 'impious' (*asebēs*). There are human courts and judges in the Old Testament, but the supreme judge is of course God. It is a fundamental axiom that as judge of the whole earth he will certainly do what is right (Gen 18: 25); and, as the context shows, this is understood to mean that he will infallibly distinguish between the righteous and the unrighteous and will hand out to each group appropriate treatment. God's own righteousness as judge will always be vindicated. Thus if by an imaginative *tour de force* God is thought of as no longer judge but as one of two litigants he is sure to win his case (Ps 51: 6, quoted in Rom 3: 4). The same thought occurs in the same forensic language in Exodus 9: 27, which does not mean (though translators have sometimes taken it so) that God is good and we are wicked; it means that God has won.

Biblical thought does inevitably tend to equate the unrighteous, the losers, with the morally wicked. This is, as I have said, a necessary consequence of the biblical belief that the judge is God and that God is a moral being. It is the wicked who lose their case (since God's law commands what is good), and having lost their case they will be punished. If God commits judgement to human representatives they are expected to behave in the same way.

Conversely, God will vindicate the innocent sufferers; they win their case and will not be treated as if they had lost. This appears most clearly in a number of passages in which righteousness and salvation appear in (nearly) synonymous parallelism.[6] This point is unfortunately lost in some modern translations which use *deliverance* or some such word instead of *righteousness*. Thus for example:

Psalm 24: 5　He shall receive a blessing from the Lord,
　　　　　　And righteousness from the God of his salvation.

Psalm 98: 2   The Lord hath made known his salvation :
His righteousness hath he openly showed in the
sight of the nations.

Psalm 103: 6   The Lord executeth righteous acts,
And judgements for all that are oppressed.

Isaiah 46: 13   I bring near my righteousness, it shall not be
far off, and my salvation shall not tarry.

There is no change in principle: God is still distinguishing between
righteous and unrighteous and treating each appropriately. Before
the Exile the Israelites were unrighteous; hence punishment, which
they deserved. Now they are (at least in comparison with the
Babylonians) righteous; hence the righteous judge, God, will deliver
them and give the Babylonians their turn of punishment. They will
go into exile (Isaiah 46). Passages in the Psalms look at this from
a personal rather than a collective point of view.

These observations of the Old Testament are important, but only
within limits. God in his righteousness saves the (comparatively)
righteous and punishes the (comparatively) wicked. He does not
save the wicked from their sin and he certainly does not acquit
them, pretending that they are good when they are not. Indeed, God
expressly declares that he will not do anything of the kind: Exodus
23: 7, 'I will not justify the wicked (the ungodly)'. For the human
application of this see Proverbs 17: 15; 24: 24 and Isaiah 5: 23.
The passages quoted above provide some background for Paul's
language (see especially Ps 98: 2 and cf. Rom 1: 16, 17), but we have
not found in the Old Testament the substance of Paul's thought.
According to Paul, God does precisely what in the Old Testament
he declares that he will never do; he is the one who justifies the
ungodly (Rom 4: 5). There is of course no one else for God to
justify; there is no one who is righteous (Rom 3: 10).

We must therefore turn to Paul himself, and see what he makes
of the Old Testament language. Undoubtedly God is judge, and he
will judge justly (Rom 2: 5, 12, 16; 3: 4–8; 1 Cor 5: 13; 11: 31, 32;
cf. 2 Thess 1: 5; 2: 12). The righteousness of God may include other
elements, but there is no question that one aspect of it is forensic
righteousness. God is a judge, and a judge of infallible wisdom and
rectitude. He will accurately and impartially distinguish between the
guilty and the innocent, and will take appropriate action. Other
elements that may be included in the range of meanings covered by
the 'righteousness of God' are the saving righteousness that we have

94

observed in the Old Testament, and the condition of righteousness in man that will satisfy God in his court. None of these possible meanings can be excluded in advance. The Gospel is the power of God leading to salvation because in it God's righteousness is revealed (Rom 1: 16, 17); it is important to know what God's righteousness is, but this can only be discovered by the study of a number of passages in the epistles, of which only a few can be examined here.

It is useful to begin with the recognition that there is another kind of righteousness, quite real and not without admirable qualities. Paul had himself possessed such a righteousness. He describes it as his own (Phil 3: 9), and he had generated it out of the Law (3: 9). He had regarded this as a credit, that is, a credit balance standing in his account with God, acquired by blameless obedience to the Law (3: 6). There is no question that this means both a high moral standard and a whole-hearted religious devotion to God, leading to scrupulous observance of commandments that had no manifest social or moral value. As a Christian Paul did not merely wipe out his credits, he converted them into debits. 'The things that were credits to me, these I have for Christ's sake counted loss' (Phil 3: 7). If Paul's language is to be taken strictly (and there is no reason why it should not be so taken) he means that this discounting of his righteousness achieved through the Law was necessary if he was to possess true righteousness, God's righteousness. 'I count all things loss on account of the surpassing excellence of the knowledge of Christ Jesus my Lord, on account of whom I suffered the confiscation, was mulcted, of all things together [J. B. Lightfoot's translation], and count them refuse, *in order that* I may gain Christ and be found in him, not having my righteousness, which comes out of the Law, but that which comes through faith in Christ, the righteousness that comes from God on the basis of faith' (Phil 3: 8, 9). This seems to mean (though some would dispute it) that Paul is thinking of alternative and contrasting kinds of righteousness, proceeding from different sources and attained by different means. Here, in Philippians, he is writing in individual terms about himself; there is perhaps more light to be had from a similar passage in which he is writing about Israel as a whole. In Romans 9, 10 he is writing about the apparently unaccountable failure of Israel to accept the promised Messiah, while the Gentiles receive him and the way of salvation he brings. The Gentiles, though they had never made righteousness (in Paul's theological sense) their aim, had attained righteousness, the righteousness that proceeds from faith.

Israel had undoubtedly taken as their aim a 'law of righteousness', but they had not achieved their aim. It is not easy to say precisely what Paul means by a 'law of righteousness'; probably a law that pointed to righteousness, pointed to the possibility of a right relation with God though without the life-giving power necessary to realize the possibility (Gal 3: 21). Israel failed in their endeavour because they sought their goal not on the basis of faith but as if it could be had on the basis of works (done in obedience to the law) (Rom 9: 30–32). Paul returns to the theme in chapter 10. The Jews have a zeal for God, but it is a zeal that is not based on a true understanding of God and his ways. They fail to recognize God's righteousness and seek to establish their own — a generalization of what Paul says in Philippians 3: 9, for, as Paul has already said, his compatriots like himself had sought to get righteousness out of the Law by works. So they had not submitted to God's righteousness, accepted righteousness on his terms. God's terms are summed up in the next verse as Christ and faith: Christ is the end of the law with a view to righteousness for everyone who believes (has faith) (Rom 10: 2–4). The meaning of the word 'end' (*telos*) is disputed. Some think it means *goal*, or *intention*. When other passages are borne in mind it is hard to doubt that it means *end*; see e.g. Romans 7: 6, 2 Corinthians 3: 7, 11, 13, 14, and Galatians 2: 19. But it is such an end as is defined in Romans 8: 3: what the law could never effect because it was weak through the flesh, God brought about when, by sending his own Son in the form of flesh which had passed under sin's rule, and to deal with sin, he condemned sin in the flesh. For sin's assault on that good thing, the Law, see above; the Law could not achieve the goal of righteousness that it suggested. Christ did achieve it for those who believed.

This study is valuable in itself, valuable also in showing a fair conspectus of the different ways in which Paul can use the word 'righteousness'.

Romans 1: 17 resembles Psalm 98: 2 so closely that it is hard to resist the conclusion that here at least (but this passage will certainly carry Romans 3: 21 with it) Paul thinks of the righteousness of God as a positive active force which is at work in the deliverance of those who are in need. The consideration however that directs it is not desert but faith. It is revealed 'from faith to faith', an obscure phrase which probably means *on the basis of nothing but faith*, faith from start to finish. This is confirmed in two ways.

First, in the next verse (1: 18) Paul continues with a closely parallel statement about God's wrath. He uses the same verb, in the same (present) tense. God's righteousness is being revealed to faith; this constitutes the Gospel of the power of God leading to salvation. But God's wrath is being revealed, not in the first instance upon the various kinds of moral wickedness described in 1: 26–31 (these are rather part of the punishment inflicted) but on the pre-moral attitude which refuses to glorify God as God and to give thanks to him (1: 21), an expression that will serve as an admirable negative definition of faith. Faith is not a collection of theological propositions but a readiness to let God be the God he means to be and to give him thanks for being the kind of God he is. God's righteousness is, as we have seen, a forensic righteousness, the righteousness of a wise and just judge who will properly distinguish between good and evil. But he has found a way of directing his acquittal, his work of liberation, by the criterion of faith. There are none so good and religious as to deserve his favourable action; all he asks is that they should be willing to receive it. The way that he has found turns upon his crucified Son, a matter to which we shall return later; but he had already in the Old Testament provided an advance model of what is involved.

This is also the second ground for understanding the use of God's righteousness in Romans 1: 17 in the way in which it is taken here. The model is Abraham, to whom God reckoned righteousness on the basis of his faith (Gen 15: 6; Rom 4: 3). Paul analyses the meaning of this Old Testament proposition at some length, distinguishing between payment given as a recompense for work done and a free—*ex gratia*—payment. He also uses a rabbinic exegetical method to show that God's reckoning of righteousness to Abraham was equivalent to a non-reckoning of sin, that is, to forgiveness.

From this, however, a further step must be taken. The righteousness that God reckoned to Abraham, gave to Abraham, is the righteousness a man must have if he is to stand before God. This is (to take up again passages we have already considered) the righteousness that comes from God (*ek theou*) that Paul receives in Philippians 3: 9; this *from God* serves to define the less clear righteousness *of God* in Romans 10: 3. Because Israel had misunderstood the Law, not recognizing that it should be responded to in faith, they failed to understand and receive God's righteousness, supposing that they had to make their own case and defence in God's court.

God's righteousness then is, in Paul's use, threefold. He is a righteous judge; his judgement is righteous judgement (Rom 2: 5); he is righteous in himself. But he has found a way (in Christ) of converting his judgement into outgoing, saving, righteousness, bestowed not on those who deserve it but on those who will receive it. This means that he gives righteousness, the status of righteousness in his court, to those who believe. If God is to be thought of in forensic terms, he is a good judge, a saving judge, and a creative judge.

At this point we must take up explicitly the theme of justification; this is forced upon us etymologically, for the verb *to justify* (*dikaioun*) and the cognate *justification* belong to the same Greek family as *righteous* (*dikaios*) and the related words; and also because it is a forensic term, the forensic equivalent of 'forgiveness' (a word Paul scarcely uses) and 'reconciliation', which he uses frequently. The latter will provide a good starting-point. The fact of reconciliation is stated clearly in Romans 5: 10: 'If, when we were enemies we were reconciled to God through the death of his Son, much more, having been reconciled, shall we be saved by his life'. This is clear; as long as man chooses to go his own way rather than God's there is an inevitable enmity between them. God finds a way of putting an end to this; the result is reconciliation. The structure of the sentence is threefold: reconciliation; by death; we shall be saved. In the previous verse (5: 9) the same fact is stated in terms of justification: much more, having now been justified by his blood, we shall be saved through him from the wrath (of God). Again the structure is threefold: justification; by blood (which of course means blood shed in death); we shall be saved. The two statements have in common two of their elements, death and salvation; it is clear that the third components, reconciliation and justification, must at the least be very closely related. Reconciliation means that by a creative act of love one of two warring parties makes peace; the adversary is no longer an adversary but a friend. He does not pretend that his former adversary is a friend; he actually makes friendship. Unless this happens there is no reconciliation; reconciliation means that it does happen. Justification sets the same situation not on a battlefield but in a court. The prisoner is accused of that disobedience to law that makes him the natural enemy of the judge, whose business it is to uphold and administer the law. The court-room image lays stress on the fact that the law is there to accuse, the witnesses are there to prove, and the judge is *ex hypothesi* 'right' (as the enemy on a battlefield might not be). The judge, again by a creative act (which, in due course, we must study, but not now), makes the enemy, his legal enemy, a friend. There is no legal fiction in this; the prisoner's status (if not at once his moral character) is actually, by the creative act, changed.

This corresponds both with the linguistic form of the verb *to justify* and with other passages in Paul's letters. Verbs of this form, derived from adjectives or nouns, are normally factitive; thus from the adjective *blind* comes the verb *to blind*. One would expect therefore on linguistic grounds that the verb *to justify* would mean *to make righteous* (as is of course accepted in the Latin behind the English *justify*). It has often been said that for Paul *to justify* cannot mean this, since it is so close to *to reconcile, to forgive*, and does not mean *to make virtuous, upright* (though it makes possible a subsequent process of moral improvement). This however is to forget the meaning of *righteous, righteousness*, which are pre-moral terms, denoting not ethical quality but relationship. God actually puts his unsatisfactory creature into a right relationship with himself.

A difficult but illuminating sentence occurs in 2 Corinthians 5: 21. Again, as in Romans 5, the context is determined by reconciliation: We beseech you on behalf of Christ, be reconciled to God; but Paul proceeds immediately to express the grounds of reconciliation in terms of the righteousness words, making clear who is in the right and who is in the wrong. He puts this in two carefully balanced clauses: Him who knew no sin he made sin on our behalf, that we might become God's righteousness in him. The balance is so important that it must be set out in parallel columns:

Him who knew no sin	we
he made	might become
sin	God's righteousness
on our behalf	in him.

Paul does not say that Christ became a sinner; rather he defines him as the one who had no experience of sin. He does not say that we have become perfectly good with a righteousness of our own. He chooses words that express relation. Throughout his ministry, but pre-eminently in his death, we see Christ occupying in relation to God a position that could normally be described as sin and the result of sin—in its alienation, separation, and liability to curse; compare Galatians 3: 13, where, as here, what Christ does he does on our behalf, for our benefit. He occupied this position that we might not occupy it. Corresponding to this objective 'Christ on our side' is the subjective 'We in Christ'—though this is not really subjective but means that we now objectively stand in relation to God in a position characterized by righteousness. This right relation is possible because Christ in his death destroyed the sinful relation which he took upon himself. He died to sin (Rom 6: 10).

This points forward not only to our next main section but also to a paragraph in Romans of such central importance and classical clarity that it must be at least briefly considered: Romans 3: 21–31. The opening sentence is closely parallel to Romans 1: 16, 17. In each, righteousness is manifested. In the new paragraph there is no reference (as there is in 1: 18) to God's wrath, a wrathful manifestation of God's righteousness. This is because the manifestation of righteousness is now defined as *apart from law*, and it is law that works wrath (Rom 4: 15). Correspondingly, this manifestation is to faith, which determines righteousness as salvation. More: it is the manifestation on the basis of faith (to all who believe) that constitutes the universality of the Gospel, both positively and negatively; there are no preconditions for faith—anyone may believe; and the distinction between Jew and Gentile is created by the Law. An operation that proceeds apart from the Law naturally encounters no distinction. The Gospel unites Jew and non-Jew, though in the first instance by declaring all to be sinners who lack the glory of God. The next verses may be passed over quickly, partly because two fundamental words—'justification' and the 'grace' by which justification takes place—have already been considered, and partly because the meaning of two other words of fundamental importance, 'redemption' and the word (*hilastērion*) by which Paul describes the crucifixion of Jesus, must be considered later. The next verses (25b, 26) must be considered now. The crucified Jesus is set forth as God's way of demonstrating (showing and proving) his righteousness. Why? Paul gives two reasons. It may be that one was a traditional reason, accepted by Paul, the other his own reason, added to the tradition. It matters little; both are important. The first relates to the past, to the fact that in the past God has passed over sins. The word ('passing over', *paresis*) Paul uses is related to the usual word for 'forgiveness' (*aphesis*), but it is not that word. It probably means not forgiveness but God's forbearing mercy, in which he has suffered men to live without either punishment or radical forgiveness (which Paul will call justification). The thought occurs elsewhere in the New Testament, oddly enough in passages in Acts which are attributed to Paul though their attribution is often doubted. Thus Acts 14: 16: 'In generations gone by God permitted all the nations to walk in their own ways'; 17: 30: 'God overlooked the times of ignorance, but now he commands men that they should all everywhere repent'. Because of the past God must now vindicate his righteousness, which otherwise would be impugned. Men might say, God does not care about sin; anyone may sin as much as he pleases and get away with it. The second reason looks to the future, pointing to the intended result of the action that God has taken. It is not enough to vindicate his past forbearance: God means to find a way of showing himself to be both a righteous judge and yet also one who can do what (as we have seen) the Old Testament declares that no just judge will do: he means to justify not the legally righteous man but the ungodly man who has faith. Why this demonstration should be made in and through the crucified Jesus is a question to be taken up shortly, though for the present very briefly.

The manifestation of God's righteousness takes place *at the present time*. This makes a double contrast, first and most obviously with the *previously committed sins* of verse 25. The present however is also contrasted with the future. God himself could no doubt afford to wait till the last judgement to demonstrate his righteousness. That men should say hard things about his government of the universe will not hurt him. But in fact, and again in grace, he chooses to act now, and the present time anticipates the final event.

God's righteousness is to be manifested not only at the last day but now, and that in the paradoxical event of the crucifixion of the Messiah, God's Son. This event was, Paul claims, a demonstration of righteousness, but to ordinary observation it could be only a denial of righteousness, not only of human righteousness but of God's righteousness, since he permitted this to happen to the one human being to whom it ought not to have happened. It could be a demonstration only to faith, that is, to those who were prepared to accept God's judgement rather than their own. But faith, in which man gives up the attempt to establish his own righteousness and submits to God's righteousness (Rom 10: 3, 4) is precisely that relation with God that makes man's pardon conceivable. As long as man is arrogant and seeks to take up an independent attitude towards God, he is storing up for himself wrath in the day of wrath and the revealing of God's righteous judgement (Rom 2: 5). When he casts himself upon God, and regards his own, law-based righteousness as not credit but loss (Phil 3: 7), and the theological wisdom in which he seeks to vindicate God's ways to man as foolishness (1 Cor 1: 20), he is in that attitude of humble and grateful receptivity in which the true relation of man to God consists—and this is righteousness (now in the sense of that righteousness that is God's gift to men, as well as in the sense of God's inherent being right and his creative righteousness—the three senses belong inextricably together). Thus it can be that the death of Jesus is a manifestation in action of the righteousness of God as it issues at once in wrath against sin and in love for man.

It remains in this section to note specifically one word that has been often enough mentioned—'faith'. Faith forms a second correlative of 'works of law' and thus corresponds with grace. Righteousness comes from God (Philippians 3: 9), comes, that is, as his gift, and this means, as the same verse says, that it is received through faith. The same point is made, as we have seen, on a large scale in Romans 10: 3, 4: Israel would not receive righteousness as a gift and sought to establish its own, that is, it sought righteousness by works and not by faith. Faith accepts grace, or mercy, as God's chosen terms of relation with man, and may be defined as the absence, or rather the repudiation of works. The alternatives are made clear in Galatians 3: 2, 5 (and indeed through the whole of Galatians 3); Romans 3: 28 and 4: 3, with the following verses up to 6. There is a comparable contrast in 1 Corinthians 2: 5; faith does not rest upon human wisdom any more than it rests upon human morals or human religion. It does rest upon the power of God (Rom 1: 16).

It has frequently been asked why Paul speaks often of faith, seldom of repentance. It cannot be said that he did not know the meaning of repentance; for example, the mourning of 1 Corinthians 5: 2 is a kind of repentance—sorrow for sin, even when the sin is not your own. So also Romans 6: 21. But for Paul faith is not essentially a matter of turning away from a bad way of life; it is equally, and at a deeper level, a turning away from a good life in which one depends on one's own achievement, one's own works done in obedience to the moral law. He himself was able to claim that his pre-Christian life had been one of perfect legal righteousness (Phil 3: 6); it was as necessary for him to turn from this highly moral existence (in which he had his own righteousness) as it was for those mentioned in 1 Corinthians 6: 9–11 to turn from their way of life. In order to believe man repudiates not only his bad morals but his good morals. Repentance is a term that would not adequately cover this.

It is necessary now to add that faith cannot be separated from morals; it involves hearing and obeying. These belong closely together; Paul knew well that the same Hebrew word (*shama'*) covered both. One example, Romans 10: 14–17, may suffice. The first stage is hearing the Gospel; the next is being obedient, that is, hearing with faith. Liberated from sin the believer is enslaved to righteousness. It is important that faith is response to a preached, proclaimed message. This leads to a further consequence. Because the preaching has a specific content (e.g. 1 Cor 15: 3–5, 11) faith also has a specific content and can be expressed in a confession of faith which is specifically related to the eschatological event of Jesus Christ, crucified and risen. In Romans 10: 9 ('If you confess with your mouth Jesus as Lord, and believe in your heart that God raised him from the dead, you will be saved') there is the confession of faith which, from the believer's responsive side, corresponds to the proclamation summarized in 1 Corinthians 15: 3–8.

CHRIST CRUCIFIED

From this point we may proceed at once to the next main division of the substantive presentation of Paul's thought. Paul sums up the Christian proclamation in traditional terms in 1 Corinthians 15: 3–8. Here it is asserted that Christ died for our sins; that he was buried; that he was raised up to life; and that he appeared to Cephas and a number of others. The subject of every verb is Christ. The content of the proclamation, which is the ground of Christian existence (15: 1, 2) is the historical event of Jesus Christ. That this is central in Paul's thought is evident, but it is also true that he does not develop it at length, mainly because it was not controversial in the sense in which such topics as sin, law, righteousness, grace, were. Of Christology we learn most from hints dropped at random as other subjects are developed. Paul and his contemporaries were not able to take over a ready-made doctrine of the Messiah, or, for example, a convenient interpretation of the Suffering Servant. Nor were they able to take over a tradition of teaching from Jesus himself which told them what they needed to know on these subjects. Paul (like the rest, but with unequalled theological insight) started not with the teaching but with the fact of Jesus, who refuses to be neatly filed away in a Jewish pigeon-hole labelled 'Messiah'; on this basis Paul proceeds to revise and rewrite the hopes, categories, and exegesis of Judaism.

It is equally true, and at this point important to add, that Paul's attitude to Jesus was not historicistic. Jesus was not the outstanding figure in history any more than he was the outstanding teacher whose every word must be treasured and recorded. Rather he was the heavenly Lord, though it was both true and important that he had recently lived a real human life and died a real human death. It is however also true and important that for Paul the recent events of the life, death, and resurrection were significant from the eschatological rather than the historical point of view. This is why for him *Lord* is a more important term than *Christ*, which for him is little more than an additional name—Jesus Christ, rather than Jesus *the* Christ, or *the* Messiah. How unimportant *Christ* is for him is shown by the fact that descent from David is mentioned only at Romans 1: 3 and 15: 12; of these, one is borrowed from Christian tradition, the other an Old Testament quotation. This is not to say that Paul is uninterested in the Old Testament or in the notion of its fulfilment. He prefers wider categories; thus 2 Corinthians 1: 20, Christ is the 'Yes' to all God's promises, and at 1 Corinthians 1: 30, all the names for what God does for and gives to men—wisdom, righteousness, sanctification, and redemption—can be applied to him.

Before we select out of many a few passages in which Paul (as a rule pursuing other matters) drops important propositions regarding Jesus it may be well to look back over ground we have already covered and consider what this may lead us to expect in the person and work of the Redeemer. This is a dangerous proceeding; we may find ourselves simply discovering what we have decided ought to be there. But to be aware of the danger is half the battle.

In the first place, Paul conceives the universe to have come under the control of usurping cosmic elements, and men's own existence to be dominated by flesh. If the human race and the universe are to have a future, if the will of God is to be done, it will be necessary that the elements should be defeated and the dominion of flesh overcome. Here we are in the realms of mythical cosmology and existential anthropology, closely related though not identical.

Secondly, according to Paul God has already placed one of his good gifts in this perverse cosmic and human situation, and, lacking the positive power to give life (Gal 3: 21), it has been perverted. This was *law*. It is good in itself, but sin has taken advantage of it, corrupted it, and made out of it another law, a different law (Romans 7: especially 10–13, 21–23). We may say, perhaps, that law, a good thing, has been converted into legalism, a bad thing. The point at which sin found a ready means of entry was the preceptual character of the law, so that any new action on God's part, any new manifestation of righteousness, must be of such a kind as to prove his love beyond dispute and leave no room for human pride.

Thirdly: Paul's basic outlook on Christian truth was eschatological; this was the natural framework of his thought. It was an established feature of apocalyptic Judaism that the good time to come should be preceded by a time of suffering which the people of God would have to endure. The righteous would have to suffer innocently before receiving their reward. Thus in an individualizing process some rabbis taught that in this world the wicked were rewarded for their few good deeds in order that their punishment hereafter might be undiluted, the righteous punished for their few sins in order that their reward in the future might be complete. Collectively this led to the notion of the messianic suffering, the so-called travail pains of the Messiah. The people (or the remnant of the people) would suffer before the glory of the Messiah was revealed. This belief Paul inherited, but for him it was complicated by the fact that there were no righteous (Rom 3: 10), none who could suffer innocently. Paul found the messianic affliction in the cross.[7] He expressed the matter in his own terms. One died for all, therefore all died (2 Cor 5: 14). The one innocent and righteous person suffered on behalf of others who were not innocent and righteous, but in such a way that they were able to enter into his suffering (Rom 6: 3–11). Jesus thus became a new Adam, founder of a new humanity. Their relation to him is described in the fundamental Pauline phrase *in Christ*. Union with Christ is described in terms of faith and baptism, and the actualization of faith and baptism in death to sin.

After all this we are still a long way from formal Christology, or a doctrine of the atonement. But we are dealing with the raw materials of Paul's thought, and it is important to see them clearly. It would be possible now to take up almost any paragraph in the epistles; there is scarcely one that would not yield results in relation to Christ and his death. It will however be better to concentrate on a small number of the most important. In some Paul seems to be building on foundations that others had laid, often revising their work — he was not the only one to set about the theological development of the primitive confession. Romans 1: 3, 4 was considered above. Similar but much more elaborate treatment is required by Philippians 2: 6–11, not only in itself one of the most important Christological passages in the Pauline literature but also one that shows very clearly how Paul worked on the tradition he inherited.

It is very widely held that Paul in this passage draws on earlier material.[8] There is some un-Pauline language, the structure is that of a prose hymn, and the material is detachable from its context.

This does not mean that it is in any way inappropriate to its context, or that it is inconsistent with Paul's thought. The fact that Paul sees fit to use it gives it his imprimatur, in the form in which he reproduces it (perhaps with some modification of a traditional text). Even if he did not himself compose the paragraph it carries his authority. Quotation is at least a reasonable hypothesis. It will be worth while to set the passage out, using the translation of the Revised Version, whose somewhat wooden literalness will be, for this purpose, helpful.

1 Who, being in the form of God,

2 Counted it not a prize to be on an equality with God,

3 But emptied himself, taking the form of a servant,

4 Being made in the likeness of men;

5 And being found in fashion as a man,

6 He humbled himself, becoming obedient even unto death,

7 Yea, the death of the cross.

8 Wherefore also God highly exalted him,

9 And gave unto him the name which is above every name;

10 That in the name of Jesus every knee should bow,

11 Of things in heaven and things on earth and things under the earth,

12 And that every tongue should confess that Jesus Christ is Lord,

13 To the glory of God the Father.

We may begin consideration of this text from one of the most famous problems, the word here translated *prize* (line 2, verse 6). It is formed from a verb that means *to seize*. It is probably passive in sense, but an active meaning cannot be ruled out. This results in three possible meanings.

1(a) It is a thing that has been seized and is thus a prized possession, which the owner might well be unwilling to let go: *a prize possessed*.

1(b) It is a thing meet to be seized, a desirable thing which one does not have but might well snatch if an opportunity presented itself: *a prize desired*.

2 An act of seizing or snatching; banditry, unlawful taking and possessing.

The problem of exegesis is made more difficult by the fact that the 'thing' we are speaking of is itself difficult to translate and interpret. In the revised version it is 'being on an equality with God'. For the moment let us call it X. We now have:

1(a) Christ did not consider X a prized possession, not on any account to be given up. That is, X was something that he possessed, but he was prepared to surrender it.

1(b) Christ did not consider X a prize to be seized by any possible means, stolen, or snatched by violence. That is, he did not have X, and though it might have seemed desirable he would take no steps in order to gain it.

2 Christ did not think of X as a matter of banditry; it was something that he possessed and to which he had a right.

1(a) and 2 are sufficiently alike in that each means that he had X. 1(a) adds that though he had it he had not made up his mind to cling to it at all costs.

But what is X? It is life lived on equality with God; not equality with God, which is something that it would be hard to give up, since you can hardly put God out of business, or, if you are God, go out of business. Life accompanied by the glory, power, and blessedness associated with deity however is something that could conceivably be given up.

On linguistic grounds we cannot exclude either 1(a) or 1(b). We must ask which makes sense of the context. Again we encounter a problem, for both do.

1(a) We begin, as Paul does (cf. e.g. Gal 4: 4), with the pre-existent life of the Son. He exists in the *form* of God (line 1), but regards this as a good, a *prize*, that may be voluntarily given up. Giving it up he became incarnate, accepting the *form* of a slave (line 3), and in this incarnate life he became obedient unto death (line 6). As a result of this God highly exalted him (line 8), restoring him to his rightful position not as slave but as Lord (line 12), acknowledged as such by the whole of creation.

1(b) We begin in a different place. Like Adam, Jesus was a man confronted by the temptation of Genesis 3: 5, 'You shall be as God'.

The old Adam, in the old story, snatching at what was above him, fell below the position of lordship that he was intended to occupy (Gen 1: 26, 28; dominion). The new Adam, content to occupy the humble role assigned to him, was exalted above his original position (Paul's word in line 8 may have a comparative force), and so became Lord.

Both of these interpretations make sense, Christian sense. It is possible that Paul, or some other very ingenious person, thought out the word *prize* as containing the necessary ambiguity and capable of suggesting both. It is more probable, if we accept the hypothesis of quotation, that the original hymn-writer understood the word in one sense, Paul in the other. We may try to reconstruct the original hymn. After an opening *who* (a common beginning for credal, confessional statements), it proceeds with lines 2, 3, 6. There is nothing here that Paul would repudiate; he himself uses the figure of Adam, and it is hard to doubt that *to be on an equality with God* was intended to evoke the story of Adam. It recalls much too clearly the temptation to which Adam fell. Life on equality with God was precisely the prospect that the serpent held out to Adam—to Eve, and through Eve to Adam. If the story of Adam is in mind it follows that Christ is being represented as the new man in whom humanity makes a new beginning. We must not (at this stage) see in lines 3 and 4 any reference to the incarnation. *He emptied himself* must not be interpreted in the light of kenosis theories; the Authorized Version's 'he made himself of no reputation' is in fact not a bad rendering of a word that was not often used metaphorically. It is defined by the next clause, *taking the form of a slave*. Whereas Adam had done his best to fill himself with knowledge and power, with a view to mastering his environment (and in the end God), Jesus humbly accepted the role of a servant. It is possible, though not very likely, that there may be a reference to the Servant of God in Isaiah 53: 12: He poured out his soul unto death.

He humbled himself is parallel to *he emptied himself*, and both refer to the humble serving life of Jesus, whose obedience did not stop short even of death, whereas Adam had sought to guarantee life for himself by eating the forbidden fruit.

The consequence of Adam's transgression had been the fulfilment of the prediction, or warning, of Genesis 2: 17. Man, created to be but little lower than God, to live immortal like the angels and to be lord over the created world, became subject to death and the slave of objects, such as the cosmic elements, of which he should have been the master. Jesus reversed Adam's sin, and the consequence was the reversal of Adam's punishment—and more. God exalted him to the position of Lord over all creation, not only over the earthly things (the beasts, whose master Adam had been in Eden), but things in heaven and things under the earth.

The figure of Christ as the new Adam appears also in Romans 5: 12-21, 1 Corinthians 15: 20-22 and 45-49; see below. In these places Paul is writing for himself, and the crudities that we shall detect in the primitive version of the Philippian hymn do not appear.

What does Paul do with this hymn which we may trace under the surface in Philippians 2? There is much in the general outline that we have constructed with which Paul could agree, but it does not meet his needs because it does not state, and is indeed scarcely consistent with, his belief in the pre-existence of the Son of God. This he must secure first of all, and does so by prefixing line 1, *existing in the form of God*. The precise meaning of *form* in this line is disputed. Paul probably took it up because he saw it used in line 3, *the form of a servant*. This meant the humble circumstances of a slave; the form of God corresponds to this and means much the same as life lived on equal terms with God (line 2). Paul is thinking in terms of functional rather than essential equality.

Line 4 now takes on a new meaning. It refers not to how Christ lived as a human being but to the very fact that he did so live, that he became man, the Son of God incarnate. Paul however still wishes to describe the human life of Jesus and takes up the thread with lines 4, 5, 6. *He humbled himself* will refer to Christ's manner of life after the incarnation had taken place. He, the incarnate Son, was obedient even unto death. The compound verb of exaltation must now lose all comparative force because he could be raised no higher than he was at the beginning, as lord over all created beings in the universe.

This is a new picture, created by Paul; and in the end it matters little (though it does matter, especially to the historian) whether he created it in the way described here, by modification of an existing Christology, or out of nothing. According to some the resulting picture is based upon Iranian mythology, and it certainly recalls the gnostic myth of the descending and ascending redeemer. In fact however it is not so much drawn from myth as leads to myth. Indeed, it is myth, but the myth arises out of Paul's developing Christology. Used in this sense *myth* is by no means incompatible with history; I shall return to this.

At this point I refer back briefly to Romans 5: 12-21, where the work of Christ is described in relation to the figure of Adam, in two ways. In verses 18 and 19 the act of Christ is the exact counterpart of the act of Adam—it is obedience, not disobedience, an act of righteousness, not an act of transgression. In verses 15–17 the expression to note is *much more*; the act of Christ is now seen to be the act not of an obedient man but of the gracious God who gives. This duality—the one act both the act of man and the act of God—corresponds to Paul's product in Philippians 2. When he looks at Christ he sees both an obedient man and a gracious God. What sort of unity these two can form is a further question that has troubled theologians from the beginning. Paul can hardly be said to deal with it, and no doubt it has always been more important to affirm both limbs of the paradox than to explain it.

The next passage to consider is 1 Corinthians 15: 20–22 and 45–49, another Adam passage. Paul's interest here is not Christological. His main theme is resurrection, together with consequences that follow from it; these are in no small part ethical. Since however for him resurrection means primarily the resurrection of Christ the passage looks in a Christological direction. Indeed the main problem with which Paul has to deal is the inclusiveness of Christ. He can easily show that the proposition 'There is no resurrection of the dead' is simply impossible for a Christian; if you affirm this you affirm that Christ did not rise from the dead, whereas this is a primary and unescapable Christian belief: so we preach and you believed (1 Cor 15: 11). It would however be possible to rejoin: Yes, of course Christ rose from the dead; he was perfect man and very God; but that proves nothing with regard to us who are human beings and sinners at that. This is why Paul takes up again the figure of Adam.[9]

In verse 20 the vital word is *firstfruits*. It is as the firstfruits that Christ has been raised; this word however is not so much an argument as an assertion. The firstfruits implies the rest of the harvest but does not actually prove that there will be a harvest; crops have been known to fail; perhaps it is reasonable to say that God's will not fail. Verses 21 and 22 are closely parallel and serve to define each other:

Since by man came death, by man came also the resurrection of the dead.
For as in Adam all die, even so in Christ shall all be made alive.

It is Adam as man who is significant, and the kind of man Adam is is representative man; similarly the kind of man that Christ is is representative man. The main point is that of Romans 5: 14 (Adam, the type of the man to come), though the rest of Romans 5: 12–21 is implied by *shall be made alive* (v. 22). It is worth while also to note in verses 25, 27 the use and combination of two Psalms, 110 and 8. Both have to do with the exaltation of a person under whose feet enemies and others will be subdued. Psalm 110 speaks of a *Lord* to whom his enemies will be subjugated. In Psalm 8 the victor is *Son of man*, representative humanity. It is as obedient man (obedient even unto death, though Paul does not say so at this point) that Christ recovers for the human race its lost lordship over the whole of creation.

One might have supposed that Paul had finished, in this context, with Adam, but Adam returns. It is not an afterthought or repetition. The point is different and arises out of the question of verse 35: 'How are the dead raised? With what kind of body do they come?' It may be a foolish question, but Paul gives it a serious answer. It is necessary to establish first the existence of natural (*psychika*) and spiritual (*pneumatika*) bodies. This Paul does on the basis of the Old Testament, but he is obliged to use the Old Testament in the same sort of way as that in which we have seen him using early Christian confessions of faith; he has to supplement it — or, as he would probably have said, he draws out from it something that is implied but not explicitly stated. He finds the necessary hint in Genesis 2: 7, where in the creation of Adam the word *soul* is used.

The first man Adam became a living soul (*psychē*).

Already, as reference to the Old Testament will show, Paul has made one or two supplements with a view to what follows. He proceeds with a parallel statement, which is not in the Old Testament but could be said to be implied by it, if it is granted that the end may be expected to match the beginning:

The last Adam became a life-giving spirit (*pneuma*).

This last Adam, notwithstanding his name (for Hebrew *'adam* means man), is placed on the side of divinity, for it is God who gives life.

The next step, which returns to the adjectives *natural* (*psychikos*, from *psychē*) and *spiritual* (*pneumatikos*, from *pneuma*) is obscure. It is not (Paul says) the spiritual that comes first, but the natural;

111

then, after that, the spiritual. This is very emphatically put, and difficult to understand unless one bears in mind the sort of exegesis of the creation narratives in Genesis 1 and 2 that had been given by Philo (an Alexandrian Jew, roughly contemporary with Paul). Like a modern Old Testament scholar Philo observed that Genesis contained two accounts of creation, including the creation of man. Instead of ascribing these to different sources Philo took the first to refer to the creation of a Platonic archetypal man, the idea of man – one might say, spiritual man (as distinct from empirical man of flesh and blood). Then in the second narrative came the creation of man as we know him – natural man, one might say, using Paul's adjectives. This is essentially Platonism, read out of the biblical narrative and fitted into the biblical framework.[10] It is essential to Philo's scheme that the 'spiritual' idea of humanity came first (Genesis 1); humanity, 'natural' man, made of the dust of the earth, came second (Genesis 2). This notion Paul flatly contradicts. One cannot say that he had read Philo; nor can one say that Philo was the only man who propounded this view. Verse 46 is so emphatic that it seems impossible that Paul did not have it in mind. It is also to be noticed that in this verse Paul uses his adjectives in the neuter (*psychikon, pneumatikon*); that is, they are in agreement not with man (*anthrōpos*, masculine) but with body (*sōma*, neuter). He is still concerned with two kinds of body and the doctrine of the resurrection. But he is still dealing with it in terms of the two men, Adam and Christ, to whom he returns in verse 47. The first line in this verse (the first man) returns to Genesis 2: 7 – creation out of the dust of the earth of dusty, earthy beings. The second line may be simply Paul's inference from the first – the second man is from heaven; but it probably has a more specific origin, equally based on Scripture (and this will account for Paul's apparently unjustified addition in verse 45). He is aware of another Old Testament passage which speaks of a man who comes from heaven – Daniel 7: 13: 'I saw in the night visions, and, behold, there came with the clouds of heaven one like unto a son of man'. Paul understood this expression and knew that it meant a human figure, a man from heaven, a heavenly man, 'Anani, Cloudman, as he would later be called. Here is heavenly, spiritual man, and he belongs not to Platonic idealism but to apocalyptic eschatology. After this point Paul drops Christology (but I shall shortly return to it) and continues with the theme which, as we have seen, he is really concerned to prove. Both men, first and last, Adam and Christ, are representative figures. From the first earthy man has sprung a multiplicity of earthy beings, all bearing the physical mortal characteristics of their ancestor. Similarly there springs from the last heavenly Man a race of spiritual beings sharing his characteristics — sharing therefore in resurrection. Here however Paul is careful to use the future tense — we *shall bear* the image of the Heavenly.

To return to Christology. It is worth observing that here Paul seems to by-pass completely the earthly life and death of Jesus, important as these (especially the latter) were to him. We must remember the strictly incidental and unsystematic manner in which the Christology is introduced. There are two points, neither of which is in itself Christological. One is the establishing of the distinction between the natural and the spiritual in an attempted explanation of the resurrection of the body. The question of verse 35 may be a foolish one, but it is not necessarily a sceptical one; the answer to it, whether we use Paul's terminology or not, must be in terms of continuity and transformation; Paul chooses to express this in terms of natural and spiritual bodies. The second point corresponds to the first and means the existence of the two humanities and their two points of origin, the first Adam and the last Adam. It is at this point that Christology enters the discussion. It is particularly important that Paul should refer to Daniel 7: 13 and the Son of man vision. This establishes a contact between Paul and the gospel tradition. It would be very odd for anyone writing Greek (and not translating or expounding Semitic idiom) to use the expression (when you come to think of it, a very odd one) the Son of man. Paul never does use it. The sense (if any) in which Jesus used it is not for discussion here — it is matter for another book.[11] It is sufficient that both Jesus and Paul appear to have had the chapter and the vision in mind. It is probable that both show awareness of the context and of the fact that the human figure somehow represents the people of the saints of the Most High (Dan 7: 18, 25, 27). That is, there is a human figure, who emerges from the world above and is presumably something more than human, who represents the elect of God and achieves their destiny on their behalf. There is a further point to make here, though it would be wrong to press it too far. In Daniel 7: 13 it is said that the human figure 'came near even to the Ancient of Days [God], and they brought him near before him'. Earlier, in verse 9, Daniel says 'I beheld till thrones were placed, and one that was ancient of days did sit'. Thrones, plural; does this mean that the human figure came to share the throne of God, to sit on a second throne, parallel and equal to God's throne? All that can rightly be said at this stage is that we know that at a later time there was in Judaism strenuous argument over the question whether one could properly maintain that there was a second heavenly—perhaps divine—being who could be said to share the throne of the Most High. It is probably not wrong to see contacts between this kind of speculation and early Christian thought. Was Paul beginning to think on these lines? It will be wise to leave that as a question. Even if the answer to the question should be 'Yes' it would still be true that Paul had done no more than cast a glance in this direction. Yet for him Christ was certainly Son of God and Lord; and we must remember 1 Corinthians 15: 25–28: Christ will sit on a throne with his enemies as his footstool; but he will be subordinate to the God who is all in all.

There remains another aspect of the person and work of Christ. Before we consider it we should review some of the points that have already been covered.

First we should remind ourselves of 1 Corinthians 15: 3, the basic form of the tradition that Paul received. It said nothing about who Christ was but concentrated on what happened to him and pointed out the relation of this to sin. Sin has so far been in the background rather than the foreground of the material we have studied.

Secondly, there is also the theme of messianic suffering. In his death Christ absorbed the awaited suffering and in his resurrection inaugurated the new age. This has the objective effect of moving on the eschatological clock, and also leads to the possibility that the individual may die and rise with Christ. This theme is integrated with the representative character of Christ. Since the death is his death, it is death to sin; since the resurrection is his resurrection, it results in living for God.

Thirdly, the study of Philippians—and here I must point ahead to what I shall say in a later chapter about Colossians, which after all may have been written by Paul—leads to something very much like the gnostic myth of the descending and ascending deity, which is a kind of doctrine of redemption. We are on the edge of gnosis, but not inside it. There is no hint of secrets, knowledge of which brings automatic salvation. The descending redeemer does not occupy himself in handing out divine secrets; he comes to practise obedience, even unto death.

A few passages will cast light on this death. One that we have skirted in the last few pages is Romans 3: 25. How (the question has already been raised) can a righteous God manifest his righteousness in justifying the sinner? He does it by grace (3: 24), and through an act of redemption; after mentioning this Paul goes on immediately to speak of the death of Jesus, whom God set forth in his blood as a means of dealing with sin (but the meaning of this is what we are about to discuss), to be received by faith.

The difficult, questionable word ('means of dealing with sin') here is *hilastērion*. The normal meaning of this Greek word and its cognates is to propitiate, to placate, to appease, to turn aside the wrath of God or man. The words however are used in the LXX as equivalents of the Hebrew *kipper*, and when this word has God as its subject, and sin, or defilement (moral or ceremonial), or the sinful or defiled person or thing, as its object, it must mean to expiate—to wipe off, to wipe clean. It is also important that the Greek, sometimes used as an adjective with a noun, is used to translate *kapporeth*, the mercy seat, or lid of the ark; that is, the place where atonement was made by the high priest on the Day of Atonement.

In Romans 3: 25 the subject is God; he set forth a *hilastērion*. It is argued that to say that 'God set him [Christ] forth as a means of propitiating himself' is an absurdity, and we must therefore accept the alternative rendering and translate, God set him forth as a means of expiation, that is, as a means of cleansing man from sin. It is true that the notion of God propitiating himself is a paradox; but it is a very biblical paradox. In fact, it states the problem, and claims to solve the problem that lies at the heart of the paradox. God in his righteousness must condemn sin; being what he is he must justify the sinner; no one else can deal with God's wrath against sin; therefore God himself must deal with it. Paul asserts that he does so in the death of Christ. At the same time, the notion of expiation is present; God not only forgives the sinner, he cleanses him from his sin.

Long ago T. W. Manson suggested[12] that the solution of the problem lay in the meaning 'mercy seat'; and he was probably right, though he may have exaggerated the four-point parallel and contrast that he drew between the Day of Atonement and the Pauline understanding of the death of Christ. He made the points:

1 God, not man (the high priest), set forth this sacrifice.

2 It was set forth openly, not secretly in the Holy of Holies.

3 The effect was received by faith, not *ex opere operato*. Here Manson probably failed to do justice to the Jewish understanding of sacrifice, the effectiveness of which was not independent of the worshipper's intention.

4 The blood was Christ's own, not an animal's.

This is probably rather too neat, but an allusion to the lid of the ark remains probable. To a Jew, this was the place where atonement was made for his people's sins and they were reconciled to God; it would be natural to apply the language and imagery to the new place of reconciliation. What we have however is a passing allusion rather than an attempt to work out a sacrificial theory. It is worth while to note the connection in thought (not in language) with the quotation of Psalm 32: 1 in Romans 4: 7: the covering of sin leads to the reckoning of righteousness.

There are other passages where there seem to be similar allusions; Old Testament language is taken up but without any attempt to work out a detailed and consistent theory.

In Romans 4: 25 there are two possibilities. The first is Isaiah 53 (which may be alluded to in Phil 2: 7; apart from this there is very little of Isa 53 in Paul). The contact would be in *was delivered up*, and *on account of our transgressions*; also perhaps in *for our justification*, but there are serious textual problems in Isaiah 53: 12, where the Masoretic (Hebrew) text and the LXX differ widely. Throughout Romans 4 it is the story of Abraham that is in mind; it is however possible that when Paul comes to apply it he turns to a recognized formula. Verse 25 is stylized and this results in a problematical double use of the preposition. Do we have to separate the *delivered up* and the *raised*? Delivered *because of* our sins and raised up *because* (now, in virtue of Christ's death) we have been justified? More probably the Greek is a loose combination; delivered and raised up are parts of one operation, and the first *for* means because of our (past) sins and the second *for* means in order that we might be justified.

Most of Romans 4 deals with Abraham, and some see in 4: 25 a reference to his (intended) sacrifice of Isaac, the 'binding (*'aqidah*) of Isaac', often referred to simply as the 'binding'. There is no doubt that Judaism came to regard this act of Abraham's as exceptionally meritorious, and Isaac as one of the greatest of intercessors for Israel. He was supposed (though this is not written in Genesis 22) to have offered himself willingly in sacrificial obedience to the will of God. That Paul was aware of what Judaism was making of Isaac and that he could have taken it over in the same allusive way that he took over other Old Testament and Jewish material may be affirmed. But is the language here close enough to support the view that the *'aqidah* contributed seriously to his thought? Probably not. Allusions to the *'aqidah* however have been found not only here but in Romans 3: 25; 5: 8, 9; 8: 32; Galatians 1: 4;

1 Thessalonians 5: 10. Of these the only one in which allusion seems at all probable is Romans 8: 32, the only passage in which there is any linguistic contact. In Genesis 22: 16 God says to Abraham 'You did not *spare* (*epheisō*) your son'; in Romans 8: 32 Paul says that God did not *spare* (*epheisato*) his Son. If there is an allusion here nothing is made of it theologically; the *a fortiori* argument (Will he not much more . . .?) will stand without it.

In 1 Corinthians 5: 6, 7 there is an allusion very similar to that of Romans 3: 25. For the image compare Galatians 5: 9. It evidently originated in Jewish Passover practice and must have been familiar. It was imperative that all leaven should be removed from every house before the feast could take place. When this process had been completed the lambs could be killed in the Temple and in the evening the meal could be eaten. Paul's point (and the context of the case of incest — 5: 1 — makes the application clear) is that in view of the sacrifice of Christ ('our Passover') we are now living in the period of the festival itself, and it is inconsistent to do this if we have not already purged out 'the old and wicked leaven'. We have to catch up with the situation that God's provision has already reached. This is perhaps the clearest of all examples of Paul's ethical principle, Become what you are. Compare Romans 6: You have died to sin; hurry up and kill it off. So much Paul means; it is doubtful whether he means any more. If a further inference is to be drawn it will be rather that we are now drinking the new wine with Christ in the kingdom of God, and might have other overtones suggesting the Christian Supper (see below). But even these are doubtful.

In this, and the other passages we have considered, Paul alludes to the sacrificial system of Judaism. He does not do more; there is no attempt to elaborate a sacrificial theory of the death of Christ. There is enough to justify the attempts of later theologians to produce such a system, but for Paul it seems dangerously easy; he works at a greater depth, and we may wind up the present discussion on the basis of one further passage.

At Galatians 3: 13 Paul takes up a verse in the Old Testament, Deuteronomy 21: 23, which declares that he that is hanged is a curse of God: an ambiguous expression and within the Jewish tradition the words have been taken in two ways. *A curse of God* means that God curses the person hanged; *a curse of God* means that the hanged person is a curse against God, the exposed corpse is an offence to him. The Greek Old Testament takes the former view and Paul follows it. Probably he had used it when he persecuted

Christians; probably those who continued to oppose the new faith used it still. Jesus of Nazareth the Messiah? On the contrary, his death proves him to be under God's curse. Here again Paul was obliged to provide a new exegesis of a passage he did not choose but whose authority he could not deny. He rewords the Old Testament sentence, probably helped by his knowledge of the Hebrew. He does not say, could not say, that Christ was cursed by God; he says that Christ became a curse, and did so on our behalf. The result is a saying closely parallel to 2 Corinthians 5: 21. In each there is the same kind of exchange—righteousness and sin, curse and blessing (the blessing is brought out explicitly in Gal 3: 14). There are two things to observe. First, Paul says that by becoming a curse for us Christ redeemed us from the curse of the Law. Behind the notion of redemption (and involved in the structure of the word) is the payment of a price in order to secure freedom. This is not developed here and we cannot be certain that Paul in this context means much more than *liberated*. The notion of liberation by the payment of a price does however occur in Paul, perhaps most clearly in 1 Corinthians 6: 19, 20, where it is developed in its ethical implications, which resemble those of 2 Corinthians 5: 15. Those who have been bought with a price are no longer their own; they belong to Christ. This being so, they will no longer live for themselves, closed to the claims and needs of others. This fits with the positive point of Galatians 3: 14; the blessing that is received is the promise of the Spirit—and for Paul this means anything but the pleasant enjoyment of religious experience; the Spirit is the divine agency that makes non-self-centred life possible. Secondly, here as in 2 Corinthians 5: 21 Paul is careful to use not an ethical but a relational word. He cannot say that Christ was actually cursed by God; he came to stand for all that the divine curse, the severing of relations, means. The only clue to the means by which the exchange of curse and blessing is effected is again the same as that which is provided in 2 Corinthians 5: 21: it takes place in Christ. Beyond this the theology is incidental. Paul is not speculating. He was confronted by an argument he had himself used in the past: the Old Testament proves that Jesus so far from being God's Messiah was under God's curse. He had himself argued that all mankind, whether under the Law or outside the Law, was under a curse. What could he do but put two and two together? The innocent took the curse that the cursed might receive the blessing.

Other passages must be passed over. One of the most important dealing with the participation of the believer in the death and resurrection of Jesus is Romans 6; something will be said about this when baptism is discussed. Another is 2 Corinthians 4. The treasure is contained in earthen vessels (4: 7) and the dying of Jesus is carried about in order that the life of Jesus too may be manifested (4: 7, 10, 11). Throughout Paul is insisting on the objectivity and subjectivity of the Gospel. The death and resurrection of Jesus constituted an eschatological event that happened *extra nos*, without our being consulted, and changing fundamentally the relation of the world to God and to its destiny in him. Yet it remains without relevance to me if I do not share in the dying and rising.

THE CHURCH

A further major topic of Paul's thought is the church. It might seem proper to begin the study of this topic in the way in which others have been approached, that is, by an examination of Paul's use of the relevant word, *church* (*ekklēsia*), but this time it will be wise to start further back. The basic problem in Paul's theology, perhaps in all theology, is that of the relation of the One to the Many. How can and does what is done and experienced by the One affect the Many? How do you move from the One to the Many? Why should there be a Many? There is only one who can properly be called the Son of God; only one who knew no sin; only one who was crucified and rose from the dead; what right have the Many to appear in the story at all? How do the unique actions of a unique person affect a plurality of persons?

Paul does not set out the problem in these terms, but he is certainly at work on it, sometimes without indicating that he is doing so, sometimes in strange terms. Thus we may look again at a passage that has been considered for other purposes. In Galatians 3: 14 Paul introduces the notion of a covenant made between God on the one hand, and, on the other, Abraham and his seed, or issue (*sperma*). Paul notes that it is not the plural but the singular, *seed*, that is used, and proceeds to identify this singular noun with Christ. This has often been dismissed as a ridiculous argument, and it is true that *seed* is a collective noun, so that it would have been impossible to use the plural. In fact Paul is here theologizing very seriously (though undoubtedly in terms that it would not occur to a twentieth-century theologian to use—and which would be wrong if he did use them). He can moreover justify himself by observing that 'seed of Abraham' is a theological rather than a physiological or racial concept; from the beginning it was not conceived in physical terms. This Paul works out in Romans 9: 6–13. It is not those who are physically descended from him who are to be recognized as seed of Abraham. This goes back to the original promise of Genesis 21: 12: 'Seed' is to be reckoned exclusively along the line of Isaac, though Ishmael, and others, were equally from the physiological point of view Abraham's seed. The next generation makes the point even more strongly; when two children emerged from one conception, 'Jacob I loved, Esau I hated'. Thus in each of the first two generations the seed was reduced to one out of a number of those who qualified physically. Why not also in the last generation? To say that at the time of End also the seed was reduced to one is only another way of stating the Pauline doctrine of the universal sinfulness of the human race, apart from Christ. The Law had precisely this effect when it shut up the whole universe under sin (Gal 3: 22). It is at this point in Paul's argument that faith is introduced, and by faith we are all children of God *in Christ* (3: 26), in whom all the various social groups — Jew, Greek; slave, free; male, female — become one person (3: 28). From this the conclusion follows in verse 29: 'You [plural] who belong to Christ are Abraham's seed, and consequently are to inherit the promise'. The word *seed* now has its proper collective sense, but this is a new collective, reached only by destroying the old collectivity of race and concentrating upon the one new Man, Jesus, and by the incorporation of both Jews and Gentiles in him.

More familiar, and sufficiently studied already, is the connection between Adam and Christ; see Romans 5: 12–21, and 1 Corinthians 15: 21, 22, 45–49. Here the relation of the One to the Many is clear.

Thus it may be said that Paul's Christology, Christology of the universal Being, itself implies the existence of a new community; it is a partial expression of this that the existence of a Messiah (in Jewish terms) implies the existence of a messianic people. The new community is continuous with the old precisely in the person of Jesus and nowhere else — a *nowhere* that Paul emphasizes over against others who found and insisted on continuity based on the Law, so that those who would join must accept circumcision and observe the commandments. This community existed by faith, and its new life was hidden with Christ in God, to be manifested only when God should choose at the Last Day (Colossians 3: 3; but the thought is found elsewhere, though less clearly set out). At the same time, the new community, bearing the image of the Heavenly Man, consisted of mortal beings of many degrees of imperfection. It is at this point that we may look at the word *church* and by this means examine the ways in which the people of God conducted their affairs in the world.

It is a close approximation to say that in the Greek Old Testament *church* (*ekklēsia*) represents the Hebrew *qahal*, which is the assembly of God's people (rather more concrete than simply 'God's people').

Paul uses the word in this sense, and with a local application; thus frequently at the beginning of a letter (1 Cor 1: 2; 2 Cor 1: 1; 1 Thess 1: 1), but also elsewhere (Rom 16: 1). A similar sense also appears in the plural: in a city there will be one church, but in a district or province there will be many (so 1 Cor 16: 1, 19; 2 Cor 8: 1; Gal 1: 2, 22; 1 Thess 2: 14). These passages all refer to the Lord's people in a particular place, or places. In the Old Testament context there is no problem; there is only one people and it all exists in one place. As soon however as the Gospel spread beyond Jerusalem, and especially as it made its way into the Gentile world, the position became more complicated. Something that truly was the people of God (at least, Paul called it *church*, *ekklēsia*, or *the saints, the holy ones, hoi hagioi*) came into existence in a variety of places, and there assembled—even in private houses (Rom 16: 5; 1 Cor 16: 19; Philemon 2). The idea of assembling is implied in the use of *ekklēsia*, and is an important part of what the word meant for Paul also. Thus he can use 'in ecclesia', *en ekklēsiai*, to mean 'in assembly', very much what we mean by 'in church' apart from the fact that he does not think of a special building.

Paul can use 'the churches' (*hai ekklēsiai*) to denote the various local churches of a district; he can also use it to mean 'the totality of churches', or at least something approaching this. This is something to which he can appeal (1 Cor 11: 16), also something for which he has a responsibility and for which he must care (2 Cor 11: 28). In modern use we employ also 'the church' (singular) to mean the same thing—'the totality of (local) churches'; is this true also of Paul's use? The answer is uncertain. The universal meaning of *the church* may occur at Galatians 1: 13; 1 Corinthians 15: 9; Philippians 3: 6; these however are all persecution passages, and it is at least arguable that Paul was never able to extend his persecuting activity beyond Jerusalem and the immediate neighbourhood; if this is so, *the church* would still be a local church. Two other passages are doubtful. In 1 Corinthians 10: 32 *the church of God* stands in parallel with Jews and Greeks and these suggest universal rather than local concepts—there may be Jews and Greeks anywhere; so perhaps the church of God may be anywhere. In fact however those

121

who received the letter would be much more likely to encounter Jews and Greeks in Corinth than elsewhere, and it may be that the church of God would be (in Paul's mind) similarly limited: be void of offence to (Corinthian) Jews, Greeks, and Christians. There is a similar ambiguity in 1 Corinthians 12: 28. Prophets, teachers, and so on, suggest the local church; this is where they were to be found. What of apostles? It depends on whether they were apostles such as Paul, or 'apostles of churches' (2 Cor 8: 23). On the whole there is some probability that here 'the church' does refer to the universal phenomenon.

For really certain examples of *church* in this sense we have to move on to Colossians and Ephesians; see pp. 144–50, 154–7. The same is true of the use of the word *body* to describe the company of Christian believers. Elsewhere it functions chiefly as an illustration, a comparison. So for example Romans 12: 4, 5: 'As in one body we have many members and all the members do not have the same function, so we who are many are all one body in Christ'. The point is clear; a human body is made up of various parts, which fit together in a harmoniously working whole. The Christian community is like that. It is not said that it *is* a body, nor is anything said about the head as a distinctive and directing part. The various gifts of service, teaching, and the like fit together. The same is true at 1 Corinthians 12: 12, where the metaphor is worked out in some detail in the following verses – hand, foot, eye, and so on; each is different, each is essential to the wellbeing of the whole, all must work together in unity. Variety is not something that has to be tolerated, but a good thing, essential for proper working; but it must be harmoniously coordinated. 1 Corinthians 12: 27 may seem to go a little beyond this, but it is really the summing up of the metaphor, and though Paul says 'You are Christ's body', we still have comparison rather than identity. When a later writer (or it could be Paul at a later stage in his career) goes beyond this and sees Christ as the head of an organism that can be described as his body it is on a Christological basis. Christ is the last Adam, the seed of Abraham; as such he is the head (the word can hardly be avoided) of a new creation, a new race. Alternatively, he is the first-born among many brothers (Rom 8: 29), continuous with all other members of the family, as the head is with the body; at the same time he is Lord over all the other members, and thus discontinuous – again, as the head is.

This leads to the question what this body looked like as a historical fact. As Paul thinks of the church, every member without exception is a minister (the word, of course, means *servant*). Thus in 1 Corinthians 12: 7 the opening words, *To each one*, must be taken quite seriously; Paul means exactly what he says. The context continues in the same vein and leads on to the image of the body, discussed above. Every part of the body, every member of the church, has its own function; anything that does not have a function is not part of the body. Romans 12: 4–6 is addressed to the whole church; we have noted the parallelism between *the grace given to me* (12: 3) and *the grace given to us* (12: 6), and the different gifts that have been distributed. None is without. It corresponds to this that Paul has very little to say about ministers as a special class. According to Acts 14: 23 Paul appointed elders (presbyters, *presbyteroi*) in every city (church); compare Acts 20: 17 (and 28). Presbyters however are never mentioned in the epistles. *Episkopoi* and *diakonoi* (which we may translate as 'bishops' and 'deacons' provided we do not make them look too much like the bishops and deacons we see today) are mentioned once only, at Philippians 1: 1. Their function is not stated, though it is evident that they must hold some special position, or rather carry out some special task, in the community. It may be that both were financial officers, who were concerned with the gift the Philippians had sent to Paul (Phil 4: 10–20). The word *episkopos* is sometimes used in secular contexts for financial administrative officers, and later at least *diakonoi* were engaged in the church's charitable work. Perhaps the *episkopoi* decided on and the *diakonoi* carried out the gift. This, it need not be added, is no more than a guess. 1 Corinthians 12: 28 is evidently important, though it contains many obscurities. Apostles (see above) may be apostles like Paul or 'apostles of churches' (2 Cor 8: 23). Prophets are doubtless people who prophesy; but does the noun indicate that there was a special group of these who were recognized as the members who regularly prophesied? It seems clear that anyone might on occasion prophesy; but it is likely that there were some who did so more frequently (and to greater effect) than others. 'Teachers' hardly needs explanation, though it is important to note that they existed. It is also important that after this word the style of the list changes and we hear no more of persons holding gifts and exercising functions, but of the functions themselves. Some of these are clear; at least two are not. Governments (*kybernēseis*) presumably refers to some kind of directing activity (those who preside?), and helps (*antilēmpseis*) to some kind of service to others. With Philippians 1: 1 in mind one might speak of *episkopoi* and *diakonoi*; but this again is guesswork. There is a similar list in

Romans 12: 6-8. Here the list changes its style in the opposite direction; it seems clear that Paul is more concerned about function than about office or order.

It is worth while in this context to note a number of unexpected silences. Thus when Paul deals with the disorder at the Corinthian supper it would have seemed natural to write, at 1 Corinthians 11: 21, 22, 33, 'Wait for the presiding minister (instead of starting to eat as soon as possible and as much as possible)'. But there is no indication of a presiding minister, and Paul can only say 'Wait for one another'. Similarly at 1 Corinthians 16: 2 it seems that there is no one to collect the funds for the collection for the poor. Each Christian saves his money week by week, and Paul himself will collect it when he comes.

To say this is not to say that the Pauline churches were simply chaotic (though on occasion Corinth can hardly have been far from this). There were leaders. To Romans 12: 6-8 and 1 Corinthians 12: 28 we may add Galatians 6: 6 — teachers were apparently paid for their services, though by those who were taught rather than by the church itself, and on the basis of sharing rather than on a fixed scale. 1 Thessalonians 5: 11-15 is particularly interesting:

11   All exhort and edify; they do this already and must continue.

12   There are some who labour, preside, and admonish. They should be recognized

13   and valued and loved for the work that they do (not for the office that they hold).

14   All the brothers are to admonish, comfort, help, be patient; that is, they are all to have an eye to discipline and pastoral care.

15   The requirement continues; the imperative is plural.

This paragraph shows very clearly that all have a responsibility for ministry, and indeed for pastoral ministry; but there are some who are outstanding in this respect. All are equal; some are more equal than others. See also 1 Corinthians 16: 15: the household of Stephanas were neither appointed from above nor elected from below. They set themselves for ministry to the saints. This certainly does not mean that they crudely pushed themselves forward in a place-seeking way; Paul would never have commended this. Rather, they saw a need, a work to be done, and set about doing it, without waiting for orders, authorization, or request.

Thus it is true that there is in the Pauline epistles, and presumably in the Pauline churches, no systematically ordered ministry; but we can observe, first, a concern for mutual service, which expresses itself under three heads, the word (prophecy and teaching), doing practical service (*diakonia*), discipline; and secondly, that in these various activities some naturally single themselves out to take the lead.

What of Paul himself as an apostle? It is natural to suggest that apostles are like the Queen in chess: they have all the moves of (nearly) all the pieces. Paul preaches and teaches, organizes relief of the poor, exercises discipline, and stands head and shoulders above everyone else. Yet in Acts he seems scarcely to be regarded as an apostle. True, he is twice described as an apostle; but at 14: 14 there is doubt about the reading and at 14: 4 it is possible to interpret: some were on the Jewish side, some on the apostolic, that is, the Christian side. These may not be very convincing explanations. As alternatives we may suggest, first, that in chapters 13 and 14 Paul and Barnabas were acting as missionaries sent out by the church of Antioch, that is, as apostles of that church (cf. 2 Cor 8: 23); after chapter 14 — and perhaps after a dispute (Gal 2: 11) — this was no longer so and Paul was a freelance; and, secondly, Paul was evidently very greatly admired by Luke, who on these occasions allows his heart to rule his head. For it must be recognized that on Luke's principles Paul cannot have been an apostle, since there were only twelve and after the defection of Judas the vacancy had been filled by Matthias. Moreover, as the story of Matthias shows, to be one of the twelve one had not only to have seen the risen Lord, as Paul claimed to have done, but also to have travelled with him during his ministry, as Paul had not done.

For Paul, his apostleship was tied up with his mission to the Gentile world (Gal 1: 16; also Rom 15: 20). And evangelization carried with it the care of all the churches (2 Cor 11: 28). It is clear (and after the evidence of Acts not surprising) that some questioned his apostleship (1 Cor 9: 2; 15: 8-10). He had nothing with which to support it except the Gospel that he preached and the fruit that it bore; 1 Corinthians 9: 2 again — how could the Corinthians doubt his apostleship since the genuineness of their own Christian faith hung upon it? The same point is made in 2 Corinthians 13: 5-10. The distrust of his fellow Christians must have added immeasurably to the troubles of a wandering and insecure life. This appears most clearly in the Corinthian letters, and a few passages will be more illuminating than a general discussion.

In 1 Corinthians 15: 1–11, the drift is clear. There is in Corinth doctrinal difficulty regarding the resurrection. It is important for Paul to show that he can build on a common Christian foundation. Hence the initial quotation of the common, primitive statement of faith, which is perhaps especially geared so as to lead up to the supplement of verse 8. There is no reason why Paul should of his own accord use the word abortion (*ektrōma*) to describe himself; he used it here because others had used it of him, probably in the sense of *freak* (he was not a proper apostle), though the sense of time (in a rather inverted way) was included. As an apostle he had been brought into the world not too soon but too late. Not only was the appearance late; he had persecuted the church. We can overhear not only 'Paul is a freak' but also 'Paul is not worthy to be called an apostle'. Up to a point he is prepared to accept all this; but his critics must not forget the grace of God.

In 1 Corinthians 9: 1–27, again criticism is plainly to be traced. Verse 3: 'my defence [*apologia*, a technical legal term] to those who examine me [another legal term, *anakrinein*] is this . . .' He insists that he has seen the Lord (verse 1); this time there is no allusion to the question of timing. As the next paragraph shows, Paul has in mind here the problem of food sacrificed to idols (see pp. 139f.); he has apostolic rights, but he does not insist on them, in Corinth has not even accepted them. In verses 19–23 Paul develops this in a way that sheds light on his apostolic ministry. A free man, he has made himself a slave to all in the interests of the Gospel — 'that I might gain the more'. Verse 20 is particularly striking: To the Jews he became a Jew; but was he not a Jew? We return here to the question of the Law (see pp. 74–87) and come to the summary in verse 23: 'all I do I do for the sake of the Gospel'. This is the determining factor and dictates his behaviour in all circumstances. What this meant in practice appears in 1 Corinthians 4: 9–13. The Corinthians were puffed up with a sense of their own importance and achievement. This is not said about apostles; they come on at the end of the gladiatorial show like the men condemned to death. The Corinthians are (or think they are) wise, strong, and highly respectable; Paul is the reverse of this.

Paul's self-portrait, which may look like a kind of religious masochism, reappears at a deeper level (which brings out its real ground), and with a contrast, in 2 Corinthians, of which almost every verse could be quoted with some degree of relevance. There were others (Paul is not thinking of Cephas and Apollos) who had invaded Paul's territory in Corinth. Here was already one difference between them and him. His principle and practice were always to break new ground, to preach where Christ had not previously been named (Rom 15: 20), but his rivals were happy to move in where the spadework had been done and to claim what credit they could get for work they had done in easier circumstances (2 Cor 10: 12–18). As they came they bore letters of commendation which introduced them to the local church (3: 1). Paul had no use for such letters; possibly there was no one who would provide them for him. It was not that there was anything wrong with the practice; he had written such a letter for Phoebe (Rom 16: 1) and there is one in 2 Corinthians itself (8: 22–24). But he had one commendation only: the double fact of the truth of the Gospel and its effectiveness. The Corinthians could deny the validity of his apostleship only at the cost of the validity of their own faith (2 Cor 13: 5). There was nothing in principle wrong in work done by others on foundations he had laid (1 Cor 3: 6). But those who had come to Corinth were not building on his work but destroying it (2 Cor 11: 1–4). Such people can only be described as false apostles, servants of Satan who only disguise themselves as servants of righteousness. Some of the historical aspects of this situation have already been sketched. All that is necessary here is to bring out Paul's understanding of his apostolic contribution to the church. His rivals boasted of their visions and of their power of speech; they exercised authority over their fellow Christians; they accepted payment for their work; they depended not on the self-validating truth of their message but on the authoritative commendations they received and the miracles they were able to perform. Paul's humble apostleship stands out all the more clearly. The authority he has is for 'building you up, not for throwing you down' (2 Cor 10: 8, and 13: 10). He has had little out of Corinth but humiliation (e.g. 12: 21) and tears. 'We are not lords over your faith, but fellow workers for your joy' (1: 24). 'It is not ourselves we proclaim as lord, but Jesus Christ, and ourselves as your slaves, for Jesus' sake' (4: 5). The theological point is not far away from this. Paul's apostolic life consists in carrying round in his body the killing (*nekrōsis*, making dead; not simply death, or dying) of Jesus, in order that the life of Jesus also may be manifested in his body (4: 10). It is easy to see and to say that an apostle will proclaim Christ crucified and risen with his speech; Paul insists that the same truth must be proclaimed by the apostle's life – and, of course, death.

This is precisely the point at which we may turn to Paul's understanding of the Christian sacraments. The background of Paul's sacramental teaching (if this is the right word – it must always be remembered that the New Testament has no word for sacrament) has been vigorously disputed. Was there a genuinely sacramental element in Jewish religion – in any form of Judaism? Did Paul's teaching and practice come from rites of initiation and cultic meals in the mystery religions? Are all of these totally irrelevant? Did Paul draw only on earlier Christian tradition? What sort of place did he assign to baptism and to the Christian meal? Arguments and counter-arguments often fail to meet each other and the debate has to some extent been conducted on the wrong grounds. It is important to begin with some historical analysis.

There is no doubt that Paul was aware of and took for granted the practice of baptism and the Lord's Supper. He assumed their importance; he assumed that everyone else knew about them; he assumed that he could argue from them as given facts. For baptism, Romans 6: 1–14 is sufficient proof. Paul can take for granted that all 'we' (Christians) have been baptized. He needs to argue from this in order to make his own point, but he can further assume that all will know ('Or do you not know . . .?' is of course rhetorical) that baptism into Christ means baptism into death; and this is a fairly sophisticated interpretation of baptism. Paul is writing in this letter to a church he had not founded, to Christians he did not know; he may have been rash in his assumptions, particularly in regard to the relation between baptism and the death of Christ. But we can hardly say less than that Christians for whose instruction he had himself been responsible would know that baptism meant baptism into the death of Christ. Other important passages are 1 Corinthians 12: 13 ('In one Spirit we were all baptized into one body'); Galatians 3: 27 ('All of you who were baptized into Christ put on Christ'). On the other hand we must not forget 1 Corinthians 1: 14–17, which can hardly mean less than a somewhat reprehensible carelessness in making up the baptism registers, and does in fact imply a real depreciation of baptism in comparison with preaching.

For the Supper see 1 Corinthians 10: 16, 17 and 11: 17–34. In the former of these passages we again see Paul arguing not *to* but *from* the practice. Something similar lies behind Galatians 2: 12, 13. The common eating of Jewish and Gentile Christians cannot fail to include their gathering for the church supper; and it is here that the problem of Jew–Gentile relations would come to a head. Again it is right to notice that the Supper can be observed in such a way that it would be better if it were not observed at all. 1 Corinthians 11: 17: 'You come together not for the better but for the worse'.

This leads to an important observation. There is no doubt that Paul knew, accepted, and practised baptism and the Supper, but his acceptance was a critical acceptance. In particular he was highly critical of the understanding and practice of the two rites that seems to have been current at Corinth. The clearest evidence of this is his adducing of the warning example of ancient Israel in 1 Corinthians 10: 1–12. It was possible to have a baptism, and to eat and drink spiritual food and drink, provided by God himself through Christ (who was the rock in the wilderness, verse 4), and still fall into sin and be punished for doing so. Hence, 'Let him who thinks he stands take heed lest he fall' (v. 12); baptism and eucharist, if practised in a merely mechanical way, will not prevent this. There are circumstances in which the Lord's Supper becomes one's own supper (1 Cor 11: 20), and this is a complete inversion of its meaning. How was this danger to be met? Paul continues by insisting on the relation between the Lord's Supper and the Last Supper, taken by Jesus and his disciples in the night in which he was betrayed (1 Cor 11: 23–25). It is often assumed that in these verses Paul was simply quoting what was in any case quoted every time one of his own churches observed the Supper, but this is by no means necessarily so. The Last Supper was, according to old tradition, the celebration of an annual event, Passover; the Christian Supper was from the beginning weekly, and the connection may have been by no means evident — a celebration of the Last Supper as such would have been part of an annual Christian Passover. The close connection between the Last Supper and the Lord's Supper may have been Paul's work. Certainly he is saying: If at your supper you recall that event, you will no longer fall into your present errors.

Paul connects baptism with the death of Jesus. This may owe something to traditional material like Luke 12: 50; if Jesus used the image of immersion to describe his approaching suffering this would be a good starting-point for Paul's thought. This connection would also confirm and use the understanding of the death of Jesus as an anticipation of the Messianic affliction; baptism would thus signify the fact that in Christ the believer shares in the messianic affliction and is thus in a position to pass through into the bliss of the age to come. Paul develops this by his description of the death of Jesus as a death to sin (Rom 6: 10). Those who in baptism share it will thus themselves die to sin. In Romans 6 Paul assumes that his readers will know the connection between baptism and death.

He does not make the same assumption in relation to the Supper. 1 Corinthians 11: 26 is his own addition to what is evidently a piece of traditional material which appears also in the Synoptic Gospels. In this verse he explains how the common meal comes to be done 'in memory of me'. This is because whenever you eat this loaf and drink the cup 'you proclaim the Lord's death until he come'. *Proclaim* (*katangellein*) does not refer to a *verbum visibile* (notwithstanding the Authorized Version's *shew*); it is used of the cultic proclamation of the myth on which the cult rests, and this gives the sense in which Paul uses the word. Whenever you meet for supper you tell the story of the Lord's death; it is this that gives meaning to what is done – and it will prevent you from taking the opportunity of getting drunk and from despising your poor brother who cannot afford as good a supper as yours.

The connection with death, in both baptism and eucharist, is essential for Paul. It was the death of Jesus that was representatively the messianic travail pains; his vindication in resurrection was the beginning of the age to come; his coming would be its consummation – hence the 'until he come' of 1 Corinthians 11: 26 and perhaps the *marana tha* ('Our Lord, come') of 16: 22. We thus have here a special part of Paul's answer to the question how the deeds of the One can affect, can become the deeds of, the Many. As we have seen, Paul can answer the question in terms of justification by faith. The righteousness of the One who knew no sin is given to the Many, who knew sin well enough; the curse that was due for the many law-breakers was borne by the One whose only fault was that he hung on a tree. The sacraments are another way of expressing the same fundamental truth: we enter into the death, and to some extent into the resurrection, of Christ himself. This means inevitably that justification and sacraments are not alternatives but correlatives; sacramental doctrine that is inconsistent with justification by faith is bad sacramental doctrine; at least, it is not Paul's sacramental doctrine. It is to be emphasized that Paul makes the connection of baptism and eucharist with death essential. For him, these are both parts of the *theologia crucis*, which he found at the heart of the Christian faith. The greatest error (to be found especially at Corinth) was to make them part of a *theologia gloriae*, pleasing religious activities by which one might be able to ascend to God. Always for him they were means by which God descends to us, and his descent means nothing less than the cross. These are ways in which he is willing to share it with us.

This suggests one further observation. Baptism (1 Cor 12: 13) and the Supper (1 Corinthians 10: 16, 17; 11: 24) are like the doctrine of the church in that both employ the word *body*. It has been maintained that the use of body in the description of the church is derived from this sacramental (especially eucharistic) use; it seems more probable that both the use of body in the sacraments and the use of body for the church have their roots in eschatology and in the primary phrase *in Christ*, which is an eschatological and ecclesiastical rather than a mystical expression.[13] Men who in real life are sinners and will surely at the end of their mortal term die, are by faith righteous and have already passed from death to life in virtue of their union with Christ in the messianic affliction and the final resurrection. The sacraments are activations of that faith that unites men to Christ, focal points of contact by which the union between them and him is effected. Of this union the church is a sign in the world. It is such a sign — a concrete, visible, audible mark — in virtue not of human religousness but of the activity of the Holy Spirit. The Spirit, with the fruit the Spirit bears, is the last topic to be handled in this chapter.[14]

THE HOLY SPIRIT AND ETHICS

It is proper to begin with the Holy Spirit. The fundamental context of thought in which Paul places the Holy Spirit is eschatology; the Spirit is the mark of the church which lives 'between the times', for which eschatology — the looked-for future — has been inaugurated but not completed. Notwithstanding a good deal of difference in terminology there is in eschatology a close correspondence between Paul and the gospel tradition. This comes to the surface in Romans 14: 17: the kingdom of God, which came near in the ministry of Jesus, is not a matter of eating and drinking (scrupulously observing or joyfully disregarding food laws); it is righteousness, peace, and joy in the Holy Spirit; that is, it is the Holy Spirit that realizes the things that the anticipation of the kingdom of God in this age means. This verse will serve as a starting-point; a fuller passage is Romans 8: 14–25, which oscillates between present and future. Being led by the Spirit Christians are (in the present) children of God. The Spirit may be described as the Spirit of adoption (or sonship), because he both effects the new relation, and gives us knowledge of it (verse 15). Note the significant Aramaic word *Abba*, borrowed from the tradition of the words of Jesus (Mark 14: 36; cf. Gal 4: 6). This may be an allusion to the use in church of the

Lord's Prayer, but, if it is, it is the Lord's Prayer said not formally but with confident assurance and arising out of a relation with God comparable with (and dependent on) that of Jesus himself. Thus the Spirit bears witness that we are children of God (verse 16); but this is not an end in itself; it points on to a further truth. If you are your father's child you are your father's heir, and may at some time expect to receive more than you already have by way of patrimony. We are thus joint-heirs with our elder Brother (cf. verse 29). This means the future; clearly we have not yet entered upon the inheritance. The present is a time of suffering, but suffering with Christ points forward to glory with Christ (verse 17). This glory is firmly fixed in the future. At present the whole creation groans, looking forward to the time of liberation that God has appointed. And this includes not only sub-human and non-Christian creation, but also us who have the firstfruits of the Spirit (verse 23). In this verse we note also the return of the word 'adoption'; we have now the Spirit that anticipates our adoption, we look forward to adoption itself at the End. Firstfruits (the word used in 1 Corinthians 15: 20) means not that we have the first part of the Spirit, with a second part of the Spirit to come in due course; it means that we have the Spirit now as a pledge and advance part-payment of all that God intends to give his people. The present however remains the time for hope (verses 24, 25).

The word 'firstfruits' (*aparchē*) has a counterpart in 2 Corinthians 1: 21, 22 and 5: 5. The (now obsolete) *earnest* translates a commercial term (*arrhabōn*) which means the first instalment of a payment — both a part of the total price, and the pledge that the rest will be paid in due course. This is perhaps the clearest of all the terms Paul uses to denote the place of the Spirit in his eschatological system.

It will be recalled that *charis, grace,* is actualized in *charismata, gifts of grace,* which enable those who receive them to do special Christian services; Romans 12: 3 and 6 are particularly good examples. Paul also uses the word *pneumatika, spiritual* (things) to indicate that these gifts are given by the Holy Spirit. The full term, *charisma pneumatikon, spiritual gift,* occurs at Romans 1: 11, and is evidently of very wide application: it can be anything that would help to establish the church. The most important passage is 1 Corinthians 12 – 14. In 12: 4 gifts, *charismata,* are not described by the adjective *pneumatika,* but they are given by the Spirit; the gifts are diverse, the Spirit is one. They are manifestations of the Spirit, that is, signs that the Spirit is present and at work, and they are given to each member of the community (12: 7). The gifts that follow (12: 8–11) were no doubt as familiar to the church at Corinth as they are in many respects obscure to us, but their relation to the Spirit is clear. We have glanced at the rest of chapter 12 in dealing with the church; it is essential that chapter 13 should follow, though love (*agapē*) is not described as either a *charisma* or a *pneumatikon*, perhaps because Paul wishes to make absolutely clear that this is not a special gift, such as speaking with tongues (13: 1), which may be given to some but not to all members of the church and is in any case of limited value. No other gift can so adequately secure at once the vitality and the unity in diversity of the whole; and it is given, or at least is on offer, to all. Chapter 14 is the fundamental source for the understanding of Paul's concept of prophecy and speaking with tongues (*pneumatika* serves as a heading in verse 1). Both are good gifts of God, and must be valued as such; Paul thanks God that he speaks with tongues more than any of the Corinthians (14: 18); he makes it clear however that in comparison with prophecy it is of little value. It is speech which no one can understand unless the complementary gift of interpretation is also given; the result is that if the whole community is speaking with tongues and strangers come in they will say 'You are mad' (v. 23). Prophecy, equally the gift of the Spirit, is intelligible and affects the conscience of the hearer (verses 24, 25). It is moreover controllable as glossolalia is not: Spirits of prophets are subject to prophets. This means that if one is prophesying, and a revelation is made to another, the first prophet can stop and sit down (verse 30). The test by which spiritual gifts may be valued is given in 12: 3: the work of the Spirit is to declare that Jesus is Lord. The more plainly a gift testifies to the lordship of Jesus the greater its value. Glossolalia bears witness to the fact that I who speak am dominated by a lord, but it does not make clear who this lord is; it might be a demon (10: 20). This observation may help towards the understanding of the obscure first part of the verse. Who could suppose that the words 'A curse on Jesus!' could be uttered in the Holy Spirit? Only one who measured the truth of what was said by the degree of inspiration manifested. But this may not be the meaning; it may be that we have to think of people struggling against a Spirit by which they do not wish to be overpowered.

That Paul clearly defined and differentiated the second and third Persons of the Trinity cannot possibly be maintained; neither however did he simply identify them. Both their proximity to each other and their distinction are shown in Romans 8: 8–11. Phrases follow upon one another in rapid sequence: 'You are in the Spirit

. . . the Spirit of God dwells in you . . . If anyone has not the Spirit of Christ . . . if Christ is in you . . . the Spirit is life . . . if the Spirit of him who raised up Jesus dwells in you . . . through his Spirit which dwells in you.' Here we note Spirit; Spirit of God (that is, Spirit of him who raised up Jesus); Spirit of Christ; the Spirit is in you; Christ is in you; you are in the Spirit. In all this it is the phrase 'Spirit of Christ' that makes it clear that Paul is not simply identifying Spirit and Christ; but it is equally clear that the two are very close together. There is in Paul's writing no clear definition of the relation of the two to each other, but it is not misleading to say that, broadly speaking, *in Christ* is objective and eschatological; that is, the believer may be said objectively to be in Christ as his property and to have passed with him through death (the messianic affliction) and to have in some degree experienced resurrection. *In the Spirit* (or *the Spirit in you*) is on the other hand the subjective outcome of this new objective existence which issues in such perceptible gifts as prophecy and healing.

In this connection 2 Corinthians 3: 17 ('the Lord is the Spirit) has been endlessly debated. Paul certainly appears to identify the Lord (Christ) and the Spirit; probably however he does not. He has been giving an interpretation of Exodus 34 and the story of the veil worn by Moses. He applies this to unbelieving Israel, on whose heart a veil lies, until it is taken away. In the last clause the verb is in the passive voice, but in 2 Corinthians 3: 16 (the quotation) the Greek verb (*periaireitai*) is probably not passive (the veil *is taken away*) but in the middle voice (whose form here is identical with the passive), *he takes away* the veil. This is supported by the Greek Old Testament. Who takes away the veil? In 3: 16 it is *the Lord* who is mentioned; it will be he who takes away the veil. But who is *the Lord*? Paul answers (in verse 17): In this quotation we must understand that *the Lord* who removes the veil is *the Spirit*. This agrees with what he says about the role of the Spirit in preaching, or perhaps rather in those who listen to the preaching: for example, 1 Thessalonians 1: 5, the Gospel came to you not in word only but also in power and in the Holy Spirit; 1 Corinthians 1: 24, 'My word and my preaching were not in persuasive words of wisdom, but in demonstration of the Spirit and of power'. The Spirit thus leads into the life of Christian obedience (cf. Gal 3: 1–5), and consequently provides a transition to the next point.

Ethics is in a sense Paul's greatest problem. To see the size of the problem is more important than to cover every specific ethical question that Paul deals with. His theology makes inevitable two shocking questions; it is to his credit that so far from concealing them he asks them in explicit terms. They are: 'Is the Law [which in Judaism is not only the guide but the ground of ethics] sin?' (Rom 7: 7), and 'Shall we continue in sin because we are not under law but under grace?' (Rom 6: 15). Paul is in no doubt about the answers to these questions; each receives a resounding 'No'. But how can he justify this answer? The questions are as awkward as they are (to an honest mind) inescapable. A variant on them (which looks at the matter from a different angle) will ask how it is that one who has already been justified, acquitted in God's court (Rom 5: 1), can be judged at the Last Day (e.g. Rom 14: 10; 2 Cor 5: 10), and notwithstanding the favourable verdict he has already received run the risk, as Paul knows that he himself does, of being declared rejected (*adokimos*, 1 Cor 9: 27). This is not only a matter of ethical principle, but also of ethical detail. That Paul should have required absolute submission to God is understandable; on what ground does he require the observance of particular lines of ethical behaviour?

The study of the Law has already brought out some basic points. The Law is to be obeyed, though since it can all be observed in obedience to one precept, 'Thou shalt love thy neighbour as thyself' (Rom 13: 8–10; Gal 5: 14), it has undergone a good deal of slimming down. This slimming down however is hardly liberalization; it is rather, like the Sermon on the Mount, radicalization. Superficially there is a paradox that in Galatians, where Paul objects most strongly to those who claim that the one commandment of circumcision forms an adequate summary of the Law (Gal 5: 3; 6: 13), Paul should claim that the one commandment of love is an adequate summary of the Law; but only superficially. It is not merely that circumcision is a ritual, love an ethical requirement; the one is inward-looking, consistent with self-centred existence; the other is outward-looking, and is inconsistent with self-centred existence — indeed, it is the definition of its opposite. God, as ever, requires this obedience; and obedience is part of faith. It is not easy to define Paul's expression, *the obedience of faith* (*hypakoē pisteōs*), but there is no mistaking the element of obedience in faith. It must be remembered also, conversely, that what the Law, rightly understood, seeks in response, is faith, which is the true form of obedience. We must recall also the ambiguity of the word righteousness (*dikaiosynē*). We have noticed its forensic and relational content; this is fundamental, and it is impossible to understand Paul's thought without it. But we have also seen that it is constantly shading into ethical meanings, whether these are Aristotelian or biblical. In the latter sense it is interesting to note that the Hebrew word for righteousness (*ṣedaqah*) came in late Hebrew to mean *almsgiving* — ethical in a precise and specific sense. To righteousness as a moral goal, object, or master Christians are expected to be obedient (Rom 6: 19). In this shift (which constantly recurs) there is an important clue to Paul's ethics. God has bestowed righteousness on those who believe. This is purely his gift; it is juridical, eschatological righteousness, the right relation with God that one may hope to have at the last judgement. It is essentially a relationship word, but there would be an internal contradiction if this relationship word was not accompanied by ethical righteousness. This is because the God with whom the justified believer now stands in a rectified relation is a moral God. He himself is holy, just, good, loving; it is impossible to remain in a right relation with him while denying the values of holiness, justice, goodness, and love. There is paradox in God's acceptance of the ungodly, but there would be more than paradox, there would be stark contradiction if the ungodly, once accepted, continued in his ungodliness (which provokes God's wrath, Rom 1: 18).

This negative consideration has a positive counterpart. A further element in the eschatological situation is the gift of the Spirit, the power of the age to come, or of the kingdom of God (Rom 14: 17), and the fruit of the Spirit, which means that human existence is no longer centred upon itself, is necessarily ethical (Gal 5: 22). The Spirit, as the earnest of the age to come, enables the believer to live, in this age, the life of the age to come. To attempt to live otherwise would, again, lead to internal contradiction.

It is on these lines that Paul is able to think of the judgement of those who have already been justified. When in Romans 14 and 15 Paul deals with the weak and the strong (see p. 140) each is warned (14: 10–12). The weak find it natural to judge the strong, who eat foods that the weak think to be forbidden; the weak condemn them as law-breakers. The strong despise the weak as mere babes in Christ who suppose that they still need to be wrapped in cotton wool and in this way protected against possible error. But all must appear before God's tribunal. This re-states what has been said in 14: 4: to his own master each man stands or falls, and his master will see to his standing. Neither the strong nor the weak has to justify his position before the other; each must do so before God. How has he applied the faith that has been given him? This is not an insignificant question, but by his God-given faith he will stand. 1 Corinthians 3: 10–17 is a very important passage. The context is that of the competing groups in Corinth. Paul's own role is clear. He was the pioneer missionary in Corinth; that is, he laid the foundation. On this, another (it makes little difference whether this is pure generalization or there is a veiled reference to Apollos or to Peter) builds, putting up course upon course of the house. This is proper; but each one who builds must take heed what he is doing. There is no question of the foundation; there is only one possibility, Jesus Christ. But in the superstructure there may be infinite variety. In verse 12 the imagery is scarcely consistent with building, but the general drift is clear, and in verse 13 the main point is reached. There will be judgement on the superstructures built into the house. The traditional imagery of fire is very suitable; at least it will distinguish between stone and metal on the one hand and wood and straw on the other. If the building stands the builder gets a reward; if it is consumed by the fire, the builder loses—his work, his pay, his reputation?—but he himself is not consumed in the fire; he is saved—just. This might seem to be all that needs to be said about judgement, but it is not quite all. It does not cover 1 Corinthians 9: 27—Paul himself rejected; nor does it cover the very difficult but important verses 2 Corinthians 13: 5-10. There is a clue in the verses that follow those that we have just considered, 1 Corinthians 3: 16 and 17. Paul has used the image of a building. What sort of building is the most appropriate to think of in the application of the image to a church? A temple. Clearly it is possible to build, even on a good foundation, a very shoddy temple; this possibility has been considered. It is also possible to destroy a temple, good or bad, that has been built. Any one who has done this God will himself destroy. The temple here is corporate, the whole body of Christians, or at least the whole company of those who meet in a particular place. Destroy this, and you bring destruction upon yourself. Compare Romans 14: 20: 'Do not for the sake of food destroy the work of God'—again, very probably, the church. There is also however an individual application of this which appears in Galatians 6: 7 and 8. *Flesh* is on the whole an individualizing concept. Sowing to flesh and Spirit is an image based on the metaphor of verse 7; the meaning is the same as that of Romans 8: 6. To return after justification to the flesh (and this can of course be done in a highly 'spiritual' way) is to invite death.

It is worth while here to note a Jewish parallel. A distinction was made between acts of disobedience to particular commandments and 'denying the root'. Exactly what this was is neither clear nor agreed, but the general sense is unmistakable. To reject, deny, or betray the very essence of Judaism was to put oneself outside the whole area of the people's life and to reject the very possibility of forgiveness. Paul seems similarly to distinguish between detailed infringements of Christian principle and destruction of the principle itself.

Once Paul's ethical thought has been set in motion in the manner described he shows himself free of the whole world of ethics, using whatever material he deems suitable for advice and for exhortation. At Philippians 4: 8 and 9 he uses the language of Hellenistic moral philosophy. If Colossians is genuine we see him there (3: 18 - 4: 1) taking up household rules, probably not of Christian origin though usable in the Christian societies—how wives, husbands, children, parents, slaves, and masters ought to behave. If we may not use Colossians we have to be content with the inconvenience of looking for the parallels here and there. The rules stand alongside specifically Christian developments such as 1 Corinthians 13.

In order to give some account of the wealth of ethical material available and to do so in reasonable compass it will be well to use 1 Corinthians, in which Paul deals with a series of ethical problems raised by the local church.

After dealing in the first four chapters with divisions and misunderstandings in the church Paul turns in chapter 5 to the first of the special problems that he has to handle. Not that chapters 1–4 should be overlooked: it appears that the Corinthians are apt to think too highly of themselves—an error with a theological root and ethical consequences which as we proceed will appear in a multiplicity of forms. But at the beginning of chapter 5 Paul starts abruptly with a case of fornication, a form of incest: One of you has taken his father's wife. This may have happened simply through what may be called natural causes; or it may have arisen through a misapplication of Jewish laws relating to proselytes—since we are now new creatures the old relationships do not hold and there may therefore now be free sexual association of those whom formerly even pagan law would have held apart. The relationship between man and mother (probably step-mother) is bad enough, but what offends most is the fact that the congregation instead of lamenting that such a thing should have happened are puffed up because they are so liberated. All things are lawful (6: 12; 10: 23)! This leads Paul to remarks about church discipline and a reference to a previous letter, which had been misunderstood. He was not giving orders that would have meant that Christians in Corinth must come out of the world; he was telling his Christians that they must exercise discipline within the community. Offenders must be excluded, but this is with a view to their ultimate salvation (5: 5). What is wrong in fornication itself will appear a little later (6: 12–20). The essence of the matter (discussed above, pp. 67f.) is that sexual intercourse, unlike eating and drinking, is an act not of one set of physical organs but of the whole person, who (in the case of a Christian) belongs to Christ.

Earlier in chapter 6 there is another point whose background is to be found in Judaism. The synagogue, not the local Gentile law court, is the place where disputes between its members should be settled. Here too Paul goes beyond the surface problem. If you have such internal disputes you ought to settle them in the right way. But you ought not to have disputes. Why not allow yourselves to be defrauded? The Corinthians are too ready to assert themselves and their rights; such self-assertion is the opposite of Christian ethics. In the same paragraph (6: 8–11) it is important to note those who will not inherit the kingdom of God, and the implied account of some of the conversions that have taken place in Corinth: 'Such were some of you; but . . .'

After dealing in 6: 12–20 with the abuse of sexual relations Paul turns in chapter 7 to deal with marriage. It is a long chapter and there are problems in it that cannot be dealt with here,[15] but at least the following points should be observed.

First, we should note the complete reciprocity between men and women, especially in verses 3 and 4. These verses amount to nothing less than a sexual revolution. Secondly, the recognition that marriage involves a physical relation and that it is foolish—and wrong—to try to suppress it; verse 5. Thirdly, the belief that if the age to come is about to come there is much to be said for not changing one's state—married or unmarried, circumcised or uncircumcised, slave or free, though Paul emphasizes from several angles that there is nothing wrong in marrying; verses 17–24. Lastly, we should note Paul's readiness to use a commandment of the Lord when one is available, and to do without when one is not; verses 10, 12, 25. What Paul has to say about the relation between men and women he sets in the context in which they were in fact likely to encounter one another, the family. To work out the relation between the sexes in, say, business or politics would for almost all his readers (but one remembers Lydia—Acts 16: 14) have been a waste of time; but what is true in one context can be transposed and applied in another.

Chapters 8, 9 and 10 deal with one question though from more angles than one and with digressions to related topics. They form a unity, though they have often served as the starting-point for theories that have divided the epistle into two or more parts. The practical question 'Is a Christian free to eat food that has been used in a heathen sacrifice to a heathen god?' is very complicated. It was considered above, but the discussion must be recapitulated here to round off the ethical material in 1 Corinthians. Does eating sacrificial food involve participation in idolatry or not? Evidently there were some in Corinth who believed that it did, and that it was therefore Christian duty to abstain from it. These strict Christians were attacked on two sides: (a) by those who took a theological line (they probably called it *gnōsis*) saying we know that there is only one God, and that meat that has been sacrificed to an idol (which is not god) is therefore no different from any other meat; it may be freely eaten; (b) by those who took a high sacramental line: the water of baptism and the bread and wine of the eucharist protect us from all possible danger and we are free to handle the materials of idolatry. The first group appear in 8: 4–6 ('We know that an idol is nothing and that there is no God but one . . .'), the latter are reflected in 10: 1–13. Paul agrees with the first group; their theological proposition is correct — as far as it goes. He does not agree with the second; the example of Israel shows that there is no automatic safety in spiritual water or spiritual food and drink. Moreover, though idols have no real existence as divine beings there are demons and one must be careful. More important for him is the theological fact that neither group considers; we are not justified by the observance — or by the non-observance — of food laws. Paul's point however is qualified by a further consideration which is more important than the matter of food sacrificed to idols in itself. You have fellow Christians who might be hurt by your exercise of your undoubted freedom to eat whatever you please. If this is so, love must prevail over freedom and you will not eat. This is the most important ethical point that arises out of the discussion of idolatry. Romans 14 and 15 make essentially the same point; the 'strong' and the 'weak' must learn not only to live together in one body but not to hurt one another. The 'weak' must not judge the 'strong' and the 'strong' must not despise the 'weak'. In 1 Corinthians 9 Paul for the moment drops the question of sacrificial food not because he cannot keep to the point but in order to illustrate it from other angles. The point remains: the voluntary abandonment of legitimate freedom in the interests of love.

This may serve to point on through the treatment of the divisions at the church's supper (11: 17–22) and the use of spiritual gifts in the church's assembly to the portrayal of love in chapter 13. It is worth noting the sequence of negatives in this chapter. Speaking with tongues is a good thing; so are theological understanding and faith; so is the charitable use of property; but all of these may be practised as a form of self-advertisement, and without love they are worth nothing. Love is not envious, does not brag, is not puffed up, does not behave in an unseemly way, does not seek its own ends, is not touchy, does not put evil down to anyone's account, does not rejoice in unrighteousness. These negatives have some positive counterparts, and they are to some extent occasioned by the kind of society to which they are addressed, but primarily they are descriptions of love as the negation of that self-centredness that is the natural form of human existence. Prophecies, tongues, knowledge: Paul returns to these, as inadequate representations of the renewal of human life by the Gospel. Love is the renewal of human life in the image of God, for the final truth about God is love (Rom 5: 8; 8: 35, 39).

Paul never had the leisure and probably never had the desire to put his thought together as a connected harmonious well-proportioned whole. The task has not been done for him in this chapter. There will be another way of looking at Paul and his theology in the last chapter; but there is another task to be undertaken first.

Notes

1   C. H. Dodd, 'The mind of Paul: II', *Bulletin of the John Rylands Library* 18 (1934); reprinted in C. H. Dodd, *New Testament Studies* (1953), pp. 83–128.

2   See C. K. Barrett, 'What is New Testament theology?' in D. Y. Hadidian (ed.), *Intergerini Parietis Septum* (1981), pp. 1–22, especially 5–8.

3   See e.g. 1 QS 3: 8, 9: 'By the humbling of his soul under all the commandments of God will his flesh be cleansed, for sprinkling with the water of purification and sanctification by the water of cleansing'.

4   For this analysis see J. A. Robinson, *The Epistle to the Ephesians* (1903), pp. 221–8; also H. Conzelmann and W. Zimmerli in *Theologisches Wörterbuch zum Neuen Testament* 7 (1973), pp. 363–97.

5   R. Bultmann, *Theologie des Neuen Testaments* (9th edn, 1984), p. 289 (my translation); cf. ET: *Theology of the New Testament* (1952), p. 289.

6 Hebrew poetry is characteristically written in lines with a regular pattern not of syllables but of stresses; very often the lines are arranged in pairs in parallelism, sometimes synonymous, sometimes antithetical, sometimes in progressing steps.

7 As I think Jesus had before him; but that is another matter. See C. K. Barrett, *Jesus and the Gospel Tradition* (1967), pp. 52, 53, 67.

8 See R. P. Martin, *Carmen Christi* (1967).

9 See C. K. Barrett, 'The significance of the Adam–Christ typology for the Resurrection of the dead' in L. De Lorenzi (ed.), *Résurrection du Christ et des Chrétiens* (1985), pp. 99–122.

10 See e.g. Philo, *Legum Allegoriae* 1: 31: 'There are two types of men; the one a heavenly man (*ouranios*), the other an earthly (*gēinos*). The heavenly man, being made in the image of God, is altogether without part or lot in corruptible and terrestrial substance, but the earthly one was compacted out of the matter scattered here and there, which Moses calls "clay" (*choun*). For this reason he says that the heavenly man was not moulded, but was stamped with the image of God; while the earthly is a moulded work of the Artificer, but not His offspring' (trans. F. H. Colson and G. H. Whitaker).

11 See *Jesus and the Gospel Tradition*, pp. 41–5, 77–83.

12 T. W. Manson, *Journal of Theological Studies* 46 (1945), pp. 1–10.

13 See R. Bultmann, *Theologie des Neuen Testaments*, p. 312; ET, p. 311.

14 On the church in Paul's teaching, see further C. K. Barrett, *Church, Ministry, and Sacraments in the New Testament* (1985), pp. 12, 13, 31–40, 63–70.

15 Many details are discussed in C. K. Barrett, *1 Corinthians* (2nd edn, 1986), pp. 153–87.

4

Pauline theology: the sequel

The above account of Paul's theology has been written on the basis of six letters: Romans, the two to the Corinthians, Galatians, Philippians, and 1 Thessalonians; Philemon has scarcely been mentioned because its theological content is slight in comparison with that of the others. There are six more that bear his name, ostensibly equally his work. These have not been used because their authorship is in doubt; see above, pp. 3–5. There is no absolute certainty in regard to questions of authorship. With reference to each of the six — Ephesians, Colossians, 2 Thessalonians, 1 and 2 Timothy, Titus — it is possible to ask the question: Which is the likelier hypothesis, that Paul in this letter for some reason wrote so much unlike himself, or that someone other than Paul wrote so much like him? We know that in some of the certainly genuine letters Paul made use of a secretary (see especially Rom 16: 22). Did he sometimes give a trusted secretary greater freedom than that of a shorthand writer, indicate the general line he wished to take, and leave it to the secretary to find the words? This might account for differences in vocabulary and style which otherwise would lead us to suspect different authorship. Again, one may ask how far Paul's beliefs, and his ways of expressing them, may have changed with advancing age. This is a proper question, but no one knows the answer. Some people change very much, others very little. The most that can be said with confidence — and it is a sort of anti-confidence — is that there are some epistles which it is unsafe to use in an account of Paul's thought. He may have written them, but there is a case against them. In regard to three, those to Timothy and Titus, it is a very strong case.

Whatever conclusion we reach in regard to authorship these epistles have a place in this book. It may be that Paul wrote them, and even if the balance of probability is against them the inquirer into Paul's thought has a right to know what they say. In any case, they remain, for a Christian, a part of Holy Scripture and carry its authority, whoever wrote them. But they have a place in a book on Paul. Granted that they are pseudonymous, they bear Paul's name. They are therefore witnesses to the importance of that name and of the man who bore it. No one wrote an epistle in the name of Paul because he thought that to be the best way to get his work thrown into the wastepaper basket. He believed that a letter bearing the name of Paul would be thought important and read. Pseudonymous letters bear witness to a certain regard for the supposed writer. Again, just so far as the thought of the pseudonymous letters differs from the thought of the authentic Paul it shows the way in which that thought developed, for those would use the name of Paul who conceived themselves to be standing in the Pauline tradition. 'If only our great teacher were living today, in our changed circumstances, this, I am sure, is what he would say.' So the writers would think, and sometimes at least they got it right and showed how Pauline thought could develop into a post-Pauline period. The same process will show how, after Paul's death, his work was understood—and sometimes misunderstood.

The understanding and misunderstanding of Paul will lead into a further part of this chapter in which, leaving behind any date at which Paul could himself conceivably have been writing letters, we ask what the church of the following generations made of him. This in turn will lead to the final chapter, on Paul and theology today.

COLOSSIANS

The Epistle to the Colossians has all the appearance of a Pauline letter; indeed, if any of the letters considered in this chapter is genuine it is this one; and a strong case can be made out for it.[1] It begins with the customary greeting from Paul, defined as an apostle and accompanied by one of his well-known assistants, Timothy; it continues with a thanksgiving for the conversion and Christian growth of those to whom the letter is addressed, and the thanksgiving grows into a doctrinal development, of which more will be said later. The doctrinal development is in part positive, in part negative, warning the readers against specious error which apparently flourished in their environment. The doctrinal section of the epistle leads into ethical instruction and exhortation, and the epistle ends with news and greetings in which the author — ostensibly of course Paul — is joined by a number of colleagues, many of whose names appear also in the certainly genuine private letter to Philemon, which incidentally could provide an occasion for writing to the Colossians. If Paul is sending a letter to Philemon he might well take the opportunity of writing to Philemon's church. Over against this general Pauline appearance is to be set, first, the style of the letter. It is wordy, with a characteristic repetition of synonyms, which does nothing to advance the thought, and a clumsy linking together of words (e.g., 'all the wealth of the conviction of the understanding', 2: 2).[2] Secondly, though it would be quite wrong to find in the epistle any trace of the gnosticism of the second century, the errors envisaged seem to belong to a more developed stage than those we meet in the certainly genuine letters, and in combating the philosophy and vain deceit of false teachers (2: 8) the writer develops a Christian application of the language of circumcision (2: 11, 12) such as is barely hinted at in Philippians 3: 3. Judaism and primitive gnostic ideas have come together. Ethical instruction is given in the form of household codes — rules for wives and husbands, children and parents, slaves and masters. None of these considerations is decisive in itself; taken together they are not decisive, for it would be possible to maintain that Paul lived long enough, or events at Colossae moved fast enough, for the developments we see in the epistle to have taken place and to have been considered by Paul. And if this was not so, the pseudonymous author has estimated with some success what Paul would have said if he had lived two decades longer than he did.

This is particularly true of the author's handling of contemporary Christology, and a sketch of this may be the best way of illustrating the contribution made by the epistle to developing Paulinism. It has often been held that Colossians 1: 15–20 is a pre-Pauline hymn which the author has incorporated in his work, no doubt because he could be confident that his readers would recognize and accept it. This is a hypothesis worth accepting at least provisionally and developing. A first glance at the hymn (if such it was) will do something to confirm the notion that Judaism and gnosis were developing in connection with each other. The list of heavenly powers in verse 6 (not only the Galatian *elements* — see pp. 57–9 — but all things in heaven and on earth, things seen and things unseen, whether thrones or dominions, whether principalities or powers) has a gnostic ring; but the hymn itself has been thought to be built on an elaborate exegesis of the opening words of Genesis 1: 1 (*in the beginning*), and though this theory is too subtle to be wholly true there are Old Testament touches in the hymn and we may suspect a Jewish gnosticizing exegesis of the Old Testament, cast in a speculative mood.

But the setting in which the author has placed the hymn is not speculative but strictly practical. He is recalling the Colossians to the fact of redemption, which he explains in terms of the forgiveness of sins (verse 14). Some have seen here a particular reference to baptism, verse 13 with 'the Son of his love' pointing to the 'My Son the Beloved' of the baptism narratives (Mark 1: 11 and parallels). But it is not necessary to see a reference to baptism every time the New Testament mentions the forgiveness of sins. The same interest returns as soon as the quotation is ended. In verse 20 reconciliation is cosmic — 'things on earth and things in heaven', but in verse 21 this is at once applied in a strictly personal fashion: 'you who were alienated and enemies . . . he has reconciled in the body of his flesh through death'. Indeed this theme is brought into the hymn itself, unless with some editors we find the end of the hymn in verse 18a.

It is sometimes said that Colossian Christology needed to be corrected because in it Christ had been displaced from his proper position of pre-eminence in cosmology, other mediatorial figures being introduced with the result of lowering his status. This does not seem to be the point. It seems rather that the Colossians, if we are to think of them as the authors (or appropriators) of the hymn, had done their best to give Christ a prominent place in the realm of cosmic speculation. What they had not done, and the editor now proceeds to do, is to recognize his earthly activity.

The hymn (or perhaps we should call it a creed; perhaps there is little difference between the two) begins with the account of Christ as the image of the invisible God. *Image* is a word that belongs to the Wisdom literature. Paul himself had used it at 2 Corinthians 4: 4. It has nothing to do with the creation of man in God's image; it refers to the revelation of the invisible God. *Wisdom* provides a means of perceiving what otherwise one could not see and would not know. A well-known passage is Wisdom 7: 26:

146

She [Wisdom] is the effulgence of eternal light
And an untarnished mirror of the working of God
And the image of his goodness.

This was a means by which Judaism could handle the problem of revelation. Greek speculation would do the same, using more frequently the word *logos, reason* or *word*. Wisdom or Word, being the image of God, constituted an epistemological bridge between man and the invisible God. There was no need here for Christians to make a fundamental change, but there was need for development. The nearer Word or Wisdom came to the invisible God, becoming his Son and of like being, the more it became a problem how they could themselves be perceived. This question is however for the present deferred.

The Mediator (Christ is of course intended by the writer of Colossians, but the non-committal word leaves open the question what may originally have been intended — Word or Wisdom or some other cosmic figure) who is the image of God is the first-born of all creation. This is the familiar translation, but there is a point here that can be most easily handled in terms of the hypothesis of quotation. The word (*prōtotokos*) translated *first-born* can also mean *first begetter* (or, used of a female, *bearing for the first time*). The Greek accent will show which meaning is intended. In the epistle as it stands before us there can be no doubt that *first-born* is correct; this is the meaning of the word in verse 18 (Jesus was the first to be raised from the dead, the first-born from the dead) and it must be the meaning here. Paul in certainly genuine Romans 8: 29 uses the word in this way. The usual translation leaves a problem: In what sense is Christ the first-born of all creation? Is he part of it, the oldest part, a creature like the rest? Or is he older and different? The alternative translation settles the matter by describing him as the first begetter of all creation, and this is a proposition that the next verses proceed to repeat and underline. In him, or by him, all things were created (verse 16a); the rest of the verse begins to list *all things*, and concludes with a repetition of the basic proposition. Verse 17 gives more detail about the relation between the Mediator and the world; not only is he first among all beings, he is the bond of unity by which all things have their coherence.

With verse 18a we come to the crucial point. A new image is introduced. The Mediator is the head of the body. If the line stopped at this point we should have what would look like a gnostic hymn celebrating Word or Wisdom as the first begetter of creation. This was essentially a unity and it had its unity in him. It was compared (and there is precedent for this) to a body. The human body was a microcosm of the universe, and each member found its directing and unifying principle in the head. This cosmic illustration is given a new meaning by the addition — grammatically an awkward addition — of *the church*, which in the text as it stands must be taken as in explanatory apposition to *the body*. Head of the body; what do I mean by body? I mean the church. This addition, reinterpreting in the first instance the word 'body', inevitably affects the way in which the propositions that follow in verses 18b and 19 are understood. This is important, but there is no space to discuss the matter here. What matters most is the development in Christology that can be traced. The intention of those who originally applied the hymn, in its original form, to Christ was to honour him. He must be given the highest place in the universe, and this was clearly that of the cosmic Mediator, creator of the universe and, as its head, both its direction and its unity. This was well meant; but it would not suffice for a writer standing in the Pauline tradition, whose concern was not cosmology, astrology, but soteriology (which we have already seen to be what is emphasized in the context). He is dealing not with an abstract and ideal cosmic unity (part of a religious philosophical theory), but with a recovered unity, the unity not of the first creation which has been hopelessly lost in the alienation caused by sin (see verse 21), but that of the new creation which in an eschatological process is now coming into being. This new unity also is indeed at present partial and obscured, but it will in due course be perfected. It is consistent with this that the word *first-born* now reappears (verse 18). Christ is the first-born from the dead, that is, the first in whom the resurrection expected at the end of time takes place; he is the origin and lord of the new creation.

It will be worth while to set this revised hymn alongside the revised hymn of Philippians 2. In Philippians Paul found material which, as it were, looked after the latter end of Christ's work. It noted his humble, obedient, sacrificial life and the glorious recompence expressed in resurrection and exaltation and consisting in the restoration of Christ, and of mankind in him, to primaeval sovereignty. Its weakness lay in the fact that Christ suddenly appears on the human scene without announcement, without anchorage in divine relationships. It looks as if we are to finish with one more divine person than we started with. Where does the new *Lord* come from? The scheme lacks cosmological background. It may not be a serious over-simplification to say that this kind of scheme was probably the firstfruits of the encounter between Jewish Christianity and Hellenism. Its Jewishness is attested by the fact that it is based on the story of Adam; the influence of Hellenism is seen in the representation of the exalted One not as the heavenly man (cf. 1 Cor 15: 47, 49) but as Lord (*kyrios*).

Over against this, the raw material in Colossians seems to have been essentially cosmological. Christ was made to fill the role of the *logos*, the head of the cosmic body, by which the unity of the cosmos and its link with the invisible God was secured. Thus the Colossian Christology had what the Philippian lacked; but in its turn it was deficient in emphasis upon the historic acts of the man Jesus. It was static and ontological rather than eschatological. This defective Christology may be defined as the result of the first Christianizing of gnosis. The essential framework of mythical cosmology was retained and Christ was simply fitted into an exalted place within it. It is however worth while and proper to emphasize that (on the hypothesis of quotation) the Philippian and Colossian hymnographers were doing their best to honour Christ, and that they did not make a bad job of it. They went as far as untrained theologians could be expected to go and since their time there have been many worse hymns. But theologians who had grasped the full content and implications of the Gospel could not be satisfied with their work.

What did the theologians produce? Essentially the author of Colossians (who may have been Paul — we cannot deny it with complete assurance) came to the same result as Paul, though because he started, as it were, from the other end, the finished product looks different. The humble life of the historical Jesus had been preceded by heavenly status; the cosmic functions of the heavenly Word or Wisdom were exercised by one who shed his own human blood on the cross. In each case, theological reflection leads to something like the myth (but here it is a fully historical myth) of a descending and ascending Redeemer. Was this the origin of the so-called Redeemer myth? It is tempting to say that it was. The problem in the usual application of this myth to the New Testament is chronological; non-biblical evidence for it is later than the New Testament. Did Paul, then, and his disciples, begin it? The difficulty with this suggestion is that it must be regarded as doubtful whether the non-Christian forms of the myth, when eventually they do arise, can be due to Christian originals. We may say however that we can trace something of the way in which Pauline influence penetrated into the developing world of gnosticism. It did not always maintain its characteristics as faithfully as it did in Colossians.

2 THESSALONIANS

The First Epistle to the Thessalonians is certainly a genuine work of Paul's. The Second, like Colossians, bears all the superficial characteristics of the Pauline letters, and goes out of its way to affirm its own genuineness: 'The greeting is written in my own hand, Paul's; this is the sign in every letter; this is how I write' (3: 17). Protesting too much? It takes up some of the thought and some of the language of the first letter, with a hint of derivativeness, perhaps. It deals with a situation that could well have arisen as a result of the first letter, which, looking into the future, contrasted those who had already fallen asleep in death with 'us', who expect to be left alive till the coming of the Lord Jesus from heaven to gather his saints together. Was it not natural on the strength of this to infer that the day of the Lord was already here? And if the day of the Lord was already here what need was there for Christian discipline, what need even to work for a living?

The second letter handles this situation firmly; with (it may seem) a greater rigidity than Paul himself would have used. It deals with it by elaborating an eschatological programme which shows that there are many things still to happen before the end comes. In the programme there is a woodenness that is (some would think) not Paul's; but there are also insights which, if not his, constitute a valid continuation of his work.

The introduction to 2 Thessalonians 2 clearly takes up themes that have appeared in 1 Thessalonians: the coming of our Lord Jesus Christ recalls 1 Thessalonians 4: 15, with identical language (except that in 1 Thessalonians we have 'the Lord' without addition); the semi-technical term *parousia* occurs in each passage; and *our gathering together to him* recalls the resurrection of the dead, the rapture of the survivors, and the promise that we shall be for ever with the Lord (1 Thess 4: 16, 17). In the second letter these are not called in question, but the writer hopes that his readers will not be disturbed by any exposition of them that might come 'through Spirit'—that is, by some inspired prophetic utterance; by word—that is, by some piece of supposed Christian teaching or preaching; or by a letter 'purporting to come from us'—a pseudonymous letter. These might claim that the day of the Lord (1 Thessalonians

5: 2—the day when these eschatological events would happen) was already here. It is not; and you must not allow yourselves to be deceived. The apocalyptic process is a long one, and as it is described here it contains a number of mysterious features. The end will not come until the 'falling away' (*apostasia*) has happened; this will involve the appearance of an antichrist figure, of whom more will be said below. This culmination of evil is at present being held off by a restraining force, expressed in Greek, in 2: 6, by a participle in the neuter gender (*to katechon*), the restraining *thing*. The *thing*, however, in 2: 7 becomes a *person*, the same participle in the masculine gender (*ho katechōn*). A mystery of evil is already in existence and secretly at work, but as long as the restraint exists it cannot be manifested. When the restraint is removed, as it will be, then the power of evil will be unleashed, appearing in personal form. This will lead to the time of the coming and presence (*parousia*) of Jesus, who will destroy the evil one with the breath of his mouth (2: 8). So there is no need to look for the coming of the Lord as long as *the restraint* is in position. And (in another sense) there is no need in this book to consider at length the question what, or who, is meant by 'the restraint'. Probably the best suggestion is that the author has in mind the power of Rome, the Empire being represented by the neuter, the Emperor himself by the masculine participle. This would be in agreement with, perhaps a development of, an important paragraph in Romans—13: 1-7, where Paul urges his readers to show respect for and obedience to the civil power, which he thinks of as part of God's providential ordering of the world. He does not assert the moral infallibility of the government, but sees it as a bulwark against human and demonic anarchy, rightly entrusted with the power of the sword. The author of 2 Thessalonians (one may say with some probability but without complete confidence) develops one aspect of this. As long as Rome persists, the powers of evil will be held at bay and the final breakdown of society will not take place.

Paul might have left the matter there: no room for complacency, no room for idleness, no excuse for rocking the imperial boat or for unnecessary provocation of civil authorities, above all no occasion for fear, or excitement, or for anything but sober-minded Christian faithfulness and vigilance. The writer of 2 Thessalonians pursues his way through his apocalypse, but, as Paul would have done, he too describes not only the events of the end but the events of the present. It is the course of the Christian mission that is in mind in 2: 11-14. There are those who reject the Gospel. They have not

151

shown the love of the truth (the Christian message) that would have led to their salvation (2: 10), and this happens not fortuitously but because God sends them a power of delusion which leads them to believe what is false (2: 11). This in turn leads to judgement, the judgement of those who do not believe the truth but delight in unrighteousness (2: 12). That this could be one consequence of the mission was well known to Paul; see 1 Corinthians 1: 18 and especially 2 Corinthians 2: 15 and 16. It did not of course apply to the members of the church, who are described in 2: 13 and 14. The Lord loved them, God chose them, and called them through the Gospel for salvation, in sanctification from the Spirit, faith in the truth, and glory.

The important point (which will be reminiscent of Paul but is also a step beyond him) is the link between this straightforward apocalyptic story and the demythologized version of it which is worked out in terms of the dialectic of a delusion that leads to destruction and faith that leads to salvation. The link lies in the story of man. The evil power is a *man*, not indeed a historical person, but a spiritual sublimation of man. He is *the man of iniquity* (*tēs anomias*), *the son of destruction* (2: 3). In 2: 8 he has become *the Wicked One*, but this term (*ho anomos*) must be equivalent to *the man of iniquity*. And, like the Lord, he has a *coming* (*parousia*, 2: 9). Over against him is the Lord, who will destroy him by the breath of his mouth and bring him to nought by the appearance of his coming (*parousia*, 2: 8). Opposed as they are to each other they have a certain community of being; the Lord who will destroy the Wicked One is, in the language of 1 Corinthians 15, the man from heaven, the heavenly man; in the language of the gospels, the Son of man. The 'man gone wrong' of 2 Thessalonians shares the literary, scriptural background that we have seen in parts of the genuine Pauline corpus, the story of the human pair in Genesis 3 who seek wisdom to make themselves equal to God and instead of achieving apotheosis are dehumanized, losing the status they were intended to enjoy. In addition the apocalypse in 2 Thessalonians is built upon the oracle on the Prince of Tyre in Ezekiel 28. God addresses the Prince, consumed as he is in his pride:

2   Because thine heart is lifted up, and thou hast said, I am God, I sit in the seat of God, . . . yet thou art man, and not God, though thou didst set thine heart as the heart of God.

3   Behold, thou art wiser than Daniel; . . .

4 By thy wisdom and by thine understanding thou hast gotten thee riches, . . .

6 Therefore thus saith the Lord God: Because thou hast set thine heart as the heart of God;

7 Therefore behold, I will bring strangers upon thee, the terrible of the nations: . . .

9 Wilt thou yet say before him that slayeth thee, I am God? but thou art man, and not God.

I have left out the topical allusions which show that the ruler of Tyre is indeed in mind; his destruction, notwithstanding the safety of his off-shore stronghold, virtually surrounded by water, came eventually, 200 years after Ezekiel's prophecy, at the hands of Alexander the Great in 332 BC. In addition to these details a further setting is provided, that of the story of the fall of man in Genesis.

12 Son of man, take up a lamentation for the king of Tyre, and say unto him, Thus saith the Lord God, Thou wast the signet of perfection, full of wisdom, and perfect in beauty.

13 Thou wast in Eden the garden of God . . .

14 . . . I set thee, so that thou wast upon the holy mountain of God; . . .

15 Thou wast perfect in thy ways from the day that thou wast created, till unrighteousness was found in thee.

17 Thine heart was lifted up because of thy beauty . . .

Ezekiel sets out the condemnation of a historical figure (or representative figure—the Prince of Tyre at present in office) in terms of the story of the fall of man from his original state and destiny. The author of 2 Thessalonians takes up the twofold picture to use it for a twofold, perhaps a threefold purpose. The man of iniquity, the son of destruction, is described (2: 4) as one who withstands and exalts himself over every one called God, every object of worship, so that he sits in the temple of God, giving himself out to be God. There may be an allusion here to the antics of a historical figure, possibly a Roman emperor; we need not pursue such allusions here.[3] The allusions certainly develop on the two lines of the eschatological figure who will be destroyed at the End by the heavenly Man and the negative reaction to the Christian mission.

153

Up to a point all this is in Pauline vein; it presents the objective and subjective, the mythological and the existential aspects of the Gospel which are essential to Paul's understanding of it. But it does not integrate them into each other as closely as he does, and it uses the apocalyptic programme in a more rigid way.

EPHESIANS

It is an attractive hypothesis that the Epistle to the Ephesians was written in order to introduce the collection of Pauline letters. We have very little knowledge of the letters except as a collection. They do not have independent textual histories, and church writers, except the very earliest, if they show knowledge of one, will usually show knowledge of all, or almost all. In the earliest lists of canonical books they appear as a group. There can be no doubt that some time in the second century someone, we do not know who, collected the letters, of which the autograph copies must have been in widely spread locations—Rome, Corinth, Galatia, and so on. They were then copied and given to the world, or at least to the churches, at a time when Paul was not a household name; the letters, addressed to various churches and dealing to a great extent with local needs and problems, needed presentation as having universal relevance and apostolic authority. In some respects Ephesians was well suited to fulfil this purpose. If this was its intention a problem in the first verse might be solved. There is strong evidence for the omission of *in Ephesus* in Ephesians 1: 1. Was the epistle written in this unusual form as a counterpoise to those that were very plainly intended for Rome, for Corinth, and so on? It is in harmony with this observation that the letter nowhere addresses specific local needs as the others do. It lauds its supposed author in a way that has always held a measure of embarrassment, and when this emphasis is reversed the reversal has an exaggerated tone; the writer professes to be less than the least of all the saints (3: 8). Again, 3: 4 ('You can, when you read, perceive my understanding in the mystery of Christ') makes sense where it stands in Ephesians taken on its own, but would make eminently good sense if it were understood to refer to the whole Pauline corpus. 'You may not know anything of this figure of a by-gone age, but if you will work through the subjoined letters you will find out how great a man he was, and how much he still has to say to us.' Again, Ephesians shows knowledge of and parallels to all the genuine Pauline letters (also and especially to

Colossians). Such knowledge would be natural in the editor of the corpus.

An attractive hypothesis, then; but probably to be rejected. It seems probable that Ephesians was in existence before the collection of the Pauline letters appeared. It never stands, whether in a New Testament manuscript or in a list, at the head of the letters; that is to say, there is no evidence that it ever served as an introduction. The references to Paul, both in his outstanding wisdom and in his humility, are part of the apparatus of pseudonymity. Various explanations of 1: 1 have been offered: the words *in Ephesus* are contained in good, old manuscripts, and may be original, or the epistle may have been intended for general use without being intended as an introduction. We can only read the epistle and ask what it intends to teach.

We may begin with a contrast, though it will be important not to exaggerate its significance. In Galatians (genuine, if any epistle is), Paul wrote '. . . the Son of God, who loved me and gave himself up for me' (2: 20). In Ephesians we read: 'Christ loved the church and gave himself up for it' (5: 25). It would be a serious error to overlook the truth that Paul regarded the church as a fact and a theme of fundamental importance, a function of his Christology. It would be equally incorrect to suggest that the author of Ephesians did not believe that Christ loved the individual Christians. Moreover, the two sayings cannot be compared unless we compare also their contexts, which evoked them and in part determine their meaning. Yet when these qualifications are made the two propositions are characteristic of the two authors and do contribute to our understanding of the relation between them.

To say that the church was more important to the author of Ephesians than to Paul would put the matter crudely, indeed mistakenly. To say that in Ephesians the church replaces the *solus Christus* of the genuine letters would be to exaggerate. A few passages will indicate what the contrast is. Thus at the end of Ephesians 1: He [God] set all things under his [Christ's] feet and gave him as head over all things to the church, the fullness of him who fills all in all (1: 22, 23). So the church is the fullness of Christ, his necessary complement, without which he would not himself be complete. Indeed some would translate: The fullness of him who all in all is being fulfilled. The church is the body of Christ, not as a subordinate organism which is under his control, the material instrument by which his will is done; it is the very substance of Christ; as it grows he himself moves to fulfilment. Again, the first section of the letter ends with a doxology (3: 20, 21):

> To him [God] who is able to do exceeding abundantly [it is hard to improve on the language of the Authorized Version] beyond all that we ask or think, according to the power that is at work within us, to him be the glory in the church and in Christ Jesus, to all generations, for ever and ever.

The same preposition (*in*) is used with both church and Christ Jesus. The obedient life of Christ gives glory to God; the obedient life of the church gives glory to God. This does not mean that Christ and church are regarded as equals; and Paul himself can urge Christians to glorify God with their bodies (1 Cor 6: 20). It is the way in which Christ and church are set down in parallel that catches the eye.

It is not hard to see what lies behind the emphasis in Ephesians. The author is profoundly impressed by the fact that Jews and Gentiles have now found in the Christian movement a unity hitherto unknown. The whole of the paragraph 2: 11–22 could be quoted here. In verse 14 the author alludes to the barrier fence in the Temple, which separated the Court of the Gentiles from the more sacred parts of the Temple to which only Jews might be admitted. Inscribed tablets from this wall, threatening death for transgression by a Gentile, are known.[4] This wall has been broken down. The result is that we both have access to the Father through Christ in one Spirit (2: 18). It follows that you (Gentiles) are no longer foreigners and aliens but fellow citizens with the holy people and members of God's household; resting upon the foundation of the apostles and prophets, with Christ Jesus as the chief cornerstone, you are built up together as God's dwelling in the Spirit (2: 19–22). It is not surprising that this happy state of things should so deeply impress the author of Ephesians and lead him to emphasize the importance of the church in which this miraculous reconciliation had taken place. Much of what he says about it is in complete harmony with Paul. It is only through Christ and in the Spirit that the unity is effected; there is no hint of any other kind of rapprochement between the two sides, nor is there any suggestion that the church has somehow organized itself so as to become attractive to both branches of the human race. The emphasis upon grace and faith has and no doubt was intended to have a Pauline ring. 'By grace have you been saved through faith, and that not of yourselves, it is God's gift' (2: 8) has often been cited as conclusive proof that no one but Paul could have written Ephesians; yet it has also been taken as the reverse of this.[5] It would have been different if the writer had used not *saved* but *justified*; that is indeed Pauline doctrine. But Paul nearly (not quite) always uses the word *saved* with reference to the future. 'Having now been justified by his blood we shall be saved through him from (God's) wrath' (Rom 5: 9). This observation is not a sufficient proof of anything, but it may serve as a pointer. Paul in the certainly genuine letters never loses the eschatological perspective: 'We are saved in hope' (Rom 8: 24); and he makes it clear in the following verses that hope is not to be glossed by any visible phenomenon. In Ephesians the eschatology almost drops out — almost, not quite. In 1: 21 there is a reference to the age to come; in the next verse Psalm 8: 7 (He has subjected all things under his feet) is quoted, as it is in 1 Corinthians 15: 27. But in 1 Corinthians 15 the quotation refers to the future: Christ must reign until all his enemies are put under his feet. The consummation has not yet happened. The author of Ephesians had witnessed a great victory of the Gospel. How widespread this was and how long it lasted are questions that could lead to speedy disillusionment, but it is understandable that he should stress what Christ had already done and — almost — forget what had still to be done, in this world and beyond it. He knew that the church must grow and develop and its members learn to express the meaning of their faith in the various stations in which they were called to live, as wives, husbands, children, parents, slaves, masters. He is more interested than Paul in the agencies by which the church grows and develops. God gave to the church apostles, prophets, evangelists, pastors, teachers; the vocabulary is mostly Pauline, and so is the task of fitting every member of the holy people for the work of ministry (4: 11, 12), but the object of these several ministries is to produce a body fitly framed and joined together, which generates its own growth in love as it lives in the world (4: 16).

THE PASTORAL EPISTLES

The Pastoral Epistles (1 and 2 Timothy; Titus) are a different proposition, designed to meet a different need and breathing a different atmosphere. Not that they are totally un-Pauline. They retain more of Paul's eschatological outlook than Ephesians does. Hymenaeus and Philetus, who teach that the resurrection has already happened (2 Tim 2: 17, 18) get short shrift. Throughout the epistles there is a persistent future outlook. Timothy is urged to keep the commandment irreproachable and without fault until the appearing of our Lord Jesus Christ (1 Tim 6: 14); Paul looks forward to receiving the crown of righteousness which the Lord, the righteous Judge, will 'in that day' give not only to him but to all who loved his appearing (2 Tim 4: 8); and Titus is reminded of the renewing power of the Holy Spirit, 'which he poured out upon us richly through Jesus Christ our Saviour, in order that, having been justified by his grace, we might become heirs in hope of eternal life' (Titus 3: 6, 7). This is a passage of great importance for several reasons. Its emphasis on hope underlines the future aspect of Christian life, but at the same time it brings out with equal force the present aspect. The Holy Spirit has been given with the result of renewal, and believers are justified, and that by grace. The emphasis on the present recurs elsewhere in the epistles. Eternal life belongs to the future but may be grasped now (1 Tim 6: 12); the Holy Spirit dwells within us, and proves to be a Spirit of power, love, and self-discipline (2 Tim 1: 14, 7). The paradox of Christian existence—a new existence within this old world (Titus 2: 12)—is here grasped: in other words the qualitative (and not merely chronological) sense of the Christian's 'between-ness' is grasped.[6] This is expressed in Titus 3: 7 with a firm grasp of Pauline terminology. Eternal life is, in the fully realized sense, a matter of hope (cf. Rom 8: 24, 25), but justification has already happened, and the positive reference in 3: 7 to justification is matched in 3: 5 by the denial that works done in righteousness contribute to the manifestation of God's mercy.

This observation points to the only aspect of the Pastorals that is relevant in this book. There is good reason[7] to think that they were not written by Paul, but they were written under his name, not as an exercise in historical fiction, or in order to boost the real author's sales. They constitute part of the history of Paulinism, not merely as witnesses to history but as constituents of history. Their author was—it might be correct to say, their authors were—profoundly concerned for the fate of the Pauline Gospel in their generation.

It was not a generation that was disposed to look on Paul with favour; those who did favour him often failed to understand him. To Clement of Rome, at the end of the first century, Peter and Paul were the great apostles, and Clement evidently knew some at least of Paul's letters. Clement meant well, and is worthy of respect, but he could write (10: 7) of Abraham that it was on account of his faith and hospitality that a son was given him in his old age, which does not put the matter in quite the Pauline manner (Romans 4). Ignatius and Polycarp were admirers of Paul, but apart from them he won little respect. Justin in the middle of the century is at best reserved; and others were plainly inimical. Jewish Christianity was strongly anti-Pauline. In the Pseudo-Clementine literature Paul appears for the most part under the name of Simon Magus (Acts 8). He is represented not as the colleague but as the evil counterpart of Peter. They form one of a sequence of pairs into which good and evil fall: Peter followed Simon (that is, Paul)

> as light the darkness, as knowledge ignorance, as the cure the disease; thus it is necessary, as the true prophet has told us, that there should come first a false Gospel, preached by an impostor, and then the true Gospel. (*Clementine Homilies* 2: 17)

It did Paul no good that he was adopted by the Gnostics and made the foundation of their systems; it made him at least a suspicious character whom it was easy to misinterpret. The epistles 'contain obscure passages, which the ignorant and unstable misinterpret to their own ruin, as they do the other scriptures' (2 Peter 3: 16). These 'ignorant and unstable' people were probably those who regarded themselves as advanced and spiritual Christians who on a Pauline basis evolved a gnostic version of Christianity.

In the middle of the second century Paul was in need of a defender. The most notable writer who took his part was Marcion, who was perhaps the first man to have a Christian Bible. The Old Testament he abandoned; it was the work of an inferior God, at the best just but not loving, a creator who created the world so badly that it had to be set right by the true, supreme, good, and loving God, who is made known in the Gospel and not at all in the law and the prophets. This was set out in a book (unfortunately lost, though fragments can be rescued) called *Antitheses*, which was followed by a New Testament, consisting of one gospel, Luke, and the Pauline letters. Both gospel and epistles were radically cut; 'Marcion criticizes with a pen-knife', said Tertullian. Old Testament references were removed, Christ was hardly a human being, and creation was viewed in a dualistic way. But the sheer goodness of a redeeming God, the centrality of Christ, and the meaning of grace and faith were grasped. A famous epigram of Harnack's is true in both its elements: In the second century, only one man understood Paul; that was Marcion, and he misunderstood him. Marcion glimpsed the radical Gospel that Paul preached as few did in the second century; tragically he came to Paul from a gnostic, dualistic angle, and got him wrong. He was a very dangerous friend to have.

It was well (humanly speaking) for Paul that he had the Pastoral Epistles, for, though they fail to represent the fire and passion of his own apostolic ministry, they defend him in ways that he could himself have accepted. It is very probable that already in his lifetime he had been attacked on the ground of his earlier activity as a persecutor of the church. He is prepared to accept the charge: 'I am the least of the apostles, not worthy to be called an apostle because I persecuted the church of God' (1 Cor 15: 9). The point is taken up:

> . . . I received mercy, because I did it ignorantly in unbelief . . .
> I received mercy that in me first Christ Jesus might demonstrate
> all his longsuffering as an example for those who were to believe
> with the goal of eternal life. (1 Tim 1: 12–16)

It is insisted that he was appointed a herald and a teacher (1 Tim 2: 7; 2 Tim 1: 11), and it is clear that the author regarded Paul not merely as an apostle but as the outstanding apostle. He was not only an apostle for his own day, but one who might properly counsel and train the new generation of Christian ministers, whom Timothy and Titus (the names taken out of the Pauline tradition) represent. They must guard the deposit of faith that has been entrusted to them. (1 Tim 6: 20, 21, with a special warning against *gnōsis*; 2 Tim 1: 14); they must preach the word, keep at it in season and out of season, reprove, rebuke, exhort (2 Tim 4: 2). They know the story of Paul's sufferings, and they must be prepared for the same experiences; all who mean to live a godly life in Christ Jesus will be persecuted (2 Tim 3: 10–12). There is more to this effect; and this is what the author is most concerned to say in Paul's name to the ministers of a new generation. He speaks about deacons and presbyter-bishops because there were such officers in the church of his day, but he is much less concerned — if indeed he is concerned at all — to propagate a form of church order than to insist that those who are the public representatives of the church should behave worthily of their calling. He was aware of the attacks on Paul from the Jewish side and was quick to rebut them, but for him Judaism was allied with gnosticism (as it is in the Clementine literature). It is Jewish myths that must be avoided (Titus 1: 14), and Jewish food laws are associated with dualism. He knew that Paul was a critic of the law, though to express the matter in that way is to fall into his own oversimplification: 1 Timothy 1: 8–11 shows no real grasp of Paul's profound dialectic.

Paul as he is represented here is not a Judaizer, not an antinomian, not a gnostic; neither does he walk riskily on the edge of these errors. Marcion took too many risks and fell over the precipice; the writer of the Pastorals avoided risks, and makes his Paul, in comparison with the historical Paul, seem tame and unadventurous. Not entirely so; for the Pastorals contain some traditions of Paul's last days, and though there is no story of his martyrdom it is brought out as explicitly as was possible in letters purporting to have been written by the martyr himself. 'I have fought the good fight, I have finished the course, I have kept the faith' (2 Tim 4: 7). Paul might have been well content with such an epitaph.

THE ACTS OF THE APOSTLES

He was to get a better epitaph; at least, a larger one. The Acts of the Apostles is not simply a life of Paul. It was important to the author (whom for brevity I shall call Luke, without prejudice to the question of authorship) to place Paul in the setting of early Christianity as a whole; that Paul was an integral part of that setting was one of the most important assertions about him that he wished to make. But there is no doubt that Paul stands out as the leading character in the book. He is introduced at the end of chapter 7 as the chief persecutor of Christians. At the beginning of chapter 9 he still holds this role, but the role is at once reversed, and he begins to preach the faith he had previously sought to destroy. He reappears in chapter 11, and from the beginning of chapter 13 to the end of the book he stands head and shoulders above all others. This is the legendary Paul, if the adjective may be used to describe a picture by no means wholly fictitious but one made, in good faith, by omissions, arrangements, and emphases, so as to present to later generations the Paul that Luke, and no doubt some of his contemporaries, wished them to see. It is not quite the Paul of the letters, and it is not quite the Paul of the Pastoral Epistles,[8] but is fairly closely related to both.

It is a question for dispute whether the most striking conversions are those of the good, who come to see their righteousness as filthy rags and recognize that good as they are they have no hope but in God's mercy, or those of the wicked, whose whole way of life is reversed in a flash. Luke succeeds in putting Paul into both groups. He is a Pharisee, and that means a good, devout man, who observes in every respect the law of God; he must learn that his goodness is not enough. At the same time, Paul is a persecutor, actively engaged in persecuting and even killing Christians, because they are Christians; he must change his way of life completely, not only ceasing to persecute, but actively spreading the Gospel, and that especially in the non-Jewish world. The first feature of Luke's picture of Paul is the outstanding convert (cf. 1 Tim 1: 16). The most pious Jew, the most depraved Gentile, can find hope in his example.

Paul the convert becomes Paul the preacher. Luke can sum up his work in a telling sentence: Paul (and Barnabas) so spoke that a great crowd of both Jews and Greeks became believers (Acts 14: 1). This success is repeated in place after place. Paul never forgot his fellow Jews and regularly began his missionary work in the synagogue, leaving it only when it became impossible to continue. That he found new settings for his work, more accessible to Gentiles, did not mean that he ceased to care for Jews; it simply broadened his scope, and under his direction the Gospel spread widely. As a result of his work in Ephesus all the inhabitants of the province of Asia, both Jews and Greeks, heard the Lord's word (Acts 19: 10). He recalls his indefatigable labour when he speaks to the elders of the church at Ephesus in Acts 20. No audience can frighten him into silence: he will speak to the Areopagus court in Athens (Acts 17: 22–31), even if some laugh at him, and is not afraid to say to the Roman governor Festus and to King Agrippa 'I wish to God that you and all who hear me this day were such as I am, apart from these bonds' (26: 29). Luke knows that Paul was not the first Christian in Rome, but his arrival in the capital is undoubtedly the climax of the book.

Paul appears also as a pastor. Unlike the gnostics, he kept back no profitable truth from those whom, as his converts, it was his business to teach, but went from house to house with his instruction; he set an example for other ministers, working with his hands so that his needs might not be a burden to others and that he might have the means to help the needy (20: 21, 34, 35). He was a fearless traveller, facing the perils of journeys by sea and land. He was a great apologist, putting the Christian case before both Jewish and Roman courts, mixing tact, argument, and defiance. He took thought for the ordering of the churches, appointing elders for the churches of the 'First Journey' (14: 23), and, it seems, for Ephesus (20: 17). He integrated disciples of John the Baptist into the church (19: 1–7).

He not only preached to Gentiles, but took thought for their membership in the whole body of the people of God. It is at this point that Luke's picture, which hitherto has had much to commend it historically, begins to run into difficulty. In Acts 15 Luke records a meeting in Jerusalem, at which Paul and Barnabas, Peter and James (the brother of Jesus), were present. It was held in order to discuss the question whether it was necessary for Gentile converts to the Christian faith to be circumcised and to observe the law of Moses; in other words, whether, in order to be Christians, they had to become Jews by the normal process of proselytization. It was decided that this was not necessary, but they must abstain from four things: the use of food that had been sacrificed to idols, blood (which may well mean the shedding of blood, though many think that it refers to the eating of meat with blood in it), animal food killed by strangulation, and fornication. To this requirement, represented as a matter of necessity (Acts 15: 28), all present, including Paul, are said by Luke to have agreed; indeed Paul is described as an active agent in circulating these decrees to the churches. Yet, although Paul argues at length and with deep feeling about the grounds on which justification and salvation may be received, about circumcision, about food offered to idols, and about fornication, he never makes any reference to the decrees, even in the letters whose authorship there is reason to doubt. Is it conceivable that he knew them? Still more, is it conceivable that as the agent of the church in Jerusalem or of a meeting of apostles, he commended them to the churches? If he had known of the decrees, would he have approved of them? It is not simply that he says plainly that (subject only to the restraint of loving concern for one's brothers) food sacrificed to idols may be freely eaten—'asking no questions for conscience' sake' (1 Cor 10: 25, 27); not simply that he clearly is on the side of the 'strong' (however loving to the 'weak') who are free to eat anything (Rom 14; 15). He could hardly make clearer than he does that grace has no conditions of acceptance except that it be accepted as what it is—grace.

Luke is not simply engaging in fiction. This is not the place (see above, pp. 7, 12, 26–30; we are here considering from a different angle matters dealt with earlier) to attempt the difficult task of disentangling the history behind his story. There was a meeting in Jerusalem (Gal 2: 1–10), and Luke did not invent the decrees; he found them current in the church and they must have come from somewhere. But he is concerned to represent Paul as an irenical, not a polemical figure. There is no conflict between him and the original apostles. Luke (unlike the author of the Pastorals) has difficulty with Paul's apostleship, on which Paul himself insisted strongly. He defines apostleship in a way that excludes Paul; when a replacement for Judas Iscariot is sought Peter declares (Acts 1: 21) that he must be one of those who accompanied Jesus throughout his ministry—a qualification that Paul could not meet. And there are in the whole book only two verses that refer, or appear to refer, to Paul as an apostle. One of these (14: 14) is textually somewhat doubtful; the other is open to different interpretations, though it is by no means impossible that Luke, who undoubtedly admired Paul greatly, forgot his definition and included both Paul and Barnabas among the apostles (14: 4). Or did he mean that they were envoys of the church of Antioch? It is part of the same picture of a pliant and accommodating colleague that when Paul finally returns to Jerusalem (21: 17) he accepts without demur the suggestion that he should (21: 23, 24) take part in the Temple proceedings by which a number of Jewish Christians were cleared of a vow. This leads to his arrest, and in all his subsequent appearances in Jewish and Roman courts he insists that as a Christian he is a good Jew, a Jew who has taken the right course for his people.

This picture of Paul the good Jew is not what one finds in the epistles. True, he never conceals his Jewishness, and he professes the deepest concern for the salvation of his people. He may have matured in this respect; in 1 Thessalonians 2: 15 he writes implacably of the Jews who killed the Lord Jesus and the prophets and persecuted us and are unpleasing to God and contrary to all, whereas in Romans he is confident of their ultimate salvation. He does however write in an extraordinary verse (1 Cor 9: 20) that to the Jews he would become as if he were a Jew—as if he were not a Jew! He had, as we have seen, a new criterion of membership of the people of God and it was neither Jewish circumcision nor Christian decrees, but Christ only. This fierce concentration of life does not appear in Acts, nor does the corresponding concentration of doctrine. This is clearest in the Apostolic Council and its outcome, but hardly less clear in the Areopagus speech. Is this popular Greek natural theology with its anonymous allusion to Jesus at the end a fair representation of the man who wrote Romans 1?

This is in fact the Pauline legend, the picture of Paul that was being canvassed towards the end of the first century, a generation after the historical Paul's death. It is important to emphasize that it is not fiction; much of it is historically true. It represents Paul as a great missionary, evangelist and pastor, who travelled widely, preached effectively if not brilliantly, founded churches, cared for their members, and did much to establish Christianity in the north-eastern quadrant of the Mediterranean. All this is true. It represents him in particular as a Jew who became the great missionary to Gentiles and their representative and defender in the counsels of the church, affirming their right to membership in the people of God without circumcision. This is true. Apart from occasional hints, it represents him as living in harmony with the church and apostles based in Jerusalem and as ready to enter compromises with them. This is true, in that he sought harmony with Jerusalem; not true, in that there were limits which he would not transgress in his quest for unity. His preaching to Gentiles is represented as taking the form that preaching to Gentiles took in Luke's time, that is, it built on the foundation laid by Hellenistic Judaism and added to it the lordship of Jesus manifested in his resurrection. This is true in that Paul evidently spoke in terms that Gentiles could understand and had a smattering of popular Stoicism; no further. It is true that Paul could see the dangers of incipient gnosticism and would have continued as an opponent of developed second-century gnosticism, but the picture is not true in that it was Paul's way to argue rather than to excommunicate. Luke was not a dealer in falsehoods, but he was a man of his own time, who was not a critical historian and did not have the theological ability fully to understand the man he so greatly admired.

There is a sense in which the legendary Paul was even more important than the historical Paul, for it was the legendary Paul—more or less, Luke's Paul—who won through in the second century. The neglect of Paul in the middle years of the second century is understandable. If he meant anything like what Marcion made of him, if he was the foundation on which Valentinus built his gnostic system, he was better left alone, and some Jewish Christians seem to have remembered clearly enough that he had opposed their founding fathers, James and Peter. It is not surprising that Justin made little use of the epistles. But at the end of the century Paul was without doubt an accepted part of the New Testament, his letters canonical literature. They appear in the early list known as the Muratorian Canon, a list contained in a Latin manuscript which shows some sign of having been translated from Greek and goes back to about AD 200. All the letters are mentioned, including those which there is some reason to think inauthentic; the letters to individuals (Philemon, Timothy, and Titus) stand a little apart from those written to churches, but they too are 'hallowed in the esteem of the catholic church for the regulation of ecclesiastical discipline'. Acts also appears in the list.

The Acts of all the Apostles [this misleading title is significant] are comprehended by Luke in one book and addressed to the most excellent Theophilus, because these different events took place when he was himself present; and he shows this clearly by his omission of the passion of Peter, and also of the journey of Paul when he went from the city [Rome] to Spain.

The reference to Acts and to its picture of what I have called the legendary Paul is important. The turning-point in the acceptance of Paul was the work of the theologian Irenaeus. Irenaeus was a good, indeed a notable and important theologian; he had read Paul for himself, and understood him better than his predecessors and many of his successors. But he approached him along the track laid down by Luke in Acts. Paul was at one with the other apostles. The Jerusalem Council, for example, is described at length on the basis of Acts (Irenaeus, *Against the Heresies* 3: 14). Irenaeus is aware of the version in Galatians 2, but uses it to show Paul's readiness to accede to Jerusalem's requests (Gal 2: 1, 2, 5), to show that he and Peter were called and used by the same God (2: 8), and that Peter and Barnabas at Antioch withdrew from table fellowship with Gentiles, thereby proving that Law and Gospel proceeded from the same God (2: 12, 13). From Acts also Irenaeus derives the principle, upheld by Paul as well as the other apostles, that the same God created and redeemed the world. Luke was right. Paul was not the odd man out, always against the government; he was one with the whole apostolic body. Marcion had got him wrong; he did not cut out the Old Testament or break the links between Christianity and Judaism. And Valentinus was wrong too; Paul was no dualist. So Paul could be used, and Irenaeus used him to some effect. But not without some emasculation of the combative polemical man, whose freedom was real freedom and who interpreted the Old Testament in terms of the New, not the New Testament in terms of the Old.

Notes

1 See W. G. Kümmel, *Einleitung in das Neue Testament* (19th edn, 1978), pp. 298–305; ET: *Introduction to the New Testament* (1975), pp. 340–6.

2 Such infelicities are apt to disappear in modern translations.

3 One thinks for example of the attempt of Caligula to set up in the Temple a statue of himself; see Josephus, *Jewish Antiquities* 18: 261–309.

4 One such inscription is given in C. K. Barrett, *The New Testament Background* (2nd edn, 1987), p. 53.

5 See H. Lietzmann, *The Beginnings of the Christian Church* (1937), p. 159, n. 1: ' . . . a proof of the spurious character of the letter'.

6 R. Bultmann, *Theologie des Neuen Testaments* (9th edn, 1984), p. 535; ET: *Theology of the New Testament*, vol. 2, p. 185.

7 See C. K. Barrett, Clarendon Bible (1963), pp. 4–12.

8 S. G. Wilson, *Luke and the Pastorals* (1979), and a few others, have maintained the view that Acts and the Pastorals were written by the same author.

5

Pauline theology today

This concluding chapter is not an attempt to rewrite Paul's theology in modern terms, nor is it an attempt to review what the theologians of today are saying in the light of what Paul once said. It is rather an attempt to take Paul seriously as a partner — a senior partner — in the theological enterprise that we have inherited from him. Or, one might say, it is an attempt (by one who is not well qualified for the task) to study him not simply as a historian but as a theologian should. One cannot assume that all the remarks of a first-century theologian will be of undiminished relevance at the end of the twentieth century. Different readers will make different selections from his work, but all will recognize that though some of his views and attitudes belong to his own day, there is a remarkable depth of thought that may need reworking but has immense potential for Christian thinkers in every period.

I have pointed out that after the death of Jesus his disciples were confronted with the task of improvising a dogmatics — not to mention a church order, an ethical system, and a liturgy. Paul was the supreme improviser, the only man capable both of plumbing the depths of the theological mine that had been opened and of bringing some sort of order into the creative mass. Even he can hardly be said to have been entirely successful in the latter task. This was no doubt in part due to the fact that the task — to begin with a quantity of refractory raw material and finish with a perfectly formed end product — was too vast even for the best of intellects, but it was due still more to the fact, which was dealt with in Chapter 2, that Paul had to fight his way from point to point with little leisure to work the points achieved in conflict into a harmonious whole. This is not to be regretted; conflict was what made Paul creative; and it is true that Christian theology must always be polemical theology; at least, it will always have a polemical element in it. This is because the theologian by the nature of his task is always called upon to do the impossible, to describe the indescribable. It is impossible to say what God is like, because there is nothing that is like him. The theologian will find himself saying, 'No, he is not like that; you have painted a picture of God that is misleading'. To take a specific, and in its way simple, example: a reader may take up the gospels and say, Jesus of Nazareth was simply a man, like any other man. No, the theologian is obliged to reply, he is not like any other man; there is something here that can only be called divine. Another reader comes from the gospels and says, Jesus was God; true, he looked like a man but this was only a matter of appearance. No, the theologian replies, this is not so; he suffered, he died; he was man. It is out of this polemical situation that there arise eventually such propositions as 'consubstantial with the Father as touching the Godhead and consubstantial with us as touching the manhood' (Chalcedonian Definition). They do not arise because making them up is a pleasant pastime; they come, as the Chalcedonian Definition did, out of ages of dispute. Paul's disputes were less sophisticated than the Christological debates of the fourth and fifth centuries, but they led to significant — and sometimes rather disjointed — results.

Along with the polemical strain in theology goes a related one, the dialectical; that is, the element of internal polemics. In any field, and not least in theology, it is the mark of a creative mind that though it welcomes questions from and debates with others, and makes profitable use of such opportunities, it is capable of generating its own questions and conducting its own debates. These may be initiated from without, but they are developed and sharpened within. The supreme example of this in Paul's theology is to be found in his treatment of the Law. There was of course plenty of external debate about the Law: there were thorough-going observants of the Law who believed that Torah was the way to God and that Gentiles who would be saved must be circumcised and observe every commandment, or at least the greater number of them. There was also the group, perhaps in practice even more troublesome, of the half-way observants, like Peter, whose line of action was unpredictable. But Paul carried the debate further in his own mind than he was obliged to do in public debate. No one brought the question to a sharper edge than his 'Is the law sin?' (Rom

7: 7), which has to be read in the context of the positive conviction that the law is holy and spiritual, the commandment holy and righteous and good, and the negative conviction that what the law produced in him was sinful passions, so that effectively it proved to be a law of sin (Rom 7: 5, 12, 14, 23). It was out of this inward debate that his dialectical view of the law, different from that of his fellow Jews, arose. Similar observations could be made with reference to other important theological themes. I have argued elsewhere[1] that in the New Testament as a whole (but this is preeminently true of Paul) the church is represented paradoxically as at once central and peripheral. It is central in that it is part of the eternal purpose of God to have a people; it is peripheral in the sense that in its present manifestation it can appear as a denial rather than an affirmation of the purpose of God. Paul knows the church as the pure unspotted virgin whom he has betrothed to Christ, and he sees it seduced into corruption. Yet it is one church, and he must wrestle with its two manifestations. One could take this further in terms of baptism, which is the sign of dying to sin and living to God (Rom 6: 1–11); yet a sign of which he can say 'I thank God that I baptized none of you — except perhaps half-a-dozen' (1 Cor 1: 14–17). In the same way he can say of the church's supper that whenever the Corinthians take the covenant blood they proclaim the Lord's death and look for his coming; and write a few verses earlier that their coming together does more harm than good (1 Cor 11: 17, 25, 26).

A theology that fails to take seriously this paradox, this dialectic, will never reach the depth of Paul's; a theologian who is afraid of a fight will never understand him. Church and sacraments are always with us, and so is law, though because it is not the Torah of Moses, but our own substitute for it, hard work has to be done on the text of the epistles before Paul's meaning can be grasped in our own idiom. In a 'post-Christian' society which has lost the standards that make judgement intelligible we are likely to approach the introspective conscience in Paul's way, as Christians, rather than in Luther's (see p. 86), and conscience may prove to be extrospective rather than introspective as we look out upon the sorrows of the world; but this makes Paul even more necessary to us than he was to Luther (if that is possible), an indispensable guide to the business of being a Christian.

An indispensable guide, or a misleading guide? That Paul misunderstood, misinterpreted, and thereby destroyed at birth the religion of Jesus is a proposition that is still maintained. It has a superficial attraction. Paul's theological vocabulary is different from that of Jesus — if indeed Jesus may be said to have had a theological vocabulary. In the gospels Jesus is most frequently referred to as the Son of man; the term does not occur in the Pauline literature (though we have seen where it seems to lie not very far under the surface). The substance of the message of Jesus is the kingdom of God, and the theme of Messiahship is handled with noteworthy reticence, especially in Mark, the earliest of the gospels. In Paul, on the other hand, the word 'kingdom' is relatively rare, and the Messianic office is so fully accepted that the word 'Christ' is virtually transformed into a second name and becomes the basic proposition of Paul's preaching: 'We preach Christ crucified' (1 Cor 1: 23). A new vocabulary is evolved, consisting of words that appear seldom in the gospels: 'righteousness', 'justification', 'flesh', 'Spirit', 'wisdom', 'grace'. Paul tells his readers very little about Jesus. He knows that Jesus was 'born of a woman'; he does not say, though he may have believed, that Jesus was born of a virgin. For him, 'born of a woman', is simply the affirmation that Jesus was truly a human being; it implies nothing like the elaborate stories of Matthew and Luke. He knows, and constantly reiterates, that Jesus died by crucifixion and was raised from the dead; again, however, this is not cast in the form of a narrative comparable with those contained in the gospels. Between Jesus' birth and death Paul refers to only one event, to the fact that in the night of his betrayal Jesus took supper, eating bread and drinking wine with his disciples. Paul does not say that this was a Passover meal. There is no more, though it has often been claimed that the words 'I beseech you by the meekness and gentleness of Christ' (2 Cor 10: 1) could hardly have been used if Paul had not had some reason to believe it historically true that Jesus had in fact been meek and gentle. This is probably a valid observation, though it is worth noting that Paul himself shows in this context little enough of meekness and gentleness: 'The weapons of our warfare are not fleshly but mighty before God, for the throwing down of strongholds' (10: 4). Little more of the teaching than of the acts of Jesus appears in the epistles. In addition to the Last Supper words Paul quotes him at 1 Cor 7: 10, 12; 9: 14; 1 Thess 4: 15; at 1 Cor 7: 25 he notes that he is unable to do so. At 1 Cor 14: 37 he claims that what he says is a commandment of the Lord, but it is not clear that this means a precept of the historical Jesus. At Rom 13: 8–10, Gal 5: 14 he picks out of the Law the same commandment of love to the neighbour that Jesus brings out at Mark 12: 31, but he gives no indication that he is quoting anything other than the Old Testament, and makes no appeal to the authority of the Lord's opinion.

It is clear that Paul was no rival to R. Eliezer ben Hyrcanus, who could be described as 'a plastered cistern which loses not a drop' of the tradition received from his teachers. He makes little or no attempt to store up in his memory and to reproduce on every relevant occasion the teaching he had received from Jesus, probably because he believed Jesus to belong to a different category from that of the teachers who had instructed him in rabbinic theology and practice. Jesus was not for him important as a teacher who had expressed infallible opinions on every conceivable subject. It was his person rather than his teaching that was centrally important, and his person was important not so much historically as eschatologically, not so much psychologically as theologically. The point may be clarified by the fact that one of Paul's references to the tradition that he received (1 Cor 11: 23) relates to the Christian supper; in fact, to two suppers, one in the past and one in the present, one that Jesus took on a specific date when he had supper with his disciples shortly before his death, and one that was taken regularly when Christians in Corinth sat down together to eat and drink. The two suppers were of course intimately related; that is why 1 Corinthians 11: 23–26 stands in the epistle. But they were not identical. Paul may well have remembered the Jewish distinction between the Passover of Egypt and the Passover of the generations that followed after. The essence of the Last Supper was eschatological, looking forward to a climax and consummation that lay ahead. 'I will no more eat . . . , I will no more drink . . . until . . .' (Mark 14: 25; Luke 22: 16, 18). Suffering is imminent, vindication lies beyond. The Lord's Supper (in Corinth and elsewhere) was observed in a new eschatological situation, 'between the times' — after the suffering, within the resurrection, before the consummation: 'You proclaim the Lord's death till he come' (1 Cor 11: 26). The two 'suppers' are on different sides of the revolutionary event of crucifixion and resurrection. You could not repeat, though you could recall, the event that belonged to past history. The same revolution affected the teaching, which no more than the supper could be literally repeated, though it could be recalled. It was necessary now to preach (as Luke in Acts saw with astonishing insight — Acts 17: 18) 'Jesus and the resurrection'. This is what Paul did, faithful to the message (the post-crucifixion, post-resurrection message) that he had received: 'If you confess with your mouth Jesus as Lord, and believe in your heart that God raised him from the dead, you will be saved' (Rom 10: 9).

This was a delicate process, leaving open many possibilities of misinterpretation. How successful was Paul in interpreting the figure of Jesus? Did he do justice to the real Jesus or not? A satisfactory answer to these questions could be attempted only after a detailed study of the traditions about Jesus as we have them in the gospels; it need not be said that such a study is impossible here.[2] It is necessary to be both selective and brief. There are three important fields of inquiry: eschatology, the Law, and Christology.

In the gospels eschatology may be taken to focus on the theme of the kingdom of God. The old question, whether the kingdom is thought of as present or future, is now often, and correctly, answered in the observation that it is both. What must be added to this bald answer is that its presentness is obscure, secret, and for the most part unrecognized. It is expressed in parables, most characteristically in parables based on the sowing and growth of seeds. The seed does indeed contain in germ the whole harvest, but at present it may be the smallest of all seeds, the mustard seed; it is hidden in the ground, disregarded by the farmer, who can do nothing to make it grow; a high proportion of the seed is lost, trodden underfoot, eaten by birds, overgrown with thorns. Even when the kingdom is (or may be) asserted to be present (Matthew 12: 28; Luke 11: 20) this is in relation to the exorcism of demons by Jesus; and it is just as easy — or easier — to say, 'He casts out demons by Beelzebul'. The kingdom is known now only by Christ-centred faith. Its manifestation lies in the future: 'Thy kingdom come'. This, though the language is different, is precisely Paul's perspective of Christian existence.

Jesus' attitude to the Law was twofold. The problems that hedge our study are here particularly severe, but he seems for the most part to have lived the life of an observant Jew, attending synagogue and reverencing Scripture; and it is not incorrect to claim that for the most part his opinions were those of a pious Pharisee. But only for the most part; and the tradition lays a finger on outstanding deviations from Pharisaic practice. His observance of Sabbath is complained of, he omits prescribed washings, he cultivates the acquaintance of people notorious for law-breaking. The last consideration is central, for it represents outsiders returning to the Father's family not by way of law — not even by way of covenantal

173

nomism — but by their relation with Jesus, who commits himself to them, the many (*hoi polloi*), the mass of men, even at the cost of death (Mark 10: 45).

In these two points we have had most of what Christology the gospels contain. The further we dig into the tradition the more unwilling Jesus appears to be to use the title 'Messiah', even though he acts with such authority as to make inevitable the question 'Could he perhaps be the Messiah?' He refers to God as his Father, using even the intimate term Abba (Mark 14: 36, picked up by Paul in Rom 8: 15; Gal 4: 6); but what does this mean? Who could not claim God as Father? He uses the term Son of man, but the background and meaning of this expression are matter of debate. The very fact of concealment — and the theme of secrecy runs deep into the tradition — is significant. There is no room for concealment if there is nothing to conceal, and the old phrase 'Messianic secret' is inadequate to describe something that may not have been by any means clear in the human mind of Jesus himself. He knew however that in him and in his ministry God was confronting the human race, and that the issue of the confrontation was of ultimate significance.

We have seen something of what Paul makes of this challenging group of puzzles and secret affirmations, which he absorbed, digested, and reformulated no longer in tales and pictures but in classical theology. It has been well seen by many interpreters that the centre of his response is the figure of Christ — *solus Christus*. He does justice to the secrecy of Jesus by his *Christ crucified*, for there is no better hiding place for a Messiah than a cross, and 'Yea rather risen' is not so much triumphalism (though Paul has indeed his own kind of triumphalism) as the affirmation that the crucified Christ eternally is, and is for ever the crucified. It is not always seen, and has from various angles been denied, that this primary affirmation carries with it the doctrine of justification by faith apart from the works of the Law. This is so, however, for if salvation is in Christ alone, it is not in religion or in any other human activity, but only in that renunciation of human activity that is faith, faith for which the Law obscurely asks, faith which is the only possible positive response to the Gospel.

Solus Christus is the substance of Paul's theology, and justification by faith is its cutting edge. The theological task that Paul has left to his successors is, first, the refinement of Christology in terms of developing philosophical and psychological concepts of being and of personality, and, secondly, the application of the principle of justification by faith to all the apparatus of Christendom —

church order, church dogmatics, liturgy, ethics—and to all those individual lives of which the church is made up. For justification by faith, hard indeed to expunge from the Pauline literature, is not an outdated concept to be abandoned, but a tool to be better used than it has been in the past.

Notes

1 C. K. Barrett, *Church, Ministry, and Sacraments in the New Testament* (1985), especially pp. 9–27.

2 See C. K. Barrett, *Jesus and the Gospel Tradition* (1967) for an indication of how the question may be approached.

Indexes

1. GENERAL

176

INDEX

2. GREEK WORDS

3. HEBREW AND ARAMAIC WORDS

*Aramaic

4. SOME IMPORTANT PAULINE PASSAGES

ROMANS

1 CORINTHIANS

2 CORINTHIANS

The
Seattle
Public
Library

A SEARING EXAMINATION OF THE DARK HEART OF MASCULINITY CONFRONTED BY A WOMEN-LED SOCIETY. *THE HANDMAID'S TALE* MEETS *HERLAND* AT A PARTY THROWN BY ANAÏS NIN.

Jonathon Bridge has a corner office in a top-tier software firm, tailored suits, and an impeccable pedigree. He has a fascinating wife, Adalia; a child on the way; and a string of pretty young interns as lovers on the side. He's a man who's going places. His world is our world: the same chaos and sprawl, haves and have-nots, men and women, skyscrapers and billboards. But it also exists alongside a vast, self-sustaining city-state called The Fortress where the indigenous inhabitants—the Vaik, a society run and populated exclusively by women—live in isolation.

When Adalia discovers his indiscretions and the ugly sexual violence pervading his firm, she agrees to continue their fractured marriage only on the condition that Jonathan voluntarily offers himself to The Fortress as a supplicant and stay there for a year. Jonathon's arrival at The Fortress begins with a recitation of the conditions of his stay: He is forbidden to ask questions, to raise his hand in anger, and to refuse sex.

Jonathon is utterly unprepared for what will happen to him over the course of the year—not only to his body, but to his mind and his heart. This absorbing, confronting, and moving novel asks questions about consent, power, love, and fulfillment. It asks what it takes for a man to change, and whether change is possible without a radical reversal of the conditions that seem normal.

"Unsettling and unashamed, *The Fortress* is a damning judgment on patriarchy, and a meditation on the labours of atonement."
—Damon Young, award-winning philosopher and author

"An imaginative exploration of the contours and confines of patriarchy, and what might lay beyond them, as immersive and thought-provoking as the fiction of Ursula K. Le Guin."
—*The Sydney Morning Herald*

USD $16.95/CAD $22.95

ISBN 978-1-64566-002-6

9 781645 660026

5 1695>

EREWHON BOOKS
EREWHONBOOKS.COM
@EREWHONBOOKS

COVER DESIGN BY MARINA DRUKMAN
COVER ART: MAN BY PHOTOALTO/ALAMY STOCK
PHOTO; BRANCH BY FL HISTORICAL M/ALAMY
STOCK PHOTO; SWORD BY PHOTO © DON TROIANI/
BRIDGEMAN IMAGES